W9-BJL-994

no d.j.

THE PIPE DREAM OF PEACE

THE
PIPE DREAM
OF PEACE

The Story of the Collapse
of Disarmament

by

JOHN W. WHEELER-BENNETT

NEW YORK

Howard Fertig

1971

HOWARD FERTIG, INC. EDITION 1971
Published by arrangement with the author

Library of Congress Catalog Card Number: 76-80601

PRINTED IN THE UNITED STATES OF AMERICA
BY NOBLE OFFSET PRINTERS, INC.

SI VIS BELLUM, PARA PACEM

COUNT BROCKDORFF-RANTZAU TO
LEON TROTSKY

PREFACE TO THE 1971 EDITION

This book aims at being an account of the General Disarmament Conference which opened on February 2, 1932, and which, more than two and a half years later, still eked out a precarious existence, living on tolerance and only continuing at all because no Great Power would accept responsibility for delivering the *coup de grâce*.

At the same time the book is a sequel to previous works, originally published in 1927 and 1932 respectively,* which traced the history of the inextricably commingled problems of disarmament and security from their inception at the Peace Conference of Paris to their then latest phase at the opening of the Disarmament Conference at Geneva.

The period covered in the present volume, therefore, is some two and a half years of European history, and I have tried to extend its scope sufficiently to include brief excursions into the contemporary history of certain states where internal events have borne directly upon the working of the central theme. For it was the political situations in France and Germany and their repercussions one on the other that complicated the situation at Geneva beyond solution, and an understanding of these events is essential if the greater tragedy of failure is itself to be understood.

The story of the Disarmament Conference was a tragic one, not only because of its record of opportunities missed and genuinely well-meant intentions misunderstood, but also because it represented the second great disillusionment which we of our generation had suffered in the postwar years. Harold Nicolson has brilliantly described how our first high hopes that a new and better world order would evolve as a result of the Great War were shattered as the course of the Peace Conference made it clear that nothing had really changed and that the old Adam of bitterness was too strong for the young spirit of understanding.

But there were many who, though they understood the

* *The Problem of Security, 1918–1926* and *Disarmament and Security Since Locarno, 1925–1931* (both to be reissued by Howard Fertig, Inc., 1971).

Peace Treaty to have been conceived and delivered in fear,
hatred and the flush of victory, believed that the mistakes
contained therein were of themselves so glaring and defiant
of reason that, in time, when the thunder of war had receded,
the Allied Powers would themselves take steps to rectify them
and to do gradually in sanity what had been impossible in the
atmosphere of Paris—build up a European structure based
upon equality and compromise. For this reason hopes were
rekindled and centered upon the success of that new Germany
which had been given birth at Weimar.

It is true that the principle of democratic government was
forced upon a Germany unprepared and, to a great extent,
unsuited for it; but, this having been done, it was hoped that
the older democracies of the West would at least extend a
helping hand, and would play their part in that policy of fulfillment which first Rathenau, then Stresemann, and then
Brüning strove genuinely and honestly to carry out.

But it was here that there came the second disillusionment.
The promises made to Germany under the Peace Treaties remained unfulfilled and, having established a democratic form
of government in Berlin, the Allies continued to treat it as
though it were composed of the most dangerous Prussian war-
lords. No measures were taken to remedy the harsh terms of
the treaty and no concession was made to Germany until it
was wrung from the Allies by the sheer inexorability of facts.
The policy of fulfillment, it became evident, was but unilateral
in character, and unilateral on the part of Germany.

Confronted abroad with cold adamant unhelpfulness, German statesmen found it increasingly difficult to meet the attacks made upon the Republic from within by the enemies on
the Right and Left, the Nationalist Reactionaries, the National-Socialist Revolutionaries and the growing force of the
Communists. Again and again, with all the eloquence and
sincerity at their command, Stresemann and Brüning warned
the Allied statesmen, and their warnings were repeated within
the Allied countries themselves, that persistence in attempting
to keep Germany permanently in subjection must inevitably
end in national revolution and all that that implied. Again
and again they assured us that it needed only a gesture of
understanding from abroad to enable them to meet this new
spirit of regeneration in Germany with an open hand, and to

control and utilize it in building up a new state of which Europe might be proud.

The warnings fell upon deaf ears. France could not, and England, apparently, would not, hear. Relentlessly they held on their same course, while in Germany the last democratic Chancellor of the Republic, Heinrich Brüning, struggled vainly to keep in check the rising tide of National Socialism.

The end came on January 30, 1933, when Adolf Hitler was appointed Chancellor and the Weimar system vanished in blood and recrimination. Suppressed too long by pressure from within and without, the spirit of regenerated crusading youth in Germany had now reached a pitch of enthusiasm which resulted in the Brown Terror and a recrudescence of the martial spirit by which Germany forfeited almost overnight all that very considerable degree of sympathy and friendship abroad which had been built up by her friends in many countries with infinite pains.

The role of Cassandra carries little satisfaction for those who play it, and now that the worst had happened and the blackest forebodings were justified, there was no time for repining. The milk had been spilt. It was worth while to try every expedient up to the last moment, but it would have been fatal to be content now to say, "We told you so."

The new situation had to be faced, and it had to be realized that the New Germany, the *Dritte Reich* of Adolf Hitler, born alike of the blindness and stupidity of Allied diplomacy and of the deep-seated passions of the revival of German nationalism, was going to rearm to the fullest degree which she considered necessary and, having done so, would set about revising the other provisions of the Treaty of Versailles which she considered unjust. Europe was faced with two alternative policies, either to take up arms in defense of the Treaty, or quietly, with such grace as was possible, to acquiesce in its violation and revision, and to watch the gradual building up of a *bloc* of states from the Baltic and North Sea to the Black Sea and the Adriatic, either politically National Socialist or having been drawn within the orbit of German influence. The Night of the Long Knives of June 30 in Germany and the brutal assassination of Engelbert Dollfuss in Vienna on July 25 showed clearly the ruthlessness which National Socialism was prepared to employ to attain its ends.

It was at this point that the present volume concluded. The ensuing years of 1934 to 1939 witnessed a tragic succession of attempts by Britain and France to appease Adolf Hitler's policies of unilateral treaty revision, culminating in a reluctant but determined stand against Nazi aggression of Poland in September 1939. Of these years I have written elsewhere.

JOHN WHEELER-BENNETT

GARSINGTON MANOR,
   OXON
June, 1969

CONTENTS

THE PIPE DREAM OF PEACE

CHAPTER I

THE BACKGROUND OF THE CONFERENCE

1

Whatever other reproaches—and there are many—which can be laid at the door of the General Disarmament Conference, that of lack of preparation is not among them. It resembled nothing so much as an overtrained athlete, who, having passed the zenith of fitness, is prone alike to nervous disorder and muscle-binding.

The Conference came as the result of twelve years of preparation by one organ or another of the League of Nations, dating from that day in November, 1920, when the First Assembly of the League had made the momentous discovery that the problem of disarmament was a political and not a technical one, and had issued instruction for it to be studied accordingly. From that moment the problem had been the subject of deep and anxious discussion by one or more of the organs of the League.[1]

At the same time, and parallel with these efforts, there had been corresponding attempts, with considerably greater success, to secure the limitation and reduction of naval armaments. The Conferences of Washington (1921-2) and of London (1930) had produced agreements which went far to curtail the armament competitions between the navies of the three great naval Powers, even if they had failed to find a formula to solve the rivalry existing between the two lesser naval Powers, France and Italy.

In addition to these agreements a variety of instruments of security had come into being since the original rather vague guarantees of the Covenant of the League of Nations had been

---

[1] It was discussed first by the Temporary Mixed Commission, resulting in the Treaty of Mutual Assistance in 1923 ; by the Fifth Assembly, which produced the Geneva Protocol in 1924 ; by a Special Committee of the Council and by a Committee of Co-ordination ; and finally, for five years, by the Preparatory Disarmament Commission which gave to the world the Draft Convention of 1930.

provided by the Treaty of Versailles.[1] All these endeavoured, albeit without success, to provide that illusive degree of security which experience had proved a necessary preliminary to the reduction and limitation of armaments.

With these continued attempts to implement the triple formula of " Arbitration, Security, and Disarmament ", and thereby to reach a satisfactory basis on which the General Disarmament Conference could build, the present author has dealt in previous works to which reference may be made,[2] but it is necessary to reconsider here the obligations which the States who came to the Disarmament Conference had undertaken, both between themselves as Members of the League of Nations, and as Allied Powers towards the ex-enemy countries disarmed under the Treaties of Peace. It was, after all, the fundamental purpose of the Draft Convention of 1930 and of the Disarmament Conference itself to implement and fulfil these pledges.

The principle of disarmament was first laid down in a legal document by the Fourth of President Wilson's Fourteen Points which formed the fundamental basis upon which Germany agreed to treat for an Armistice. Point Four ran as follows :—

" Adequate guarantees given and taken that national arma-ments will be reduced to the lowest point consistent with domestic safety."

This principle was given more definite shape in the first paragraph of Article VIII of the Covenant of the League of Nations, which was also Article VIII of each of the four Treaties of Peace concluded at Paris :—

" The Members of the League recognize that the maintenance of peace requires the reduction of national armaments to the lowest point consistent with national safety, and the enforcement by common action of international obligations."

So much for the mutual obligations which the States Members of the League had entered into *vis-à-vis* one another. There was, however, a further series of pledges, even more explicit

[1] The Locarno Agreements (1925) ; the Pact of Paris (1928) and its unexpected sequel the Litvinoff Protocol (1929) ; the General Act (1928) ; the Convention for Financial Assistance (1930), and the Convention for Improving the Means of Preventing War (1931), as well as a host of bi-lateral agreements for Non-Aggression, Neutrality, Alliance, and Pacific Settlement.
[2] See *The Reduction of Armaments*, by J. W. Wheeler-Bennett (Allen and Unwin, 1925) ; *The Problem of Security*, by J. W. Wheeler-Bennett and F. E. Langermann (Allen and Unwin, 1927) ; and *Disarmament and Security since Locarno*, by J. W. Wheeler-Bennett (Allen and Unwin, 1932)

in nature, which the Allied Powers had given to Germany and, *mutatis mutandis*, to Austria, Hungary, and Bulgaria. These specific promises were incorporated as a preamble to the very sections of the Treaties which contained the provision for the disarmament of the ex-enemy States. The preamble to Part V of the Treaty of Versailles reads as follows :—

" In order to render possible the initiation of a general limitation of the armaments of all nations, Germany undertakes strictly to observe the military, naval, and air clauses which follow."

The promises were further emphasized in the official Reply of the Allied and Associated Powers to the Observations of the German Delegation on the conditions of peace, which was handed by M. Clemenceau to Count von Brockdorff-Rantzau on 16th June, 1919. Part V of the Note dealt with disarmament in the following words :—

I. The Allied and Associated Powers wish to make it clear that their requirements in regard to German armaments were not made solely with the object of rendering it impossible for Germany to resume her policy of military aggression. They are also the first steps towards that general reduction and limitation of armaments which they seek to bring about as one of the most fruitful preventives of war, and which it will be one of the first duties of the League of Nations to promote.

II. They must point out, however, that the colossal growth in armaments of the last few decades was forced upon the nations of Europe by Germany. As Germany increased her power, her neighbours had to follow suit unless they were to become impotent to resist German dictation or the German sword. It is, therefore, right, as it is necessary, that the process of limitation of armaments should begin with the nation which has been responsible for their expansion. It is not until the aggressor has led the way that the attacked can safely afford to follow suit.

III. . . . Germany must consent unconditionally to disarm in advance of the Allied and Associated Powers [1] . . .

It is difficult to over-emphasize the importance of the bearing of this document on the deliberations of the Disarmament Conference, for not only did it form one of the principal *raisons d'être* of the Conference, but also the basis of the German claim for equality which finally wrecked the whole concern in the winter of 1933.

[1] It is, however, important to note that this famous document also contained the following passage, which, if taken in conjunction with German demands for equality of method in disarmament, assumes an added significance : " No deviation from the organization in armament (*la constitution de l'armament*) laid down in the present Treaty can be permitted until Germany is admitted to the League of Nations, which may then agree to such modifications as may seem desirable."

2

For a moment one must consider what steps were taken by the drafters of the Disarmament Convention of 1930 to meet these two sets of obligations. In writing of the Convention in 1931 the present author re-echoed a comment made in the French press at the time : " *Ce document a une grande vertu qui est d'éxister,*" [1] and in the passage of time it would still seem that this is the kindest criticism which could be made. For though its degree of achievement was considerably greater than might have been expected from the previous drafts prepared, this achievement was so hedged about with reservations and caveats as materially to lessen its practical value.[2] On the other hand its lacunæ were so glaring that it was impossible for them to be overlooked or glossed over.

On a credit and debit basis the Draft Convention comes out badly. On the one hand it secured qualified agreement on six main heads ; the acceptance of the principle of budgetary limitation ; the acceptance of limitation of the period of service ; the establishment of a Permanent Disarmament Commission ; the limitation of a number of effectives in land, sea, and air forces ; the acceptance of the method of naval limitation embodied in the London Agreement of 1930 ; and the renunciation of chemical and bacteriological warfare.

On the other hand, no provision was made for the inclusion of trained reserves in the totals of effectives of conscript armies ; nor for the direct limitation of material of armies or navies ; nor for the limitation of cost of material of air forces. In other words, even if the Convention were universally accepted, a State signatory to it might still have unlimited trained reserves over and above the limited regular army for which the Convention provided. It could also supply both the regular army and trained reserves with an unlimited amount of war-material to the cost of which no limit was set, and, in addition, although its air force might be limited, it could provide that air force with any amount of material the cost of which was also unrestricted, and further, no prohibition was placed upon the construction or adaption of commercial machines for military purposes.

[1] See *Disarmament and Security*, p. 102.
[2] For text of the Convention of 1930 and the reservations made thereto, see *Documents on International Affairs, 1931*, edited by J. W. Wheeler-Bennett (Oxford University Press, 1932), pp. 18–39.

Viewed in the light of the obligations undertaken by the Members of the League amongst themselves and of the pledges given by the Allied Powers to Germany and her former Allies, it will be admitted that these provisions of the Draft Convention went no very great distance towards fulfilment, but there was one further provision of the Convention which made the whole instrument inacceptable to Germany.

Article 53 consisted of two paragraphs, the first, the outcome of British proposals to ensure that the undertakings given in the Washington and London Naval Treaties should in no way be diminished ; the second, representing the only condition upon which France and " vassal " States would agree to the Convention. The text of the Article was as follows :—

" The present Convention shall not affect the provisions of previous treaties under which certain of the High Contracting Parties have agreed to limit their land, sea, or air armaments and have fixed in relation to one another their respective rights and obligations in this connection.

" The following High Contracting Parties . . . signatories to the said treaties, declare that the limits fixed for their armaments under the present Convention are accepted by them in relation to the obligations referred to in the preceding paragraphs, the maintenance of such obligations being for them an essential condition for the observance of the present Convention."

Speeches made by the French,[1] Belgian, Polish [2] and Little Entente delegates, and finally by Count Bernstorff, on behalf of Germany, in connection with the adoption of this Article by the Preparatory Commission, showed quite clearly that both sides interpreted it as being a reaffirmation by Germany of the disarmament obligations imposed upon her by the Treaty of Versailles, and in view of this the German delegation made the following formal reservation to the Convention as a whole :—

" That in so far as it (Article 53) does not refer to the Washington and London Treaties, the German delegation would vote against the Draft Convention as a whole. The draft, as drawn up by the majority of the Preparatory Commission, excludes essential

[1] " By the Text (Article 53) the Powers concerned define the conditions under which they accept the figures for limitation to be inserted, in regard to themselves, in the Convention. It is a reservation, if you will, but one of which the other signatory Powers will be cognizant in advance and which will thus become for these Powers who submit it an essential condition of the obligation they accept." (M. Massigli in the Preparatory Commission, 27th November, 1930.)

[2] " My Government consider the maintenance and strict observation of the disarmament obligations incurred by certain Powers in the Peace Treaties of 1919 as a prerequisite condition for the acceptance . . . of the present Convention by other Powers." (Gen. Kasprzycki, in the Preparatory Commission, 27th November, 1930.)

elements from the limitation and reduction of land armaments. Instead of leading to real disarmament, this draft would serve only to conceal the real state of world armaments, or would even allow armaments to be increased. To accept it would be tantamount to a renewal of the German signature to the disarmament clauses of the Treaty of Versailles." [1]

Thus at the conclusion of five years' work, the Draft Convention, as adopted by the Preparatory Commission at the close of 1930, had done little to implement the pledges of the Covenant and the Treaties of Peace and had convinced Germany—and particularly the then young and growing Nazi Party—of the intention of the Allied Powers not to fulfil them. The Draft Convention gave as much satisfaction to a weary and waiting world as did the Red Queen's dry biscuit to a tired and thirsty Alice in Wonderland.

3

At its session in January, 1931, the Council of the League of Nations set aside the request of Germany that the Disarmament Conference should be convened in the following November [2] and ordained that it should open on 2nd February, 1932. The reason for this decision was that at least a year was required for the final preparations for the Conference, but every additional delay diminished the chances of success when the meeting actually took place.

The Council at its next session in May unanimously named the then British Foreign Secretary, Mr. Arthur Henderson, as President-elect of the Conference. Mr. Henderson had many excellent qualities which fitted him for the position. He had behind him a long experience of international labour and trade union congresses, so that the technique of conferences was not new to him. His natural urbanity and ability to find a formula of compromise were essentially in his favour and, in addition, he had the immense prestige of his official position of Secretary of State for Foreign Affairs.

Yet this in itself was a drawback. Much might have been done in the twelve months prior to the opening of the Conference by the President-elect visiting the capitals of Europe with a small secretariat, and endeavouring to find a basis of agreement beforehand between the divergent and conflicting theses which

[1] See *Disarmament and Security*, pp. 97–100.
[2] This request had also been made to the Preparatory Commission which had refused to incorporate it in its Report.

had been the outcome of the discussions of the Preparatory Commission. Had such an exploration been made, it is not impossible that at least a tentative agreement might have been reached, and this would have appreciably increased the opportunities and scope of the Conference.

The very arduous duties of one of His Majesty's Principal Secretaries of State, more especially during a period of the greatest diplomatic activity and complexity, could not, it is clear, be combined with these preliminary duties of a President-elect of the Disarmament Conference, and much valuable time and opportunity were, therefore, unavoidably lost. Not a little ironical was the sequel. As a result of the economic and financial crisis in Great Britain, the Labour Administration resigned on 24th August,1931, and Mr. Henderson led the majority of the Labour Party into opposition to Mr. MacDonald's National Government. Thus, when he finally came to preside over the Disarmament Conference in the following February, Mr. Henderson was only a private citizen after all, and the position was further complicated by the fact that the President of the Conference was politically at daggers drawn with the first Delegate of Great Britain.

It had been confidently hoped that the year 1931 would provide a period of progressive development and preparation towards the great moment—when the general Disarmament Conference should convene on 2nd February, 1932. In effect, however, it would be difficult to find a year in which occurred more events calculated to render sterile the efforts of such a gathering.[1] But from this maelstrom of international politics there emerged very definitely three distinct schools of thought in regard to disarmament, the German, the French, and the American. To Germany, disarmament was presented in a different aspect from that in which it appears to the other Powers. Alone among them Germany stood disarmed, and, militarily speaking, helpless, her volunteer army of 100,000 men without reserves, without heavy artillery, tanks or military aircraft ; her navy, strictly limited in number, category and tonnage, without submarines. To Germany the question of disarmament was not theoretical but practical ; disarmed herself, she was eager to see other nations follow suit.

Ever since Germany became a Member of the League of Nations in 1926 her representatives, both in the Assembly, the Council, and the Preparatory Commission, had urged on the other Powers the necessity of honouring their pledges given to Germany in

[1] For a survey of the year 1931, see Appendix I, p. 250.

the Treaty of Versailles and subsequently. Disarmament was the keystone upon which Herr Stresemann based his policy of fulfilment, and only in the belief that disarmament could be best brought about by this means was he able to bring Germany into the League.

The prevailing influence in the German attitude towards disarmament was that of inferiority ; hence, as a natural corollary, came the demand for equality. Either let the ex-Allied Powers disarm to Germany's level, or, if they were unwilling to do this, let Germany be allowed to re-arm to a certain point to which the ex-Allies agree to reduce. This briefly was the German argument, and in either case the stigma of inequality would be removed.

This attitude explains the deep disappointment and resentment felt in Germany at the adoption of the Draft Disarmament Convention of 1930. In this document Germany saw the perpetuation of the *status quo* in armaments established in the Treaty of Versailles, and a reaffirmation of the doctrine of one law for the victor and another for the vanquished. Such being the case, she had no choice but to reject the Draft Convention.

It was to this doctrine of equality that France showed herself to be so implacably opposed, and let it be known that one of her primary conditions of disarmament was the respecting of treaty obligations by Germany. In other quarters, however, there had been an increase of sympathy for the German thesis, especially in regard to equality of method in disarmament, and this was well illustrated by the fact that the Conference of the International Federation of League of Nations Societies, held at Budapest in July, 1931, adopted a resolution declaring it to be " indispensable that the League of Nations should officially recognize the principle of equality in disarmament between the ' vanquished ' and the ' victorious ' Powers, and that the 1932 Conference must begin to effect such equality ".

They considered, however, that such equality should be effected not by increasing armaments already reduced under the Treaties, " but by the proportionate reduction of those of other States." In addition they recorded their opinion that the principle of limitation and reduction of armaments should be the same for all States, and that consequently each State should be bound to limit the amount budgeted for its army, navy, and air force, and that the prohibition of certain material, naval, land, or air, enjoined in the Treaties, should apply to all States signatory to the Convention.

The French thesis was, largely speaking, the antithesis of the German, and for this the reason is not hard to find.

In speaking on 29th June, 1931, on the position of France with regard to disarmament, the Prime Minister of Great Britain requested the House of Commons to use its imagination. This was really unnecessary. A mere recapitulation of the facts of history was sufficient to explain the French mentality.

Three times within a hundred years, and twice within living memory, France has been invaded and bled white, each time by the same Power. As a result of this repeated experience France has become obsessed with a sense of insecurity. The most illuminating example of the power of this obsession was the Treaty of Versailles, whereby France sought at last to obtain her security against Germany. For a variety of reasons, the provisions of the Treaty have in the course of years undergone modification. France had, therefore, been forced to fall back to a great extent upon her own resources to guarantee her security. In the summer of 1931 she had reached a position, politically, militarily, and financially, in which she could justly be said to dominate Europe. She had at last achieved national security by dint of her own efforts and was unwilling to abandon this possession of power except on her own terms.

The national attitude was clearly set out in the French Government's Memorandum published on 21st July, 1931. It was based upon four fundamental principles :—

(1) No action could be taken towards disarmament save with the general idea of common action.

(2) The progress of disarmament must be correlated with that of security.

(3) Respect for the disarmament obligations imposed by Treaty on certain States was the very basis of all work for disarmament.

(4) It did not follow from this necessary respect for Treaties that one should *a priori* adopt the methods and statistics used in the Treaties for the purpose of securing disarmament.

In effect these conditions meant that France would only disarm if the perpetuation of the present state of German armaments was recognized and if some kind of general guarantee of security was accepted similar in nature to the Geneva Protocol.

The principal line of disarmament adopted by France had been the reduction of the period of compulsory service with the

colours. In 1923 this period was reduced from three years to
eighteen months and, later, in 1928, to twelve months.

On the other hand, the cost of the French army had, during the
last six years, 1924-1930, increased by over £20,000,000, and the
cost of the navy by £10,000,000. This additional expenditure
might partially be accounted for by the growing rivalry of Italy.
Strategically speaking, France regarded Italy as a potential
ally of Germany in the event of war, and she must therefore
maintain a fleet and army equal to the combined forces of these
two States.

There was also a tendency amongst even the highest French
political and military opinion to advance the dangerous and
unfortunate argument that French armaments were the last
bulwark against Bolshevism. As has often been demonstrated
by leading citizens of the Soviet Union, the greatest factor in
favour of Bolshevism would be a universal financial breakdown,
and one of the causes most calculated to bring such a disaster
about was precisely the existing burden of armaments.

Of all States participating in the Disarmament Conference,
France was in the position to make the greatest contribution to
its success or failure.

The United States occupied a somewhat unique position
with regard to disarmament. She was under no international
obligation to disarm, and yet it was on her initiative that the
first two post-war Disarmament Conferences—the Washington
Conference of 1921-2 and the Geneva Conference of 1927—were
summoned. There had always existed in America, long before
the Great War, a very real and genuine desire for disarmament.
This feeling became intensified after the War and was fortified
by a growing nationalism that cried out for naval parity with
England. Was this parity to be achieved by building up to
England's strength or by mutual reduction ? For the time it
seemed as if the first course was to be followed and that a second
armaments race would be initiated. Thanks to a display of
conciliation and real statesmanship on both sides of the Atlantic,
such a misfortune was avoided and the Washington and London
Naval Agreements of 1922 and 1930 obviated to a very great
extent the danger of further rivalry.

America had therefore achieved her own immediate aim and
could afford to approach the problem of European disarmament
with a refreshingly impartial outlook. The approach was,
however, guided and influenced by one very important factor.
The United States was the great creditor nation of the world.

Debts and reparations had repeatedly been said to be at the root of the present state of world-wide depression. Was the United States willing to extend for an indefinite period the offer contained in Mr. Hoover's historic proposal of June, 1931 ? Here lay the strong and intimate connection between War Debts and armaments, and the United States was unwilling to consider any scaling down or postponement of the inter-Allied War Debts which might release large sums of money in Europe for additional armaments.

The most cogent force, however, which drove the United States itself towards disarmament was that of economic pressure. The deficit for the fiscal year closing on 30th June, 1931, was $903,000,000 (£180,600,000 at par exchange) as compared with a surplus of $184,000,000 (£36,800,000) for the year ending 30th June, 1930. The second quarter of the fiscal year 1931-2 closed on 31st December, 1931, with a deficit of $1,500 millions, which by the close of the year 30th June, 1932, had increased to the colossal figure of $2,886 millions.

To bridge this enormous gap in the national budget, the most drastic economies were proposed, including a " cut to the bone " amounting to over £12,000,000 in naval expenditure. Amongst the proposals for effecting this curtailment were the laying-up of a fifth of the United States Navy ; the reducing of personnel by from 4,000 to 5,000 and the closing of a number of naval stations.

It was, therefore, with these three warring creeds that the Disarmament Conference had to deal, and the chance of ultimate agreement depended on a judicious and subtle amalgam of the three.

CHAPTER II

THE FIRST WEEKS

1

Ironic contrast has never been far distant from the deliberations of the League of Nations. Perhaps the greatest irony was the circumstance of its birth at the Peace Conference in Paris, in an atmosphere so charged with hatred and suspicion that it is surprising that any good thing could come out of it. Then, again, the umbilical connection of the Covenant with the Treaty of Versailles, the one an instrument of peace, the other no less clearly a creature of war and fear, is ironical in the extreme.

But never was irony so clearly apparent as in the course of the Disarmament Conference. At the moment when Mr. Henderson was calling the first plenary session to order on the afternoon of 2nd February, 1932, the Japanese fleet were concentrating upon the Chinese city of Shanghai the fiercest artillery operation which had been conducted at any time since the Armistice of November, 1918. The superstitious might have been forgiven for seeing an ill omen in the fact that the meeting of the Conference had to be postponed for an hour while the Council of the League met to discuss the Sino-Japanese dispute. Mr. Philip Noel-Baker, Private Secretary to Mr. Henderson, suggests that this may not have been merely a tragic coincidence.

> " I know people in responsible positions . . . who believe that the conquest of the Manchurian provinces of China was determined by the Japanese military leaders after consultation with the armament manufacturers of Europe ; and that the date of their invasion was so arranged that it would present the Disarmament Conference with the League of Nations Covenant in ruins when it met. I should not myself care to take responsibility for that assertion. But there are certain facts which make it impossible to dismiss it as absurd." [1]

A year later, when the second session of the Conference was gathering, the Japanese armies, in defiance alike of the demands of the Council and the Assembly, were sweeping towards the

[1] See *Recovery*, 10th November, 1933, p. 12.

" forbidden " city of Jehol, and the Japanese spokesman at Geneva was placidly giving notice of his country's intention of withdrawing from the League altogether.

Even as Gibbon dates the Decline and Fall of the Roman Empire from the reign of the first Emperor, so did the decline of the Disarmament Conference begin at its opening session.

Nothing could have illustrated more clearly than did these marked contrasts the great gulf which was fixed between the atmosphere of the Disarmament Conference and the practical realm of things as they are. Indeed there were moments when it seemed as if the Delegates at Geneva had lost all relation with reality, so academic had their debates become, and it was only when some alarming crisis of extraordinary gravity penetrated the curtain of oratory and rhetoric that the Conference itself was recalled to the realization of the fundamental problems which it was called upon to consider.

The crisis, for example, of the German claim to equality of status and the crisis of the Nazi Revolution had at least the effect of withdrawing the interest of the Conference as a whole from the technical disputations of the Commissions, and of focusing it anew on the essential facts and problems of disarmament and their relation to the national and international policies pursued by individual nations in other fields.

2

Fifty-nine nations out of the sixty-four invited were represented in that dreary building, the *Bâtiment Electoral*, on the grey morning of 2nd February ; the Dominican Republic subsequently promoted their " observer " to delegate, the absentees being Ecuador, Nicaragua, Paraguay, and Salvador. The difficulties of the Disarmament Conference can hardly be regarded as due to these failures to attend.

When the Conference met it had before it the Draft Convention drawn up by the Preparatory Commission. In theory the Conference had only to fill in the blanks which had been left wherever figures should have appeared as to the levels to which the nations of the world were prepared to reduce their navies, armies, and air forces. But the Conference was also to reconcile the irreconcilable differences of the amendments, or amendments to amendments, which marked almost every clause of the Draft Convention. Sir John Simon in his first speech suggested that the Draft Convention should be taken as the basis for discussion, and this proposal was eventually adopted, but in practice the Draft Convention was rapidly forgotten in the maze of new plans and proposals which were tossed from Committee to Committee.

Mr. Henderson, in his opening speech, defined the three objectives of the Conference as being :—

> (a) To arrive at a collective agreement on an effective programme of practical proposals speedily to secure a substantial reduction and limitation of all national armaments.
>
> (b) To determine that no armaments should be maintained outside the scope of the treaty by which all nations represented at the Conference would make the achievement of universal disarmament their common aim.
>
> (c) To ensure continuity of advance in disarmament, without detracting in any way from the fullest measure of success of the immediate effort of the Conference, by arranging for similar conferences to meet at reasonably short intervals of time.

The remainder of the speech was a review of the previous work of the League with regard to the various plans for disarmament and security.

The next few days were taken up in the examination of the credentials of delegates and the election of further vice-presidents who automatically constituted the Bureau of the Conference under the chairmanship of Mr. Henderson. The countries represented on the Bureau were : France, Italy, the United Kingdom, the United States of America, Germany, Sweden, Japan, Spain, the Argentine Republic, Belgium, the U.S.S.R., Czechoslovakia, Poland, and Austria. A general Commission was set up on which each country was entitled to one delegate.

It had been agreed that the general debate should open on 8th February with a speech by Sir John Simon, the British Foreign Secretary, but the French Government realized the value of having the first—as well as the last—word. At the end of the formal session on 5th February, M. Tardieu, the French War Minister, announced that the proposals of his Government would be circulated immediately, and in a few minutes they were in the hands of the delegates and the Press. They were obviously the offspring of " the marriage of true minds ", the parents being the French plan for an international police force, submitted to the League of Nations Committee of the Peace Conference in 1919, and the Geneva Protocol of 1924. The chief points were :—

> " (I) The internationalization of civil aviation. Subjects of signatory States would be allowed to construct non-military machines, of a tonnage below a figure to be agreed upon ;

machines of a heavier tonnage would be confined to continental, inter-continental, and inter-colonial organizations under the auspices of the League of Nations. Only the League should have the right to dispose of heavy bombing machines. In case of ' flagrant aggression ' a State that was the victim of an aerial bombardment should have the right, upon the sole condition that the League be notified, to use all its air forces, even those earmarked to be at the disposal of the League.

" (2) Batteries of long-range artillery, vessels carrying guns of more than 8-inch calibre or of over 10,000 tons, and submarines of more than an agreed tonnage should be at the disposal of the League.

" (3) An international police force should be created to prevent war and, if necessary in case of aggression, to provide a first contingent of effective troops to come to the aid of the attacked State. This force should be at the disposal of the League, which should organize its command.

" (4) With these measures there should be an acceptance of compulsory arbitration, and ' aggression ' should be defined. Precise guarantees should also be provided to ensure rapidity of decision by the authorities controlling the international force, and to facilitate the bringing of this action into conformity with international law (which is still insufficiently precise, but of which the permanent and binding elements result from international treaties and pacts). Provision should also be made for international control of the execution of all agreements concerning armaments."

All the above proposals are intended to be taken as a whole.

" New rules for the protection of civil population are also to be adopted, including prohibition of the use of aircraft or artillery, of projectiles containing poisonous gases, etc., and prohibition of bombardment from aircraft or by artillery at more than a specified distance from the front line.

" The plan concludes by affirming the necessity of laying stress upon the provisions for mutual assistance contained in the Covenant, which have always been interpreted along the line of least resistance."

As a result of these French proposals, the Delegates spent an agitated week-end. It was feared that the fresh attempt to " tie " a disarmament convention to the enforcement of sanctions would alienate the United States, while at the same time it would meet with the unwavering opposition of the British Government. France found her only supporters to be her *cortège habituel*, the Members of the Little Entente, Belgium, and Poland. The general international public gathered in Geneva, always liable to panic, talked openly of the Conference having been torpedoed before it began, and made haste to demonstrate the general popular support for disarmament.

The session of 6th February was devoted to the reception of petitions and manifestoes in favour of disarmament from organizations all over the world.   The petition presented by certain women's associations had alone over five and a half million signatures.

The scene was described by an enthusiastic onlooker :—

> " The President began by summarizing his collection of telegrams, each with its message expressing the hopes of so many millions or hundreds of thousands of people throughout the world. Then the women.   Miss Dingman spoke in a clear American voice ; then turned and handed up to Mr. Henderson a great sheet bearing the petition figures from I forget how many countries. Eight million, three hundred thousand signatures.   Then came the visible sign, the petitioners with packages and books from all round the world.   There were only four packets out of the British lot ; only a sample out of 2,100,000.   But even so the pile rose higher and higher and began to topple ; the packets were carried off in relays in baskets.   The President leant over from his dais and smiled as the mountain grew.   The procession ended at last, and everyone felt that the President did well in his brief speech at the session's end to offer a special word of grateful cheer to women who had made this moving testimony possible."

To-day, samples of these monster petitions moulder dusty and forgotten behind the glass doors of the cupboards at the end of the corridor outside the temporary committee rooms.

3

In opening the general debate on 8th February, Sir John Simon made a polite but extremely perfunctory reference to the French proposals, which he said would be studied with the most sympathetic attention by the British Delegation. He went on to declare that the British Delegation " accepted as a foundation the general scheme of the Draft Convention— that special attention must be directed to such prohibitions as would weaken offensive weapons and so remove the temptation to aggression ".   He then submitted the following proposals :—

> " The Government accepts as the basis of future discussion the Draft Disarmament Convention.
> " It accepts in general the method of limitation by reference to the establishment of maxima contained in that Convention.
> " It supports the establishment of a Permanent Disarmament Commission.
> " It urges the abolition of submarines, and of gas and chemical warfare.
> " The abolition of conscription being a very controversial

subject, it urges the limitation of effectives by the most practical course.

" It is ready to co-operate in every method of agreed reduction in the size of warships and maximum gun calibre, and will agree to prohibit land guns above a certain calibre.

" It wishes special attention to be paid to such prohibition or limitation of arms as would weaken the power of attack and so remove temptation for aggression.

" It is ready to study the French plan with every care, and in general will support any changes which will really contribute to a reduction in armaments ; and, as regards naval armaments, it believes that the Conference will find it well to accept the work of the Washington and London Agreements, building upon them and framing the general convention upon their continued operation."

M. Tardieu immediately returned to the charge, undeterred by the attacks on his proposals in the German and English press. His *leit-motif* was " back to the Covenant ", and disarmament faded into the background as he enlarged on the need for a fresh interpretation of certain clauses and for providing the League with " the means for securing the execution of its decisions "—in other words, sanctions backed up by an international force.

Knowing that Mr. Stimson, United States Secretary of State, had informed the American Delegation before it left that the United States could not become entangled in the political problems of Europe through security guarantees, the speech of Mr. Gibson, the chief American Delegate, was awaited with curiosity and anxiety. Would the attempt of the French to force the issue induce the American representatives to retire into their shells ?

After another polite and pressing promise that the French proposals would be examined by his Government " with an open mind ", Mr. Gibson went on to emphasize the need to abolish weapons devoted primarily to aggressive war. His nine points showed an advance in the American readiness to co-operate, as in 1930 the Government of the United States were not prepared to accept budgetary limitation, which now figured as the ninth point [1] :—

" (1) Consideration of the Draft Convention as containing the outline of a convenient basis for discussions, the United States at the same time being willing to give full consideration to any supplementary proposals ' calculated to advance the ends we all seek.'

[1] For the previous policy of the United States with regard to Budgetary Limitation, see *Disarmament and Security*, pp. 72 and 94.

" (2) Prolongation of the Washington and London Naval Agreements, the London Agreement to be completed by the adherence of France and Italy.

" (3) Proportional reductions from the figures laid down in these two Naval Agreements on naval tonnage ' as soon as all parties to the Washington Agreement have entered this framework '.

" (4) Total abolition of submarines.

" (5) Protection of civilian population against aerial bombing.

" (6) Total abolition of ' lethal gases and bacteriological warfare '

" (7) The computation of the numbers of the armed forces on the basis of the effectives necessary for the maintenance of internal order, *plus* some suitable contingent for defence. The former are obviously impossible of reduction ; the latter is a question of relativity.

" (8) Special restrictions for tanks and heavy mobile guns for those arms ' of a peculiarly offensive character '.

" (9) The United States is prepared to consider a limitation of expenditure on material as a complementary method to direct limitation, feeling that it may prove useful to prevent a qualitative race if and when quantitative limitation has been made effective."

Mr. Gibson's last point was in some respects the most interesting, for it showed a change in the attitude of the American Government. Prior to the meeting of the Conference the United States had been opposed to any attempt to limit armaments by any form of control of expenditure in material, but the Chief Delegate now accepted this method as supplementary to " qualitative disarmament ".

It had been feared that Germany would carry her opposition to the Draft Convention to the extent of refusing to accept it as the basis of discussion at the Conference, but this anxiety was allayed by Dr. Brüning's statement that his Government was prepared to regard it as a " point of departure ". " The Draft," he declared, " does not meet the needs of the moment. It is marred by certain omissions and passes in silence over certain essential points. The German Delegation reserves its right to lay before the Conference proposals for remedying this defect." This was done on 18th February, when the German plan was circulated. This included both qualitative and quantitative disarmament, being based in great part upon the military clauses of the Treaty of Versailles, which had determined the disarmament of Germany, and accepting the implied definitions contained therein of aggressive and defensive warfare. Heavy artillery, tanks, and military aircraft were to be prohibited, and also " fortresses which might constitute a direct menace to other nations ". Capital ships, submarines, and aircraft carriers were to be abolished, international control to be applied to all countries, " and a limitation and control of the trade in arms and of their manufacture, both private and public."

By far the most important part of Dr. Brüning's speech was that which dealt with Germany's demand for " equality of status ". Dr. Brüning's actual words were :—

" The German Government and people ask that their own disarmament should be followed by general disarmament. This is Germany's legal and moral right, which no one can contest. The German people is counting on the present Conference to find a solution of the problem of general disarmament on the basis of equal rights and equal security for all peoples."

It was strange that this clear statement aroused no public reactions. Whether it was tacitly decided to ignore it, or whether his hearers did not realize the importance of his words, it was only referred to by implication in the subsequent speeches, although similar claims were made by other Powers whose armaments are limited by the Peace Treaties.

For the German Chancellor, more than for any other statesman at the Conference, disarmament was a matter of the gravest importance. Almost alone in Europe, Dr. Brüning had foreseen the dire and inevitable consequences of an unsuccessful Conference or, which would be almost as bad, a protracted series of long drawn out debates. With the knowledge that the growth in the country of the influence and popularity of the Nazis had only been held temporarily in check by his statement on 9th January that Germany could pay no more reparations,[1] it was all too clear to Dr. Brüning that his own political position, and perhaps even the maintaining of the peace of Europe, were lost unless he could take back to Germany at an early date some substantial measure of satisfaction for the German claims. Unfortunately it seemed that only his Italian colleague was able to appreciate the gravity of the position and the essential need for despatch.

Signor Grandi on 10th February showed the Italian weariness with the unceasing French arguments about security. " To go on arguing whether security produced disarmament or vice versa is just the kind of sophistry that we must leave behind us." He considered that the French plan raised juridical,

[1] See *The Wreck of Reparations*, pp. 176-8.

political, and technical problems affecting the very structure of
the Covenant. Italy would not hesitate to examine any proposal
which aimed at strengthening the institutions of the League,
provided it was likely to result in an effective reduction of
armaments.

The Italian Government in determining the policy of Italy
laid emphasis on two essential points ; equality of rights between
States and an equitable reduction of armed forces to the lowest
possible level.

The Italian proposals were :—

" The guiding principle of the Government's policy is equality
of rights between all States, and the equalization of armaments
at the lowest possible level. Its concrete proposals may be summarized under the following seven heads :—

" (1) The simultaneous abolition of capital ships and submarines.

" (2) The abolition of aircraft carriers.

" (3) The abolition of heavy artillery of all kinds.

" (4) The abolition of tanks of all kinds.

" (5) The abolition of all kinds of aggressive means of chemical
and bacteriological warfare ; and

" (7) The revision of the laws of war so as to ensure a more
complete and effective protection of civilian population."

M. Matsudaira, the next speaker, declared that Japan had
already reduced her army by four divisions and by 35 per cent
of effectives since 1913. But her proposals were less drastic
than those of Italy :—

(1) Acceptance of the draft Disarmament Convention as the
basis of discussion.

(2) Limitation in the use of submarines by adherence of other
States to the London Declaration on the subject. Japan thinks
that " wanton use of the submarine ", which is inhuman, is not
inherent in its nature. Surface craft can be just as inhuman.

(3) Reduction in the size of battleships and calibre of guns.

(4) Reduction in the tonnage of airplane-carriers, and the total
abolition of airplane landing decks.

(5) Abolition of " aerial bombardment " and the use of poison
gas and bacteria.

(6) A fair and equitable limitation and reduction of armaments
compatible with national safety.

The Polish Minister, M. Zaleski, supported the French plan,
accepted the Draft Convention as a basis of discussion, and
pleaded for " moral disarmament ", on which subject his
Delegation circulated a memorandum on 13th February. This
memorandum dealt with " a class of actions incompatible with

satisfactory international relations and dangerous to the peace of the world ", which were to be punishable offences under the laws of the various States. The spreading of false or distorted reports, inciting public opinion to warlike sentiments, propaganda aimed at inducing the State to violate international law, etc., were cited as some of the dangers to be dealt with. Special consideration was to be devoted to the Press, education, broadcasting, cinemas, and the stage as means of influencing public opinion.

The memorandum ended by suggesting that the question of moral disarmament should be referred to a sub-committee.

On 11th February the most important speech was that of M. Litvinoff, who once again returned to the U.S.S.R. advocacy of total disarmament, the " only infallible remedy ", which he had so fully and eloquently expounded to the Preparatory Disarmament Commission in 1919.[1] Failing this his Government was prepared to proceed by stages, beginning with the abolition of aggressive weapons and the prohibition of chemical and bacteriological warfare. On 18th February M. Litvinoff followed up his demand for " general and complete disarmament " by circulating a draft resolution and the draft convention of 1929, which was immediately rejected when submitted to the General Commission at its session on 25th February.

The speeches, to the number of fifty, continued without intermission until 25th February, and it is useless to attempt any description of the variations on the main theme proposed by the smaller Powers. The " Satellite Nations "—i.e. those under French influence—Belgium, Czechoslovakia, Poland, Rumania, and Yugoslavia, all supported the French plan with varying slight additions. The Scandinavian group, the Netherlands and Switzerland, showed no enthusiasm for the French plan, except in the case of M. Motta, who declared that it was logical but impossible—if such an opinion can be regarded as support for an international police force.

The disarmed Powers, supported by Italy and the U.S.S.R., Spain and Sweden, with Anglo-American sympathy, stood for what has come to be called " equality of status ".

On 24th February Mr. Henderson made a speech summarizing the general debate. He considered that there was a very considerable measure of agreement which gave the greatest encouragement for the future success of the Conference. Agreement seemed probable, especially in regard to the control,

[1] See *Disarmament and Security*, pp. 234–9.

limitation or abolition of offensive weapons of all kinds and the suppression of chemical and bacteriological warfare, as well as the necessity for taking steps to protect, as far as possible, the civilian population from the most brutal results of war.

Also it seemed likely that all countries were likely to accept budgetary limitation and the creation of some form of supervisory machinery.

4

There were, as has been said, two organs of the Conference in existence, the General Commission on which all the States were represented, and the Bureau. The former was concerned with the general discussion, the latter with the procedure to be followed.

The Bureau had met on 23rd February and recommended a resolution (adopted by the Conference) that all the drafts and proposals submitted to it (numbering about fifty) should be studied by the General Commission and co-ordinated with the Draft Convention, and suggested that the General Commission should " constitute as and when the need arises such commissions, sub-commissions or committees as it may consider desirable, and in particular the Military, Naval, Air, and National Expenditure Commissions ".

At its meeting on the afternoon of 24th February the Commission invited the ingenious M. Beneš, who has drafted more agreed Genevan formulae than any living man, to act as *rapporteur*. He prepared a synoptic table showing in four columns the various chapters and articles of the Draft Convention, all proposals directly connected with them, questions of principle raised by the Draft Convention, and the proposals and observations as to time or method of referring various questions to the special or Technical Commissions.

The table was adopted by the Bureau as a working basis, and M. Beneš then drew up a scheme by which the various questions were dealt out to the appropriate Commissions.

At the same meeting the General Commission had before it a resolution moved by Sir John Simon that it should conduct its discussions within the framework of the Draft Convention. This aroused a certain amount of opposition until it was subsequently explained away to the point of allowing *any* delegate to make *any* alteration in the Draft Convention which he chose.

It was then agreed that the first business was to clear the

U.S.S.R. resolution for the total abolition of armaments out of the way, which was done on the morning of 25th February, only Turkey and Persia supporting the proposal.

The next move was with France. It had been suggested by the Secretariat that four technical commissions should be set up—military, naval, air, and expenditure, but M. Tardieu immediately proposed the creation of a fifth—political—otherwise when or where could " Security " be discussed ? How could Peace be organized ? The average delegate thought that political questions were so important that they would be dealt with by the General Commission. That did not satisfy M. Tardieu, so a fifth commission was duly created and Mr. Henderson became its Chairman. It may be doubted whether this was part of the French plan.

While M. Beneš wrestled with his task from which Hercules might well have shrunk, the League turned to other matters. The Disarmament Conference adjourned and the Special Assembly met to deal with what the Japanese Delegate once so far forgot himself as to describe as the " war " between China and Japan. (The unfortunate word was hastily erased from the *verbatim* report of the proceedings.)

On 8th March the synoptic table was ready, also the list of questions to be discussed by the General Commission and the Technical Commissions. Then began two vast, interesting and ingenious games. The first was that of battledore and shuttlecock. What is a question of principle and what is a technical question ? The Air Commission, which was instructed to consider the " abolition of military aviation (with or without the internationalization of civil aviation) ", returned the shuttlecock over the net to the General Commission with the observation that this was a question of principle to be decided by the General Commission, which sent it back again saying that what was needed was the opinion of the experts as to whether it was possible, not whether it was desirable.

The Military and Naval Commissions found themselves in the position of the party of people who once decided to tell the truth but were unable to decide what the truth was to be. They were quite unable to agree as to what they meant by the word " effectives ". Both Commissions fell back on the well recognized way out of any Geneva dilemma, they appointed sub-committees, the Naval Commission hitting on the further refinement of appointing itself as its own sub-committee. It was apparently considered that this would assist its members in clarity of thought.

Abandoning the question of "effectives" for the moment, the Naval Commission adopted resolutions to the effect :—

(a) That war vessels should not be replaced till they have reached a certain age.

(b) That a country engaged in war should not have the right to use any warship under construction in its own territory for the Navy of another Power.

(c) That a country should not acquire or construct for another Power any war vessel exceeding the limitations of displacement or armaments agreed upon under the Convention.

(d) That the gift, sale or transfer of any vessel for use as a vessel of war in the Navy of a foreign Power is to be prohibited.

The Political Commission had a general discussion on the Polish proposal for "Moral Disarmament" and referred the question to a sub-committee.

The Budgetary Commission decided to set up a sub-committee of eleven experts to examine the replies received from Governments regarding their armaments expenditure and technical questions relating to the limitation and publicity of this expenditure.

This study in devolution produced one of the many periods of suspended animation of the Conference. While the Committees and Sub-Committees disputed amicably together the grains were running out in the German hour-glass.

5

At this point the Conference adjourned for the Easter recess—19th March to 11th April. The most important and outstanding developments of these first weeks had been the general interest aroused by the proposal for the abolition of military aircraft, coupled with international control of civilian aviation and the support for the abolition of "aggressive" weapons. Each nation continued to consider every proposal in the light of its own special interests and problems. The United States and Great Britain urged the prohibition of submarines, but clung to their battleships ; the smaller naval Powers denounced battleships and declared that submarines were defensive ; France still demanded security before disarmament ; Germany wished for the prohibition of all capital ships over 10,000 tons, a tonnage which would enable her to retain the *Deutschland* ; while the wrangle as to the definition of "aggressive" weapons was well begun. Curiously enough, it had not seemed to strike anyone except Dr. Brüning and Signor Grandi that " aggressive " weapons had been simply and easily defined by the framers of the Disarmament Clauses of the Versailles Treaty.[1]

[1] An analysis of the different proposals and statements shows that 14 countries supported the abolition of heavy long-range artillery ; 11 favoured the abolition of tanks ; 13 the abolition of bombing aircraft ; 7 the abolition of all military aircraft ; 7 the abolition of all capital ships ; 6 the abolition of aircraft carriers ; 10 the abolition of submarines ; 26 favoured the prohibition of chemical and bacteriological arms ; while eight expressly asked for prohibition of all preparation or manufacture of chemicals which might be employed in time of war.

Chapter III

APRIL   TRAGEDY

1

Though the Easter recess was short, it was sufficient to allow the world at large to realize that, though the Conference had been in session nearly two months, it had achieved not the slightest measure of agreement and had merely relapsed into that same welter of expert committees and sub-committees which had characterized the sessions of the Preparatory Disarmament Commission. The subjects which had been so ardently debated by that body for seven years were now re-discussed with equal ardour and with an equal lack of progress.

Nowhere was this situation more fully realized in all its aspects than in Germany, where Dr. Brüning's position was becoming increasingly precarious. The fact that definite action by the European Powers in the matter of a final reparation settlement, consequent upon the Basle Report, had been postponed until June had materially weakened the Chancellor's stand against the Nazis, since he had nothing to offer the German people in return for the continually increasing burden of taxation and economics which he was compelled to place upon them. These burdens, bringing with them discontent and despair, provided ample grist for the Nazi mills. The General Election of 1930 had returned the Party to the Reichstag with 107 seats ; by the close of 1931 it numbered a million registered members, and successive state elections showed that in all classes the reasoning of despair rather than a belief in Nazi policy was leading the German people in an avalanche towards the Right.

The same was true of the growth of the Communist Party which had made large additions in the recent elections. Both Communists and Nazis were recruited mainly from the same discontented elements of the working- and middle-classes. There was a constant interchange of membership between both. For both were opposed to a democratic form of Government such as existed in the Reichstag. The proportional representation system prevented the younger men from getting into the Diet and the Reichstag, and their only hope was in the new Parties who, therefore, though at opposite ends of the political poll, had nevertheless much in common.[1]

But this was by no means the only care which troubled the Chancellor. The increasing weakness of his position in Germany was attributable to other reasons besides these. The very composition of his Cabinet, during this period of Presidial Government, made for weakness rather than for strength. It included Dr. Wirth, a Centre Party man and a Rhinelander, but suspected of too great friendship for the extreme Left policy, including friendship for Russia, and also a tendency to coquette with the Social Democrats. Herr Stegewald, the Minister of Labour, represented the Trades Union element in the Cabinet, but he was becoming increasingly unpopular with his followers owing to the Emergency Decrees, the lowered wages, and the increased contributions from the workers for social services which had become a necessary part of the Government's programme. The Finance Minister, Dr. Dietrich, was a representative of a small and insignificant group in the Reichstag, and his policy had been unable to avert the breakdown of July, 1931. His influence, therefore, was very definitely weakened. Dr. Brüning's original Foreign Minister, Dr. Curtius, never had the support of his own Party, who were continually intriguing against him, and he had eventually been forced to resign owing to the failure of his proposed Austro-German Customs Union. There remained the Minister of Economic Affairs, Herr Treviranus, a former naval officer who had begun his political career as a member of the Nationalist Party, but had led a revolt against the dictatorship of Dr. Hugenberg. He was frankly regarded as being somewhat irresponsible though personally devoted to the Chancellor. And, finally, there was the Minister of Defence, General Groener, who, though he was perhaps the most valuable of Dr. Brüning's lieutenants, had lost, through the intrigues of his subordinates, the confidence of both the *Reichswehr* and of the President.

It was a minority Government with the strongest Party in it the Centre—a Catholic Group—and, though for some time it had managed to command a majority in the Reichstag, this was always rather a matter of good fortune and of careful political manœuvring.

Further problems which harassed the Chancellor were the

---

[1] It must be assumed that the increase of the Hitler poll at the second ballot for the Presidency—April, 1932—was largely due to the Communists voting for him against the nominee of the Social-Democrats, Centre, and fraction Parties.

lowered standard of living of the workers following the economic
breakdown of 1930 ; the bankruptcy of large estates in East
Prussia, attributed to the dumping of Russian agricultural
produce which the Government had failed to prevent ; the
industrial depression in the heavy industries in Westphalia and
the Rhineland consequent upon the dumping of British coal at
a price far lower than that ruling in Germany, and the lowering
of world demand for steel and iron.

The Chancellor had thrown himself, with even more than his
accustomed vigour, into the Presidential election campaign, in
the interest of Marshal von Hindenburg.   On his shoulders
Dr. Brüning bore the greater part of the burden of securing the
old veteran's re-election, sparing him every possible effort,
and disclosing himself for the first time as an orator and having
the ability to appeal to the people.

But, before the Disarmament Conference had adjourned, had
come the news that the first ballot on 13th March had proved
ineffective, and that, though the Marshal had only failed to
attain the necessary two-thirds majority by half a million votes,
a second ballot was necessary.   This was held on 10th April,
the day before the Conference re-assembled, and though
Marshal von Hindenburg was assured of election, his opponent,
Herr Hitler, had increased his votes by two million between the
first and second ballot, receiving in the latter 13' million votes,
more than double the voting strength of the Nazi Party at the
Reichstag elections of 1930.

It may be imagined with what hopes and fears Dr. Brüning
watched the re-assembly of the Disarmament Conference on
11th April.

2

And at first it almost seemed as though the hopes would be
realized, for no sooner had the Chairman concluded his opening
remarks at the re-assembly of the Conference, than Mr. Hugh
Gibson was on his feet and urging that there should be an
immediate discussion of an American proposal for the abolition
of weapons of a nature peculiarly offensive against land defences.
" I am convinced," said he, " that in the abolition of these
weapons lies the key to the whole difficulty in the way of
disarmament, that of removing fear and providing security."
He thereupon proposed that the General Commission give their
immediate attention to a draft resolution of the following
provisions :—

I

(a) That the following weapons are of a peculiarly aggressive value against land defences :—Tanks, heavy mobile guns, and gases, and as such shall be abolished ; and

(b) To request the Land Commission to draw up and submit to the General Commission a plan for scrapping tanks and mobile guns exceeding 155 mm. (6·2 in.) in calibre and for the abolition of gases in war.

II

(a) That an undertaking by the States not to avail themselves of the above-mentioned weapons in the event of war is equally essential ; and

(b) To request the Political Commission to draw up and submit to the General Commission texts for these purposes.

This proposal went at least some long way to meeting the German claims for equality and was eminently practical. It was supported as such by the British, German, and Italian delegations, Sir John Simon suggesting that, if a little time were consecrated to this definite proposal, the Conference would be " moving out of a world of sometimes vague and impalpable conceptions to a discussion of actual, and, I believe, practical proposals ". Corresponding questions in the range of naval and air armaments would have to be considered with equal definiteness, but " Remove these instruments of attack and you remove fear, which is the parent of insecurity ".

But opposition arose from an expected quarter. M. Tardieu claimed that his own plan went much further in the direction of providing for security than did Mr. Gibson's proposals which contained no provision for supervisions or sanctions, and applied only to land armaments, whereas the French plan laid stress on the interdependence of all armaments, and included the pro-hibition of bombing planes, large submarines, and cruisers of more than 10,000 tons, together with a proposal that " offensive weapons " should be placed at the disposal of the League. He therefore opposed the separate discussion of the American resolution, suggesting that it should be discussed with the French plan as part of the problem as a whole, and he won his point.

After listening to some further proposals by the Soviet and Italian delegations, the General Commission took no further action on the American resolution and passed a further week in discussing " general principles ". Thus a further opportunity was lost of reaching some concrete result, and it took all the united energy of Sir John Simon and Mr. Gibson to persuade the General Commission to take any action at all. Three

resolutions were, however, passed ; the first, unanimously, on
19th April, to the effect that the reduction of armaments should
be achieved progressively by means of successive revisions at
suitable intervals " after the present Conference shall have taken
the first decisive step for the reduction of armaments to the
lowest possible level ".   The second resolution, passed on the
following day with one negative vote, that of M. Litvinoff, was
a corollary of the first, and provided that the Disarmament
Convention should apply the provisions of Article 8 of the
Covenant, and that consequently armaments should be reduced
to the minimum compatible with national security and with
the execution of international obligations, account being taken
of the geographical situation and the special conditions of
each state.

Finally, on 22nd April, the third resolution, proposed by
Sir John Simon, was unanimously adopted, stating that
" without prejudice to other proposals, the Conference declares
its approval of the principle of qualitative disarmament in the
selection of certain classes of weapons, the possession or use of
which should be absolutely prohibited to all states or inter-
nationalized by means of a general convention ".

This measure was only achieved, however, after considerable
difficulty, and was only saved by the skill of Sir John Simon
in modifying the terms in which it was expressed in such a way
as to disarm the opposition of France.   Speaking on 20th April,
M. Paul-Boncour showed serious alarm lest the wording as at
first drafted should exclude the right of France to ask that her
plan should be discussed.   He hastened to add that he did not
wish to exclude qualitative reduction as a principle, but he
could not agree to exclude the adoption of certain other
proposals, and he repeated the arguments as to the interdependence of all arms and the necessity of providing for effective
international supervision.

As at first submitted by the British Foreign Minister, the
resolution called for the prohibition of such weapons as should
be classified as primarily offensive in character, but, in view of
the French attitude, the provision for internationalization as an
alternative to abolition was inserted, and this enabled it to get
through the Committee on 22nd April without a dissentient
vote, though M. Litvinoff expressed the opinion not inappro-
priately that the real meaning of the amended resolution was the
postponement of a decision, and Herr Nadolny criticized it as
not going far enough.

3

Nor indeed did the April resolution go far enough to meet the demands of the ever-increasing Nazi influence, of which a further indication was provided two days later. On 24th April elections were held in Prussia, Bavaria, Württemburg, Anhalt, and Hamburg, in all an area amounting to four-fifths of the whole Reich, and the results therefore being almost tantamount to those of a general election. In Bavaria the Nazis increased their representation by 34, securing 43 seats in the new Diet, while in Hamburg, Anhalt, and Württemburg they made enormous advances. In Prussia they increased the number of their seats from 9 to 162, their gains being mostly at the expense of the other Parties of the Right, including those splinter-Parties which had previously supported the Brüning policy. It was the last warning vouchsafed to the Allied Powers that, unless they gave some definite indication of their intention to fulfil their side of the disarmament pledges of Versailles, a new and awakened Germany would take steps to rectify and readjust the unequal position thus created.

Dr. Brüning saw the position only too clearly. He realized that, though the Nazis were in the ascendant, they were as yet neither strong enough nor sufficiently well organized to take over the government of the country. They were still a malleable quantity, capable of being controlled, and if he could secure some specific agreement that when the Disarmament Convention was finally drawn up it would definitely be substituted for the inequalities of the Treaty of Versailles—if he could take back this achievement to Berlin, then he might realize his long cherished dream of bringing the Nazis into the Cabinet on his own terms and making them share the responsibilities of government. On the other hand, the Chancellor was equally aware that failure now would sign his own political death warrant and would throw the Nazis into the arms of that small *camarilla* of the palace led by Dr. Meissner, the President's Secretary of State, General von Schleicher, and Colonel Oskar von Hindenburg, who were already planning his defeat and turning the mind of the aged President against him.

In view of these facts, Dr. Brüning decided to go to Geneva and to make a definite offer to the Great Powers on the matter of equality. The moment was a propitious one. There were already at Geneva the British Prime Minister, the American Secretary of State, and Mr. Norman Davis, Ambassador-at-large, and also the Italian Minister for Foreign Affairs.

Mr. Stimson, considerably perturbed at the slow progress of the Conference, had conferred with Mr. MacDonald in London, and together they had arrived at Geneva to give if possible a further injection of activity into the Conference proceedings.   M. Tardieu, it was true, had left to take part in the campaign for the French general elections to be held on 8th May, but it was felt that, if a basis of agreement was in sight, he could be called back to Geneva in an emergency.

Accordingly, on 26th April conversations took place between the British, American, and German statesmen.   Dr. Brüning proposed that, in return for an undertaking given by Germany not to increase her armaments for five years, or until the second Disarmament Conference, she should be permitted to reduce the twelve-year period of *Reichswehr* service to five years ;   to organize a militia which should not exceed the number of 100,000 men which the Treaty allows the *Reichswehr*, and a release from the restrictions imposed by the Treaty on the purchase of war material.   He also asked that the prohibition of the Reich's possession of weapons of offence (tanks, aeroplanes, etc.) should be abrogated, but said that Germany was prepared to renounce these on condition that all other Powers did the same ; alternatively Germany would be satisfied with " samples " of these weapons.

The Chancellor in addition made a detailed *exposé* of the German position with regard to her demand for equality of status, and maintained that the Convention which the Disarmament Conference would finally adopt should be substituted, as far as Germany was concerned, for Part V of the Treaty of Versailles.

Mr. MacDonald and Mr. Stimson emphasized the fact that the substitution of any new regime for Part V must be made by general consent of the Powers and not by unilateral action on the part of Germany, but there was general agreement that the German contention was both justified and reasonable, a view which was shared by Signor Grandi when the proposals were communicated to him.   A formula had therefore been found which satisfied four out of the five Great Powers, and Mr. Stimson asked Mr. Davis to telephone this good news to M. Tardieu and to beg him to hasten back to Geneva.

Almost it seemed as if the chief barrier to the success of the Conference had been removed and that the peace of Europe had received a fresh guarantee, for Dr. Brüning had utilized his time in Geneva to get into personal touch with other European

statesmen and to discuss with them on an amicable basis some
of the mutual problems which they shared with Germany.

And then, just when the thirsty travellers were pressing
forward to the shimmering oasis of agreement, it vanished into a
mirage. In Berlin the *camarilla* had also not been idle, and that
Feld-graue Eminenz of the *Reichswehr*, General von Schleicher,
had met the French Ambassador at an evening party at a
private house and had tendered advice to the French Government not to negotiate with Dr. Brüning, whose fall was already
virtually accomplished and whose successor, whom he named,
would be more amenable to deal with.   As a result,
M. Tardieu made more of his attack of laryngitis than he
otherwise might have done and regretfully refused the
invitation to return to Geneva, and with this refusal the hopes
of success for the Conference became moribund.

But, despite this blow to their hopes, the statesmen of the
Powers might have attained a measure of success had they
but realized how important it was, not only to success of the
Conference, but to the success of their own policies, that
Dr. Brüning should remain in office. It appears, however, to
have occurred to none of them, save perhaps to Signor Grandi,
that it was impossible to repeat the manœuvre of the previous
June and send the Chancellor home empty-handed.

In this latter case Dr. Brüning had been expected in Germany
on his return from the Chequers Conference to declare a reparation
moratorium. On the advice of the British Ministers he did not
do this, and a violent political crisis resulted ; indeed, it is
questionable whether the Brüning government could have
remained in power, had not the whole situation been
miraculously changed by President Hoover's famous proposal
of 20th June.[1]

Now, however, the same situation had arisen in regard to
disarmament, but with conditions in Germany considerably
more dangerous. The Allied Powers were sending Dr. Brüning
back to Germany with empty pockets, and were apparently
unaware either that they were encompassing his defeat or of
the fact that he would be succeeded by men of very different
character.

What a chance was here for statesmanship, what an
opportunity for the British Prime Minister to take the lead
in Europe. Had Mr. MacDonald, in face of M. Tardieu's refusal
to return to Geneva and discuss the German proposals, persuaded

[1] See *The Wreck of Reparations*, pp. 37–81.

his colleagues to make public the nature of Dr. Brüning's offer, together with the fact that his contention was considered justified and reasonable by the British, American, and Italian delegations, the French Government would have been placed in an untenable position by reason of the very fairness of the German proposals, and the plans of the *camarilla* in Berlin would have received a decided check. For, even in Germany, public opinion must have realized the fact that the Chancellor had made a bold bid for *Gleichberechtigung*, and the world at large could not but be impressed by the frank honesty and reasoned fairness of the German offer.

But the opportunity was lost and, instead, the details of the April Conversation were kept shrouded in mystery, and Mr. MacDonald regarded any subsequent reference to them almost as a personal affront. Dr. Brüning returned empty-handed to Berlin to face the inevitable, and on 30th May was dismissed by President von Hindenburg, whose re-election a month before he, more than any other man, had brought about. But the aged Marshal had become the *Pas-prisonnier-mais* of Rostand's phrase, and the *camarilla* had triumphed. Her von Papen succeeded to the Chancellorship and the curtain rang up on the " Prelude to Hitler ".[1]

Nor was this the only April tragedy at Geneva. On the proposal of the Bureau of the Conference, the General Commission decided on 26th April to suspend work until the reports had been received from the various Technical Commissions on the subject of the most offensive weapons. This meant that all consideration of Mr. Gibson's proposal of 11th April, and incidentally of the French plan, was indefinitely postponed, and, on account of the political situation in France after the general election in which M. Tardieu went down ingloriously to defeat, no discussion on question of principle took place for a further six weeks, by which time the Lausanne Reparation Conference had monopolized all international attention.

And yet, before leaving Geneva on 30th April, Mr. Stimson was able to tell the representatives of the American Press that the conversations he had had with the leaders of numerous delegations had given him confidence in the final success of the Conference.

---

[1] This is not the place to tell in detail, as the author hopes one day to do, of the fall of Dr. Brüning. Suffice it to say here that no European statesman of modern times has been so basely betrayed and ungratefully treated. The story savours more of medieval intrigue than of twentieth century politics, for one has to go back to the period of Machiavelli and Cesare Borgia for a parallel.

CHAPTER IV

LAUSANNE AND GENEVA

1

Throughout the early summer of 1932, while the discussions and adventures of the leading statesmen were occupying the attention of the world, the technical committees of the Disarmament Conference were pursuing their quiet work of obstruction in the background. To all appearances entirely detached from and unaware of the storm clouds gathering about them, the experts continued to wrangle and dispute as once the medieval philosophers of Bologna had wrangled and disputed as to how many angels could stand on the point of a needle, and kindred important subjects. Rapidly the Conference was becoming a *chose-à-rire*.

The Naval Commission was the first to get to grips. Spurred on by Mr. MacDonald's statement that he attached the greatest importance—that he made it the acid test—" as to whether the London Naval Treaty, which has been signed by three Powers, can be made a general treaty," and his very plain hint that, failing this, the British Government would have to consider having recourse to the safeguarding, or " escalator ", clause (Article 21) and build in excess of the tonnages allowed by Part III of the Treaty, the Naval Commission settled down to a discussion of " offensive weapons " which immediately demonstrated the entirely antithetical views of the Naval Powers.

The battle raged most fiercely over the question of capital ships and submarines. The British and Americans supported the view that capital ships were not primarily offensive weapons ; one of their chief duties was the protection of convoys, and they were not able to take aggressive action by bombarding shore fortifications with any prospects of success. The German delegate very naturally took another point of view ; he pointed out that capital ships were offensive weapons, as they had been employed for the blockade of Germany during the world war. He made

¹ All the major documents referred to in this chapter will be found in *Documents on International Affairs, 1932*, ed. by John W. Wheeler-Bennett (Oxford University Press, 1933), pp. 12–24 and 169–183.

a *beaugeste*, for he stated that Germany was willing to scrap her " pocket battleships " (in commission or building) provided the other Powers would do the same. Japan was non-committal in her attitude, one of her delegates supplying the answer to the question—" When is a battleship a defensive weapon ? When it flies a British or American flag."

The submarine as usual divided the Commission between " rich men, poor men ", the French leading the party for its retention as a defensive weapon for those nations which could not afford capital ships.

The varying standpoints may be summarized as follows :—

(*a*) Great Britain and the United States claimed that no single type of warship is offensive, but urged the abolition of the submarine on humanitarian and financial grounds.

(*b*) Japan claimed that aircraft carriers are offensive and should be abolished, but that submarines are defensive and should be retained.

(*c*) France supported Great Britain and the United States as regards capital ships and aircraft carriers, and the Japanese point of view regarding submarines.

(*d*) Italy and Germany demanded the abolition of surface vessels of a displacement in excess of 10,000 tons, aircraft carriers, and submarines.

A report showing the impossibility of arriving at any agreement on these questions was presented to the General Commission on 22nd April.

The Land Commission found itself in exactly the same position with regard to guns and tanks. With regard to the first, the discussion turned on the maximum calibre of guns which may be classed as not specifically aggressive, and the Commission divided into four groups :—

(1) The ex-enemy Powers, Italy and the smaller States, who set the figure at about 100 m.m. (3·9 inches), which approximates to the 77 m.m. (3 inches) limit of the Versailles Treaty.

(2) Great Britain and the United States, who set the figure at about 155 m.m. (6·1 inches).

(3) Japan, who set the figure at 220 m.m.

(4) Russia, who set the figure at 250 m.m.

A report on these lines was presented to the General Commission, but ultimately the Land Commission arrived at an agreement that all artillery over 220 mm. (8·5 inches) were offensive weapons.

Tanks presented two distinct problems—first of all, what is a tank ? Is an armoured car or any mechanically propelled vehicle a tank ? Secondly, when is a tank an offensive weapon ? It was eventually decided that all mechanically propelled vehicles should rank as tanks provisionally, and it was proposed by the British delegation that the " offensive–defensive " definition should be made by weight. This was eventually adopted and the weight was fixed at 70 tons.

The Air Commission appropriately and most unfortunately found itself unable to take off, and in consequence never did more than bump about the ground. It became involved in a discussion as to whether the control of military aviation or the internationalization of civilian aircraft should be dealt with first. Spain proposed a scheme for the international organization of civilian aviation on the lines of the Universal Postal Union, which proposal received a certain amount of support from France and Sweden. The Germans wished to see military air-craft abolished entirely, but this received only the votes of Italy and the U.S.S.R. The British were concerned in trying to devise a plan which would prevent the use of civil aircraft for military purposes. The United States delegates were of opinion that the problem was an exclusively European one, and were prepared to agree to any scheme which was adopted. In the end the only conclusion on which the Air Commission was agreed was that " All aircraft, without alterations of any kind and whatever their tonnage, may constitute a danger to civilians whether used directly to attack civilians or against military objectives situated in densely populated areas ". Otherwise their report consisted of such illuminating observations as " air arma-ments were at present ineffective against permanent fortifications, though aircraft carrying 5,000 to 6,000 kg. would be capable of producing serious results " ; " the general usefulness of aircraft depended on the weights they could carry and their range of action."

The Naval and Military Commissions having failed in their endeavours to agree on a definition of the word " effectives ", the General Commission set up a committee to consider :--

(a) The methods of comparing effectives of the various countries (a process which was impossible owing to the different ways in which statements are prepared).

(b) The American proposals for a formula to determine the effectives required, based upon allowances for the maintenance of internal order, security of frontiers and policing of overseas possessions.

Another committee was also set up composed of representatives from the Naval, Military, and Air Commissions, to consider chemical and bacteriological warfare. This proved to be the only committee which produced a unanimous report ; it was agreed that chemical and bacteriological warfare should be prohibited, but, as most of the members of the Conference were already bound by the Geneva Protocol of 1925 not to make use of these weapons, this was hardly regarded as a notable advance.

On 6th June the Committee on Effectives announced that it was unable to agree as to any definition. Well might Signor Grandi, in summing up the progress of the Conference before the Senate in Rome on 3rd June, remark, with his usual brevity and clarity, that the Naval Powers wanted land disarmament, the Land Powers wanted naval disarmament, and the delegates at Geneva wanted a new mentality.

When the Bureau met on 14th June it had before it the reports of the Committees and was fully able to appreciate the measure of disagreement that had been reached. As every Committee had found itself unable to decide what was the line of division between offensive and defensive weapons, the German delegate once again suggested the very simple method of being guided by the disarmament chapters in the Versailles Treaty. M. Herriot took note of this proposal.

Mr. Henderson proposed that delegations " should resume their private conversations with a view to the elucidation of certain political questions of principle . . . in order to facilitate the discussion of the reports by the General Commission ".

2

Meanwhile, at Lausanne, the statesmen of the Powers were gathering for the opening on 16th June of the 35th and " final " Reparations Conference. Political activities in Paris and Berlin had caused changes in the French and German delegations. M. Herriot, whose Socialist idealism, allied with that of Mr. MacDonald, had parented the Geneva Protocol of 1924, had replaced M. Tardieu, and in the room of Dr. Brüning came the new German Chancellor, Herr von Papen, and his Foreign Minister, Baron von Neurath.

Herr von Papen is to-day perhaps the most pathetic figure in international politics. As a cavalry officer he had a gallant war record which had been justly rewarded with the Iron Cross. Unfortunately his diplomatic career had not been so unblemished. As Military Attaché in Washington he had been expelled from the United States in 1916 with his naval colleague, Captain von Boy-Ed, for organized *sabotage* of munition works and other activities incompatible with the position of a diplomat in a neutral country. A fearless horseman, he carried into political life something of the dash and flourish of a *Herrnreiter* with the usual results consequent upon rushing one's hedges.

As a member of the Centre, Dr. Brüning's own party, he had taken office with two objects in mind, first to harness the Nazi Party and to build up a strong government based upon the Right and the Centre, and, secondly, to negotiate a military alliance with France. The first of the objects received a crushing blow when the Centre, not unnaturally after the part he had played in Dr. Brüning's fall, expelled him from the Party, and the second he never had any chance of attaining. He is assured of a place in history, though not one that he would have wished, for he will always be remembered as the man who played a willing Kerensky to Hitler's Lenin in the Nazi Revolution of 1933. *Par excellence* he is a monument to the valour of ignorance.

With him in his cabinet was Lieutenant-General Kurt von Schleicher as Minister of Defence, a man whose name describes most eloquently his character and tactics,[1] and who had already earned the reputation of having more " notches on his gun " than any political gun-man since Holstein. Every Chief under whom General von Schleicher had served was sooner or later eliminated from the political arena, a fact which Herr von Papen was to learn to his cost, and, though he too, as Chancellor, was to fall a victim to political intrigue, he had been sufficiently long in power to ensure a Nazi majority to succeed him.

The somewhat sinister complexion which the records of the Chancellor and the Defence Minister gave to the new German Cabinet was to some extent counteracted by the personalities of the Foreign Minister and the Minister of Finance. Baron von Neurath, a Württemburg nobleman, cool-headed, cynical, witty, and phlegmatic, had been a popular Ambassador in Rome and London, but entertained a lively and deep-rooted dislike of the League of Nations as constituted by the Treaty of Versailles. His colleague, Count Schwerin von Krosigk, a former Rhodes Scholar, was a professional civil servant and had impressed his fellow experts at the Basle Committees of August and December, 1931, with his efficient and clear-headed handling of economic and financial problems.

Such then was the new German team, of whom the Chancellor, Baron von Neurath and Count Schwerin von Krosigk came to

[1] The German word *Schleicher* is translated as " Creeper " in English.

Lausanne, leaving General von Schleicher to hold the fort in Berlin.

3

By reason of the fact that the Disarmament Conference and Reparations Conference were being held simultaneously at opposite ends of the Lake of Geneva, and, further, that the American delegates to the first Conference might not, at least in their official capacity, attend the second, a considerable amount of time was spent on the roads between Geneva, Lausanne, and the obscure Swiss village where Mr. Hugh Gibson, the leader of the American delegation, thought it wise to take up his post of vantage.

Mr. MacDonald was anxious to make a successful conclusion of the Lausanne Conference coincide with a definite step forward in the Disarmament discussions, and with this object in view both he and M. Herriot revisited Geneva on 19th June, but while the latter took the definite step of withdrawing the original French proposal for an international force, Mr. MacDonald lunched with Mr. Hugh Gibson. The sequel was swift and dramatic. On the following day, 20th June, Mr. Gibson and M. Herriot, each with a lieutenant, met at Morges, on Lac Léman, midway between Lausanne and Geneva. Mr. Gibson there laid down the position of the United States with regard both to Disarmament and War-debts, pointing out America's anxiety to see something real accomplished at the Disarmament Conference, and saying that this should be done by means of reducing effectives. M. Herriot replied that any form of quantitative reduction was inacceptable to France and a reversal of the policy accepted in the April Resolution which had declared in favour of qualitative disarmament, whereupon Mr. Gibson frankly told him that if, as a result of the Lausanne Conference, an appeal was made to the United States to make a sacrifice in the shape of a reduction of War-debts, public opinion would be unalterably opposed to the granting of any such appeal if Europe continued to spend on armaments enough money to pay the services of those Debts.

The next move came, with equal suddenness and drama, simultaneously from Geneva and Washington. The General Commission of the Disarmament Conference, which had not intended to meet again until 1st July, was hastily summoned in special session to hear certain new proposals made by Mr. Gibson on behalf of the President of the United States, which were issued as a manifesto from the White House on the same day. Mr. Hoover prefaced his proposals by the statement that they were based on certain definite principles—that all nations of the world by signing the Kellogg Pact had agreed to use their arms solely for defence ; that reduction of armaments should be carried out not only by means of broad general units, " but by increasing the comparative power of defence through decreases in the power of the attack "; that, as armaments had gone up in mutual relation to each other, such relativity should generally speaking be preserved in their reduction ; that reduction must be real and positive, effecting economic relief ; and, finally, that in considering the question of reduction all three branches of armaments, land, sea and air, were interconnected and could not be dissociated one from another.

With this prelude the President proceeded to make proposals affecting all three branches. As regards land armaments his scheme provided that the armed land forces should be divided into two categories : those necessary for police work and those for defence against foreign invasion. The land forces of the first category, the " police component ", would be calculated upon the basis of the effectives permitted to the defeated nations by the Peace Treaties, while, as to the " defence component", there should be a reduction of one-third in the strength of all armies over and above the police component. In addition, all tanks, large mobile guns, bombing aeroplanes, and all means of chemical and bacteriological warfare should be abolished, and all bombardment from the air prohibited.

As regards naval armaments, Mr. Hoover proposed that the Washington Treaty number and total tonnage of capital ships should be reduced by one-third, and the total Treaty tonnage of aircraft-carriers, cruisers, and destroyers by one-fourth ; also that the total Treaty tonnage of submarines should be reduced by one-third, while no nation should be allowed a total submarine tonnage in excess of 35,000 tons, with no single vessel exceeding 1,200 tons. For the purpose of this proposal, the French and Italian cruiser strength would be calculated as though those Powers had adhered to the Treaty of London, 1930.

In his statement amplifying these proposals Mr. Gibson said that, as to cruiser strength, the intention was that the 25 per cent reduction of the aggregate tonnage of the United States and Great Britain should be calculated on the existing total London Treaty tonnage of Great Britain, i.e. 339,000 tons. Furthermore, the total tonnage allowed under that Treaty for 8-inch gun cruisers

should be limited to 150,000 tons each for the United States and
Great Britain, and to the proportionate 90,000 tons for Japan.
As to submarines, in order to make the acceptance of so large
a reduction possible, the proposal was based on the principle that
no nation, whether or not party to the existing Naval Treaties,
should retain an aggregate tonnage exceeding 35,000 tons, or
more than 40 units.

In conclusion, the American delegate pointed out that the
proposals represented a sacrifice for the United States of over
300,000 tons of existing ships and the abandonment of the right
to build a further 50,000 tons. On land they would scrap over
1,000 heavy guns, 924 tanks, and over 300 bombing aeroplanes [1] ;
and the total cost of all the armaments to be scrapped, land, sea,
and air, was estimated to be over $1,000 million.

The first reply to the American proposals came from Sir John
Simon, who, however, confined himself to what he described as
preliminary and provisional observations, made, as they were,
prior to a close study of the proposals. The British delegate
welcomed the breadth of view which characterized the President's
communication, and said that all the proposals as regards land
forces would be examined promptly by the British delegation
" with careful attention ".   As regards the naval proposals,
however, he doubted whether they were, in some respects,
adequate, and in others appropriate, to the varying circumstances
of the different naval Powers. Great Britain wanted submarines
to be abolished entirely and, in respect of capital ships,
Mr. Hoover's proposals made no prospective provision for
reducing their present " monstrous size ". In conclusion, he
asked whether it would be possible to agree to a much lower
limit in tonnage and gun calibre in the case of construction still
to be undertaken.

M. Paul-Boncour was suspicious of the extremely simple
character of the plan ; a uniform reduction might, for instance,
constitute a fundamental injustice towards the smaller Powers.
In any case he asked that the French proposals of security should
first be considered as concrete suggestions designed to serve
as a basis of discussion. Descending to details, he said that, as
far as the land proposals went, France had already proceeded
to a more considerable reduction than that recommended by
Mr. Hoover, and she was consistently reducing her military

---

[1] The cash values of these three weapons have been estimated at $150
million, $15 million and $27,600,000 respectively, a total of $192
million odd.

budget. As for the provision of the Kellogg Treaty to which the President had made a reference (when he said that they should be guided by the principle that the signatories had " agreed that they will use their arms solely for defence "), the French delegate returned to the old question as to whether the United States could be relied upon to take any action against a State which violated this undertaking. Suppose, said M. Paul-Boncour, that a State used for aggression the means left to it for defence, they were back at the position where something in the nature of the French plan for security was the first thing at which they should aim. An equal degree of caution was shown by M. Herriot when commenting on the proposals in a statement to the Press in Paris. He pointed out, among other things, that they took no account of the possibility of coalitions among the Powers, a danger against which the French plan was especially calculated to guard, since it implied and included international organization and control.

The German and Soviet delegations welcomed the proposals, and Signor Grandi said that Italy would accept them, as a whole and in their details, without conditions of any kind. The Japanese delegate looked upon them in a very different light, but for the moment contented himself with pointing out that the distribution of naval tonnage provided for by the London Treaty of 1930 had been accepted by Japan on the understanding that it should remain in force until 1936. From statements made in Tokyo it was evident that the plan had no chance of acceptance ; a cut of one-third was considered to be too much at one stroke, and the Foreign Office pointed out that Japan's policy was governed by other factors than those operating between Washington and Geneva. The solution of the Manchurian question on lines which would ensure her security was a vital factor, as were her relations with the U.S.S.R., and her army and navy were the only guarantees she had against China's millions or Russia's unknown future.

Other pronouncements of an official character both in Tokyo and Geneva would seem to suggest that the American proposals were regarded with something not short of alarm. The Japanese Minister of War issued a written statement explaining that the application of a uniform rate of reduction in armaments to countries whose defence problems might be entirely dissimilar was incompatible with the principle that reduction should not impair the national security, and when asked whether the army could agree to the abolition of tanks, mobile howitzers, and bombing aeroplanes, he replied that it was impossible to say that some weapons were right and others wrong, since each case demanded special examination. Naval officials, on their side, considered that, if fleets were to be drastically reduced, the smaller ones should receive a greater degree of equality ; also that cruiser and submarine strength could not be reduced indefinitely by an island nation with trade routes to keep open and strategic points to defend. In short, in their opinion, the plan suggested would strengthen the United States fleet at the expense of the Japanese, and in the instructions sent to the naval delegates at Geneva it was understood that the view was put forward that the reduction proposed would perpetuate the existing degree of inferiority *vis-à-vis* the American fleet, an inferiority which up to the present existed on paper rather than in fact. Finally, in case any doubt should still exist as to their attitude, on 2nd July the delegates at Geneva quite openly stated that their instructions were that the Hoover plan was not regarded by the Japanese Government as a practical basis for discussion.

From these national reactions of the Five Great Powers, it will be realized how small were the prospects that the Hoover Proposals would be accepted, even with considerable modifications, and these prospects were not increased by the statement made in the House of Commons by Mr. Baldwin on 7th July. This statement represented the considered verdict of the British Government on the American proposals, and nothing that the Leader of the House could say as to the policy of the Government being in close sympathy with Mr. Hoover's views could hide the fact that Great Britain was not prepared to accept the chief points of his proposals.

But, if the Great Powers were cool in their reception of the Hoover Plan, the smaller States seized upon it as an opportunity of getting something done. A number of lesser Powers had resented Mr. Henderson's policy of handing over the decision of matters of general principle to political conversations outside the Conference and, as a revolt against being left to revolve, as it were, in a vacuum, a group was formed consisting of the delegates of Spain, Sweden, Norway, Belgium, the Netherlands, Switzerland, and Czechoslovakia, led by Señor de Madariaga, of Spain. This group was christened—or christened itself—" The Straight Eight," the antithesis being " The Crooked Five "— Great Britain, France, Italy, Japan, and the United States.

When it became clear that " The Crooked Five " would not, as such, accept the Hoover Proposals, " The Straight Eight " called on Mr. Arthur Henderson and urged the necessity of the Conference achieving some definite results before the adjournment, which all felt to be imminent. They considered that agreement might be reached on at least four points—the prohibition of bombing from the air, together with all training and preparation for this purpose ; the prohibition of chemical and bacteriological warfare ; a measure of budgetary limitation ; and the setting up of a Permanent Disarmament Commission. Their request was referred to the Drafting Committee of the Bureau and bore fruit later when the final Resolution, prior to the adjournment, was framed.

4

At the other end of the Lake the discussions of the statesmen at Lausanne had gone from Dan to Beersheba, and from China to Peru, in an effort to reach a general settlement. A number of cognate subjects had been canvassed and amongst them disarmament and war-guilt.[1]

Having failed to persuade M. Herriot to agree to the policy of a " clean-slate " in the matter of war-debts and reparations, Mr. MacDonald suggested that the scope of the Conference should be widened to include the settlement of the questions of war-guilt and the inequality of status in armaments. He proposed that a statement should be included in the final Protocol of Conference definitely abrogating Article 231 of the Treaty of Versailles (the War-guilt Clause) and that some precise agreement should be reached as to Germany's armaments. In return for this Germany must agree to the principle of a final payment, and to this end Mr. MacDonald produced the Bergmann Plan for a bond issue to meet such a payment.[2] After some discussions both Herr von Papen and M. Herriot agreed to accept this as a general principle upon which the final agreement should be based.

Both the Chancellor and the French Premier were imbued with this spirit of agreement when each left for his respective capital on the night of 23rd June, and it was in this same spirit that Herr von Papen gave his celebrated interview to the *Matin* just before his departure. " I am the first," he said, " to

[1] A full account of the Lausanne Conference and the " Gentlemen's Agreement " will be found in *The Wreck of Reparations*, pp. 210–253.
[2] See *The History of Reparations* by Carl Bergmann (Ernest Benn, London, 1927), pp. 317–327.

acknowledge France's right to compensation for the remuneration of reparations. France has a guarantee that Germany will endorse any Franco-German Agreement that I sign. In contrast to my predecessor, I represent all the nationalist forces of Germany."

On arrival in Berlin the Chancellor found he had aroused a storm of obloquy which brought down on him more scathing comments than had been passed on Dr. Brüning. The Nationalist Press flatly contradicted his claim to speak for them. The *Deutsche Allgemeine Zeitung* declared that he had laid the onus of making proposals on Germany and had thus put his country in an unfavourable tactical position which all efforts had been exerted to avoid. " The Chancellor is wrong in saying that all Germany would endorse his signature. Germany would not follow him on this path." The *Tageszeitung* remarked acidly that Herr von Papen's references to reparations " are not what national Germany expects from a national Chancellor ".

Not all the Chancellor's protestations and explanations served to appease the Press and the general forces of German nationalism, and, although the Cabinet approved the attitude of the Delegation at Lausanne and its future intentions as put forward by the Chancellor, the Chancellor himself was severely criticized by his ministerial colleagues and principally by General von Schleicher. Nevertheless, Herr von Papen was informed that he had the support of the heavy industries for concluding an agreement as outlined.

In Paris M. Herriot also met with severe opposition from the Right. His position was weaker than that of Herr von Papen's in that he was dependent on a parliamentary majority. He had, therefore, to accept the terms of the Right and returned to Lausanne refusing any concessions in the matter of war-guilt and disarmament, and insisting on the principle of a final payment. Somewhat to his surprise he found an unexpected ally in Mr. MacDonald.

The reason for the British *volte-face* is interesting. Over the week-end Mr. MacDonald had had an opportunity to ponder fully the Hoover Disarmament proposals of 22nd June and had found them, particularly with regard to naval armaments, inacceptable to Great Britain. The result was to drive him into the arms of M. Herriot, whose support he needed in rejecting the American proposals and whom he was prepared to support in return. " In face of this diplomatic *coup à l'américaine*," wrote M. Bérenger, Chairman of the Foreign Affairs Committee of the Senate, in the *Revue de Paris*, " Mr. MacDonald turned without hesitation towards France, and thus a Franco-British *rapprochement* was achieved. It had been in the air, of course, for months, and in logic for years ; but, all the same, let us be thankful for the ' unilaterality ' of the Hoover message which gave us the MacDonald–Herriot ' bilaterality '."

In the final Declaration of 9th July, therefore, there was mention neither of war-guilt nor equality. The signatories averred that there would transpire from the deliberations of Lausanne " a new order " permitting the establishment and development of confidence between nations in a mutual spirit of reconciliation, collaboration, and justice. The Declaration concluded with the statement that " this new effort in the cause of real peace . . . can only be complete if it is applied in both the economic and in the political sphere and if all possibility of resort to arms and violence is rejected ". The signatory Powers also undertook somewhat cynically to make every effort to resolve the problems which existed at the moment or which might arise subsequently " in the spirit which has inspired the present Agreement ". One might almost say that this is what has happened !

The German delegates made every effort to gain something which they could take back as a palliative against the general resentment which would inevitably arise when it became known that the principle of a final payment had been accepted, and the legal validity and continued existence of The Hague Agreements and the Young Plan recognized. What Mr. MacDonald told them in this connection is unknown, but there is no doubt as to the impression left by his remarks in the minds of the German delegation. This impression certainly was that Mr. MacDonald would make before the House of Commons a statement to the effect that, as far as Great Britain was concerned, the question of war-guilt was abrogated along with the termination of reparations, and the consequent fact that Part VIII of the Treaty of Versailles had ceased to function,[1] and, further, that if Germany made a claim in proper terms to equality of status in armaments the British Government would accord it their support. Neither of these things happened, and when a few months later a British daily newspaper made reference to them Mr. MacDonald denied them with the utmost vehemence.

[1] Article 231 containing the War-guilt Clause was the first article of Part VIII of the Treaty, which provided for the payment of reparations.

5

Nor was this to be the only blow which German and also Italian diplomacy received at Lausanne.[1] At one moment in the discussions the French revived the old proposal, which they had made more than once to Dr. Brüning in 1931, of a " political truce "—aimed at obtaining a temporary cessation of German propaganda in the matter of the Polish frontier and the Corridor— and this the Germans were prepared to discuss under the title of a " consultative pact ".

In the hope that it might appeal to the French view, the British delegation prepared a draft declaration of good intentions, followed by an agreement for a wide and friendly exchange of views, either periodically or whenever the prospect of disturbing disputes rendered it desirable. To the Germans this proposal was more acceptable than that of a " political truce ", in that it provided opportunities of raising grievances instead of imposing a five or ten years' silence, which would, in their view, strengthen the basis of the *status quo*, which Germany had never accepted and had only agreed under the Eastern Locarno Pact not to upset by force of arms.

After a full discussion the whole idea was dropped at the request of M. Herriot on the grounds that it might be prejudicial to the League of Nations. No reference was made to it in the final Declaration and it was considered to have disappeared into the limbo of " historical might-have-beens ".

With what surprise, therefore, did the German and Italian Foreign Offices learn of the statement of Sir John Simon in the House of Commons, on 13th July, that there had that morning been signed in Paris, by M. Herriot and Lord Tyrrell, an Anglo-French Accord " having ", he assured the House, " no organic connection with the Lausanne Convention or the Gentlemen's Agreement . . . ," but being an attempt " to formulate the expression of the new political spirit which was illustrated at Lausanne, and which will be so valuable if it can be preserved in the future ".

The Text of the Accord was as follows :—

" In the declaration which forms part of the Final Act of the Lausanne Conference the signatory Powers express the hope that

[1] In addition to the blows mentioned above, there was the " Gentlemen's Agreement " of 2nd July, by which the Creditor Powers agreed not to ratify the Lausanne Agreement until they themselves had negotiated satisfactorily debt agreements with America, Herr von Papen was not informed of this Agreement until after he had accepted the Creditors' terms.

the task there accomplished will be followed by fresh achievements. They affirm that further success will be more readily won if nations will rally to a new effort in the cause of peace, which can only be complete if it is applied both in the economic and political sphere. In the same document the signatory Powers declare their intention to make every effort to resolve the problems which exist at the present moment or may arise subsequently in the spirit which has inspired the Lausanne Agreement.

" In that spirit His Majesty's Government in the United Kingdom and the French Government decided themselves to give the lead in making an immediate and mutual contribution to that end on the following lines :—

" (1) In accordance with the spirit of the Covenant of the League of Nations they intend to exchange views with one another with complete candour concerning, and to keep each other mutually informed of, any questions coming to their notice similar in origin to that now so happily settled at Lausanne, which may affect the European regime. It is their hope that other Governments will join them in adopting this procedure.

" (2) They intend to work together and with other Delegations at Geneva to find a solution of the Disarmament question which will be beneficial and equitable for all the Powers concerned.

" (3) They will co-operate with each other and other interested Governments in the careful and practical preparation of the World Economic Conference.

" (4) Pending the negotiation at a later date of a new commercial treaty between their two countries they will avoid any action of the nature of discrimination by the one country against the interests of the other."

There was evidently more than a little perturbation in the mind of the Foreign Secretary in making his announcement, for he was at considerable pains to explain the inoffensiveness of the new pact, and indeed it was the object on all sides of such fervent apologies that one is tempted to wonder why it was ever negotiated at all. " Indeed it is no substantive agreement at all," said Sir John, " but we hope all the leading European Powers will respond." It was in no sense—apart from the fourth paragraph—special or exclusive, and, in the case of the first three paragraphs, the invitation was general to the other countries in Europe " to declare their adhesion to the rule that they will endeavour to promote political appeasement in Europe by open and friendly discussion on all grounds of difference by seeking a solution at the Disarmament Conference that shall be *beneficial* and *equitable* "—Sir John Simon laid special stress on these two words [1]—" and by co-operating in the preparation for the all-important World Economic Conference . . . in con- nection with which we hope to have the advantage also of American assistance." It was strongly emphasized that in no sense was there an intention of forming, on the one hand, an Anglo-French *bloc* against Germany, or, on the other, of creating a united European front towards America.

In order to clear up any misapprehension that might remain, an official statement was issued from 10 Downing Street on 14th July, pointing out that other Governments had been invited to adhere to the Declaration and that there was " no truth in any statement that it is applicable to the question of British debts to the United States. The use in the Declaration of the words ' European regime ' expressly excludes from its purview any questions affecting non-European countries." [2]

That such a statement was necessary may well be judged from the fact that the Accord was to be subject to a somewhat different interpretation on the other side of the Channel. M. Herriot's remarks before the Foreign Affairs and Finance Committees of the French Chamber were significant. Describing it as a revival of the *Entente Cordiale*, and as the opening of a new era in Franco-British relations, he said that in future no problem affecting the interests of the two countries would be treated separately. Its immediate consequence would be that Great Britain could not, as in 1923, undertake in future to make payments to the United States for the settlement of debts without previously consulting the French Government. A certainty, he added, of a concerted attitude was henceforth an acquired fact, which would facilitate success in the negotiations with Washington. While, in the course of a communication to Sir John Simon, referred to by the latter on 14th July, M. Herriot stated that he did not regard the initiative as a contribution towards an Anglo-French Pact, but purely as a plan of European procedure, his first statement above may be taken as a significant indication of the manner in which French policy would like the Accord to be interpreted.

While the Belgian and Italian Governments immediately

---

[1] In drafting the wording of the new Accord considerable difficulty occurred over the word *equitable*, which the British insisted on including as a gesture towards Germany and which the French wished to omit as binding their future decision at Geneva.

[2] This reassurance was emphasized by the British Ambassador, Sir Ronald Lindsay, in a personal call at the State Department in Washington on the same day.

gave their adherence to the Accord—the latter noting, without laying undue stress upon, the divergences of interpretation— and the Polish Government adhered on 18th July, the German Government was more critical. A clear interpretation of the aims of the " consultative pact "—as Germany preferred to call it—was considered essential, as also was an assurance that it would not be exploited for the formation of a " united front " against either the United States or Soviet Russia, and would not in any way limit Germany's freedom of action or the raising by her of political issues and the questions ventilated at Lausanne. Inquiries in this sense were made at the Foreign Office on 19th July.

The German Government was naturally surprised and annoyed to find a plan, which they themselves had proposed and which had been discussed and rejected in the course of the Lausanne negotiations, suddenly revived as an Anglo-French proposal without previous reference to Germany herself. Moreover, Germany was sceptical of the wording of that part of the Accord which referred to disarmament, and scented in it an Anglo- French agreement not to disarm. Their suspicions received confirmation when Sir John Simon's resolution was introduced into the Disarmament Conference on 21st July. The German delegate, Herr Nadolny, vehemently opposed the resolution as making no concession towards Germany's claim to equality, and finally voted against it when the Conference adjourned on 23rd July. A further cause of German dissatisfaction was the multilateral nature of the new Accord. The German proposal had been for a Four-Power Pact of Consultation, or at most a pact including the Locarno Powers. Since the main object of the Accord was to provide a method of discussing Germany's difficulties with her neighbours, it seemed unnecessary that all Europe should be included.

Nevertheless, Germany adhered on 26th July. Had it been possible to produce a Four-Power Pact immediately, the effect would have been better in every way and would at once have reassured the fears of Germany and Italy that they were being excluded. Such a proposition was rendered impossible by reason of the new British orientation towards France which resulted from the MacDonald–Herriot *rapprochement* at Lausanne, a change of policy which had its repercussions in various European capitals.

The first immediate effect was in Italy, where, on 20th July, Signor Grandi, Minister for Foreign Affairs, resigned from the

Cabinet. Ever since he succeeded the Duce at the Palazzo Chigi in 1929, Signor Grandi had based his foreign policy on co-operation with the League of Nations and friendship with England. The failure of the Disarmament Conference to reach any decisive degree of agreement completed the process of disillusionment, or alternatively of cynical disbelief, of Italy towards the League, and within the Fascist Party there had for some time been considerable dissatisfaction at Signor Grandi's continued belief.

The abandonment by Great Britain at Lausanne of the policy of the "clean slate" which she shared with Italy, and the consequent resuscitation of the *Entente Cordiale*, dealt a heavy blow at the Anglo-Italian friendship which Sir Austen Chamberlain had been at such pains to build up, though he himself damaged it severely in excluding Italy from the Anglo-French negotiations regarding the Naval Compromise of 1928. Now a similar situation had arisen. Italy felt that she should have been consulted in the first place in regard to the new consultative Pact, and her susceptibilities were hurt through being left out in the cold. Hence, though she adhered to the Pact on 14th July, Signor Grandi considered that his policy had failed, and that he had lost the confidence of his colleagues and his party. He therefore resigned after three years of office and was succeeded by Signor Mussolini in person.[1]

It was difficult to see what good could be served by this new Accord or Pact which roused suspicions in Germany and the United States, and cost Italy one of her, and Europe's, ablest statesmen. Why was this new product of the united sentimentality of Mr. MacDonald and M. Herriot, the same combination which produced the Geneva Protocol of 1924, necessary, since it was expressly stated that it was neither to supplement nor supplant any existing agreement ? In the Covenant of the League of Nations, the Locarno Treaties, and the Pact of Paris, the world had ample opportunity and machinery for the discussion of its problems if the will to discuss was there, and if it was not there no amount of consultative pacts would create it. A change of heart and not a multiplication of treaties was what was needed then as now.

---

[1] Signor Grandi was appointed Ambassador in London on 21st July, in succession to the late Signor Bordonaro. The appointment gave general satisfaction in England, where Signor Grandi had made himself deservedly popular during the London Conference of 1930.

6

Neither the reception which the Great Powers had accorded to the Hoover Proposals of 22nd June nor the outcome of the disarmament discussions at Lausanne gave any vestige of encouragement for a successful conclusion of the first session of the Disarmament Conference. Time had been wasted, opportunities lost, and now that the time had come to take a view of the profit and loss account of the Conference there was little to record on the credit side.

The Bureau of the Conference met on 5th July to consider the programme to be placed before the General Commission before its adjournment, and to Sir John Simon was allotted the task of putting on the best face possible and of drafting a resolution setting out all the points upon which all the Governments represented were in approximate agreement. Such a resolution, it was agreed, would form the basis for a definite programme of work for the autumn session.

If the supporters of disarmament retained any hopes that such a programme of work would include at least any material measures of armaments reduction, they must have been bitterly disappointed when the text of the resolution appeared. Sir John Simon's task was, of course, an exceedingly difficult one, since he had to produce a text which would meet with general acceptance, contain all the points on which there was general agreement, and, in spite of the fewness of these, produce nevertheless a document which registered progress. He heard statements by most of the Governments represented—on 8th July alone the delegates of eighteen States expressed their views on the Hoover plan—and received a communication from the Soviet delegation on 14th July, warning him very clearly that they would accept no resolution which did not provide for a deduction of at least one-third in existing armaments. On 20th July the text was completed and presented to the General Commission and simultaneously published. It was discussed for three days and on 23rd July adopted by 41 votes to 2, with 8 abstentions.[1]

The Preamble gave hope of something better than actually followed, for it stated that :—

" The Conference . . . profoundly convinced that the time

[1] The two negative votes were those of Germany and the U.S.S.R. The eight abstentions composed a *bloc* led by Italy, and included Albania, Afghanistan, Austria, Bulgaria, China, Hungary, and Turkey.

has come when all nations of the world must adopt substantial and comprehensive measures of disarmament . . . firmly determined to achieve a first decisive step involving a substantial reduction of armaments . . . welcoming heartily the initiative taken by the President of the United States of America . . . decides forthwith and unanimously . . . (1) that a substantial reduction of world armaments shall be effected to be applied by a general Convention alike to land, naval, and air armaments ; (2) that a primary objective shall be to reduce the means of attack."

There followed the " Conclusions of the First Phase of the Conference ", and these may be summarized thus :—

(1) Air attack against the civilian population shall be absolutely prohibited. (2) The High Contracting Parties shall agree as between themselves that all bombardment from the air shall be abolished, subject to agreement with regard to measures to be adopted to render effective the observance of this rule.

These measures shall include a limitation by number and a restriction by characteristics of military aircraft and the submission of civil aircraft to regulation and full publicity.

The Conference agrees that (a) all heavy land artillery between limits to be determined shall be limited in number. (b) The limitation of calibre of land artillery shall be fixed by the Convention. But different maxima may be fixed (i) for guns in coastal defence, (ii) guns in fortress defensive systems, (iii) mobile land guns.

The maximum unit tonnage of tanks shall be limited.

Chemical, bacteriological, and incendiary warfare shall be prohibited.

A Permanent Disarmament Commission shall be established.

The Bureau was requested to continue its work during the adjournment of the General Committee, and to draft texts concerning questions on which agreement had already been reached. The first of these questions related to effectives, and a strict limitation and a real reduction of effectives were to be brought about, taking into consideration President Hoover's proposals in this regard.

On resumption, the Conference was to decide on a system of limitation and publicity of expenditure on national defence.

The Bureau was to set up a special Committee to submit proposals to the Conference in regard to regulations to be applied to the trade in and private and State manufacture of armaments.

The Conference invited the Powers parties to the naval treaties of Washington and London to confer together as to further measures of naval reduction which might become a part of the general programme of disarmament. The Conference further invited the naval Powers not signatory to the above treaties to consider the degree of naval limitation they were prepared to accept.

Rules of international law would be formulated in connection with the provisions relating to the prohibition of chemical warfare and bombing from the air.

The Bureau would keep delegations informed of the progress of its work and was to fix the date of the next meeting of the General Commission with one month's notice. The Bureau would meet about 19th September, 1932, and the General Commission not later than four months after that date.

The Conference recommended the Governments to renew for a period of four months from 1st November, 1932, the armaments truce provided for in the resolution of the League Assembly of 29th September, 1932.

A more wholesale admission of failure and incompetence it would be difficult to find. After six months' deliberations the only concrete achievement of the Conference was the agreement to abolish chemical and bacteriological warfare, an agreement which had been reached as early as 1925. The true and lamentable nature of the Resolution was clearly reflected in the speeches of the representatives of those countries who voted against it or abstained from voting at all.

For Germany the Resolution of July spelt nothing but disappointment and defeat. The seven years which had elapsed between the opening meeting of the first session of the Preparatory Disarmament Commission on 18th May, 1926, and the closing of the first session of the Disarmament Conference, had seen no progress towards meeting the German claims for equality of status, and Herr Nadolny found himself in the same position as Count Bernstorff when in December, 1930, he rejected the Draft Convention on behalf of Germany.

In his speech to the General Commission of the Conference, Herr Nadolny outlined once more the position of Germany, pointing out that much goodwill and courage had been needed for the decision to participate at all in the Conference after the Preparatory Disarmament Commission had adopted Article 53 of its Draft Convention, which refused equal rights to Germany and which intended to perpetuate against the whole world the exceptional regime imposed upon her by the disarmament clauses of the Treaty of Versailles. Despite this, however, the German Delegation had constantly endeavoured to arrive at an understanding with the other Delegations without regard to its own sensibility or prestige, it had collaborated in all measures adopted by the Conference, and had itself made positive proposals and had carefully avoided differences of opinion which might offend susceptibilities. In a word, they had done all that was humanly possible to co-operate with other Delegations and to expedite the work of the Conference, which, after all, was also a Conference for the liquidation of the past, having as its task the ending of a further chapter of post-war history which should have been ended long ago.

Herr Nadolny went on to review the many proposals that had recently been placed before the Conference, those submitted by President Hoover, by the British Government, by the Italians, and by the Government of the U.S.S.R., all of which had awakened great hopes throughout the world, in which the German people had shared. But against all goodwill, and against the excellent intentions which had found expression at the Conference, negative forces had arisen in a regrettable manner and had so far impeded the work by tenacious counter-effect in details. The general public of the world, and particularly of Germany, was convinced that the process of exchanging opinions, of preparations, and of preliminary work must have an end at last and that it was high time for the Conference to enter into a period of practical results. There was little hope that the Resolution was capable of initiating such a period, for, after all, any achievement that it might record had already been adopted in the Resolution of 22nd April, when the Conference had decided on the principle of qualitative disarmament, and had done little towards taking account of this principle. The German Delegation, therefore, was not in a position to regard the Resolution as satisfactory from the point of view of the disarmament measures contemplated by it, and Germany could never fix her signature to a Convention which was not based upon the principle of juridical equality. The German Government had, therefore, commissioned its Delegation to make a final declaration as follows :—

" The German Government is ready to continue its collaboration in the work of the Disarmament Conference in order to contribute by all means in its power to the endeavours now being made to achieve a really decisive step towards general disarmament within the meaning of Article 8 of the Covenant. Nevertheless, its collaboration is only possible when the subsequent work of the Conference is carried out on the basis of a clear and definite recognition of the principle of equality of rights as between nations. Equality of rights is the fundamental principle upon which the League of Nations and the community of States in general rests.

" If the Conference were to draw up rules and principles for general disarmament of States excluding at the same time Germany or other States, and subjecting any State to an exceptional and discriminatory regime, such an attitude would be incompatible with the feelings of national honour and international justice. It would also be contrary to the treaty rights which Germany holds and which it cannot abandon. To its great regret the German Government notes that the present Resolution takes no account of that view. The work of the first phase of the Conference, and in particular the conversations of the last few days, have, on the contrary, given the impression that this necessary condition has not yet been understood or accepted by all Governments. The German Government is of opinion that this uncertainty regarding one of the fundamental questions of the problem of disarmament makes it impossible for useful work to be done. It must therefore press for its doubts to be dispelled by the recognition without delay of equality of all States as regards national security and the enforcement of all provisions of the convention.

" So far as the various questions which arise out of the application of the principle of equality of rights might need to be investigated, the German Government is ready to enter at once into negotiations with the Governments concerned. The German Government must, however, point out at once that it cannot undertake to continue its collaboration if a satisfactory solution on this decisive point for Germany is not reached by the time the Conference resumes its work." [1]

Almost in these same terms had Count Bernstorff rejected the Draft Convention in December, 1930, but with this difference ; at that time the nationalist movement in Germany was only in its awakening period ; but it had become firmly established and fiercely combative of the unequal position which Germany occupied. In 1930 the spirit of Herr Stresemann's policy was still visible ; in 1932 it had vanished, and its place had been taken by a new spirit antagonistic, implacable, and desperate.

The position was not improved by the next event, which occurred in Paris on the following day (24th July). M. Herriot

---

[1] This declaration was made in the nature of a warning. The first withdrawal of Germany from the Conference was not actually effected until 14th September, when Baron von Neurath informed Mr. Henderson, on the occasion of the meeting of the Bureau, that, as no " satisfactory solution " had been found, Germany could no longer collaborate in the work of the Conference. See below, p. 67.

had experienced considerable difficulty in balancing the French Budget, and had met with serious opposition from the Left in regard to the military estimates, and in particular to those which provided for the cost of completing and maintaining the new chain of fortresses which France had erected along her Eastern frontier. In an attempt to justify this expenditure, M. Lamoureux, the *Rapporteur General* for the Budget, had pointed to the fact that these defences had achieved for France the security which she had fought for so long. The work of construction, by its extent and by the technical difficulties which had had to be overcome, was without precedent in the history of the nations. The German army, he declared, be it never so powerful, brave and tenacious, would break, should the occasion arise, on those passive defences. They were proof against the heaviest and most efficient artillery. The artillery and machine-gun fire they could produce were so well combined and so powerful that no adversary could resist it. This system of fortification thus gave to France the fullest security against an invasion similar to that of 1914. The very nature and object of the fortifications illustrated the defensive attitude of France.

True though these claims might be, they were at complete variance with the attitude adopted by the French Delegation at the Disarmament Conference, which had consistently pleaded the continued insecurity of France as the reason for the impossibility of further disarmament.

It was impossible both for reasons of policy and of human nature for the German Government to allow to slip such an opportumty as that presented by M. Lamoureux' declaration, and on 26th July Lieut.-General von Schleicher, Minister of Defence, took full advantage of it in a broadcast address transmitted by all German stations. The speech, lightened by blithe attacks on France and supported by quotations from Mr. Lloyd George, gave blunt intimation that Germany would look after her own security if equality in arms were denied her. The naked fact, said General von Schleicher, was that " no other European land possessed in so small a degree the security for which, paradoxical though it sounded, precisely the strongest military Power in the world incessantly clamoured."

" But sometimes people in France let the cat out of the bag," said the General, and proceeded to quote at length M. Lamoureux' statement. " Compare this Report," he continued, " with the attitude and proposals of the French Delegation in Geneva ; international courtesy forbids me to characterize this attitude,"

Continuing, General von Schleicher said that there were two ways by which Germany could attain her security ; either the other Powers could disarm to Germany's level, as they were legally and morally bound to do, or, alternatively, Germany could organize her armed forces by reorganization, not by extension —*umbauen nicht ausbauen*—so that they would give at least a certain degree of security, and he wished in connection with the German declaration at Geneva to leave no doubt that they would take this course if full security and equality of rights were further withheld from them. He concluded with a wholehearted eulogium of military virtues, appealing to the youth of Germany to school itself by physical exercises, by enduring hardships and by voluntary discipline, and thereby conquer *der innere Schweinhund*.

On the following day, 27th July, the Chancellor, Herr von Papen, in an interview given to the United Press, declared that Germany insisted upon both moral equality and the right to possess modern military implements.

As may be imagined, the reaction in France to these two statements was one of grave concern. The French Ambassador was instructed to ask for an explanation, but was informed by the Foreign Minister, Baron von Neurath, that General von Schleicher had expressed the united views of the entire German Cabinet. In the French Press there were revived all the old mistrusts of Germany, though there is doubt as to whether this had ever subsided, but in some quarters there was almost relief that at last the mask was off. " Von Schleicher's trenchant words," said the *Echo de Paris*, " are more welcome since they cut short the equivocations which the representatives of the United States and Great Britain have tried to develop." The *Journal des Débats* declared " we are back in the same situation as that of 1914, aggravated this time by frightful demoralization in the international sphere " ; and *l'Intransigeant* averred that " Germany's leaders grip the masses with the idea of a war of revenge, and they dare to give their preparations for attack an appearance of self-defence against our aggression ". Other journals, too, expressed their disillusion in the new turn of German politics. " General Schleicher," cried *le Temps*, " has publicly proclaimed the determination of Germany to repudiate the military clauses of the Treaty of Versailles and to re-arm." *Le Journal* preferred " this frankness to Stresemann's deceitfulness ; at last we know where we stand ". *L'Homme Libre* asked derisively if there were any countries " which still entertain

illusions as to Germany's desire for peace ", and pointed out
that they should now be enlightened and would have no excuse
if they did not take action in consequence. Finally, the *Echo
de Paris* phrased the French case in a nutshell, " Germany wishes
to be able to do in the full light of day that which she has been
doing in secret for the past ten years."

The official reaction to the German declarations of policy may
be found in the speeches delivered by M. Lebrun, President of
the French Republic, and Marshal Petain at the inauguration of
the great ossuary at Douaumont on the battlefield of Verdun
on 7th August. " France," said M. Lebrun, " must not be asked
to stop thinking of her security so long as the spirit of peace is
not present everywhere " ; and the Marshal added, " let us not
abandon the means of defending our soil for the sake of an ideal
of peace, the practical application of which is still uncertain."

Just so much reliance does France place upon her elaborate
Eastern defences in a time of crisis, and President Lebrun's
words are merely a re-echo of those spoken at Nice by his predecessor, M. Doumergue, in April, 1931. The only change brought
about in the national attitudes of France and Germany as
a result of the first session of the Disarmament Conference was
a hardening of the several positions which they had taken up
since the Peace Conference.

7

It was not in Germany alone that there was dissatisfaction
over the work of the first session of the Disarmament Conference.
Both Italy, the Soviet Union, and the United States expressed
their grave disappointment at the small degree of achievement
which had been attained. Analysing the Simon Resolution point
by point, M. Litvinoff admitted that it contained only one concrete
recommendation—the prohibition of chemical and bacteriological
warfare—a decision already contained in the Geneva Protocol
of 1925 ; on all other fundamental questions the Resolution did
not contain one concrete decision either for qualitative or
quantitative disarmament, and, in effect, went no further than
the Resolution of 22nd April. The whole essence of the Simon
Resolution was to postpone the taking of any definite decision
for a further six months, and the whole history of the problem
of disarmament under the auspices of the League of Nations
had been one of a continuous series of postponements, pro-
crastinations and references to private negotiations and private

conferences. It was high time, he urged, that disarmament ceased to play the part of a tennis ball buffeted from one commission or sub-commission to another, from one conference and from one session to another. In six months' time the reply of the Government would be exactly the same as to-day, and there was no need to postpone it ; for this reason the Soviet delegation could not accept the Resolution.

Even more trenchant were the comments of General Balbo on behalf of Italy, who declared that it was not enough to lay down principles which were in themselves inadequate, and that the Conference had made no marked progress towards the effective attainment of disarmament. He then made the following declaration :—

> " The Fascist Government now deem it necessary to state that it is not enough for the Powers here assembled to make a declaration of goodwill couched in general terms in order to make an impression on the peoples of the world, who are seeking and waiting definite and positive results. The Italian Delegation, after having sincerely and unsparingly collaborated to secure the triumph of those principles which, within the general framework of armaments, would have enabled the Conference to secure positive results, is compelled to state that the effort made has been a vain one and entirely inadequate when compared with the wishes and hopes of the world."

But this did not conclude the Italian attack on the work of the Conference. In an article in the *Popolo d'Italia* for 31st July, General Balbo made a caustic criticism of the League in general and a condemnation of the Disarmament Conference in particular, defending Italy, Germany and the Soviet Union as against " the dominating Powers at Geneva, Great Britain, France, and the United States of America ".

The League, said he, was no more than " a limited liability company under the control of England, France, and indirectly America ", and Italy might leave the Disarmament Conference, since all decisions taken at Geneva bore the trade mark of this group. The Conference was a perfect example of this, and amongst the members of its Bureau there was not an Italian, a German, or a Russian, or " any Delegate suspected of friendliness towards any independent Power ".

He claimed that while Italy began with a frank call to disarm, France, Britain, and the United States had no intention of disarming, or, at most, desired only relative disarmament, such as would strengthen their individual decisions or weaken those

of the others.   Before coming to the Conference Britain and the
United States had increased their naval armaments in view of
possible reductions, and France had strengthened her land
armaments so that the premise of the Conference was " an
even madder race to arm ".

The opposition of some ten Powers to the Simon Resolution
had, he added, been promoted by Italy's example, and the
so-called High Contracting Powers must take note of this precedent if they wished to keep alive " that monstrous factory
of delusions and traps for the ingenuous which goes by the
name of the Disarmament Conference ".

In the United States the worst possible impression had been
made by the reception accorded to President Hoover's
proposals of 22nd June and the failure to embody any of them
in the July Resolution.   On the same day that the proposals
were made, a report reached Washington that, in the private
conversations at Geneva, the French delegates had brought
forward proposals for the conclusion of a security pact, and the
State Department accordingly issued an announcement the
next day that in no circumstances would the Government
consider entering such an agreement.   The failure of Geneva
to make any progress towards disarmament, however, impressed
both the President and the Secretary of State with the necessity
for going as far as possible in the direction of meeting the French
view, with the result that Mr. Stimson made a definite gesture
of collaboration in the speech he made before the Council on
Foreign Relations on 8th August.   Before dealing with this, it
may be of interest to notice that both the Democratic Party
Convention and the Republican Convention published their
programmes in June, and that they both included among the
planks of their platforms a proposal that measures should be
enacted by Congress authorizing the Government to call or
participate in an international conference in case the Kellogg
Treaty was violated.   Also, on 11th August, Mr. Hoover claimed
that the Government, under his administration, "had given the
leadership in transforming the Kellogg Treaty from inspiring
the outlawry of war to an organized instrument for peaceful
settlements, backed by a definite mobilization of world public
opinion against aggression ", and he went on—

" We shall, under the spirit of that Pact, consult with other
nations in times of emergency to promote world peace.   We shall
enter no agreements committing us to any future course of action,
or which call for the use of force to preserve peace."

This last statement may be read as an addition to and a rounding off, primarily for the benefit of France, of the detailed and circumstantial definition of American foreign policy given by Mr. Stimson in his speech before the Council on Foreign Relations on 8th August. In that speech the Secretary of State described the implications of the Kellogg Treaty as understood in the United States, and, no doubt with the desire to assist the work at Geneva, went as far as he could do towards meeting the French thesis regarding security and the necessity for providing means for dealing with violations of the Kellogg Treaty.

The Treaty, said Mr. Stimson, had changed the whole doctrine of neutrality, and it had also provided a means for mobilizing the opinion of the world against war. Although there was no provision in it for consultation between neutrals, consultation was implicit both in the Treaty itself and in the use which had been made of it in the Far Eastern disputes of 1929 and 1931. Not only this, but it was a Treaty which contained definite promises and conferred benefits, while those who accepted it accepted a positive obligation to direct national policy in accordance with its pledge.

After reviewing the steps taken by the U.S. Government in doing its share to mobilize world opinion in connection with the Sino-Japanese dispute, the Secretary of State said that another phase which followed this development of the Treaty was that consultation between the signatories, when faced with the threat of its violation, became inevitable, since " any effective invocation of the power of world opinion postulates discussion and consultation " ; and that the American people subscribed to this view was made clear by the fact that each of the platforms recently adopted by the two great party con-ventions contained plans endorsing the principle of consultation. Such a view of the Treaty had the advantage that it combined the readiness to co-operate for peace and justice, " while at the same time it preserves the independence of judgment and the flexibility of action upon which our people have always insisted ".

The reception given to this pronouncement in France was a good one, M. Herriot taking occasion to inform the Press of his approval of the thesis that the Kellogg Treaty should not be regarded as a mere declaration of good intention, but as an obligatory instrument. At the same time the fact was not lost upon French opinion that both Mr. Stimson and Mr. Hoover

had made special reference to the need for preserving independence of judgment and of avoiding any agreement committing
their country to any future course of action. The French
Government, M. Herriot assured the Press, would examine
means of ensuring that the solemn engagements of the Treaty
should not be transgressed, and he pigeon-holed Mr. Stimson's
remarks for future reference.[1]

8

Thus at the close of the first session of the Disarmament
Conference the position was infinitely worse than at the
beginning. Disarmament was further away than ever, Germany
had left the Conference and, in another sphere, Japan was
openly defying the League of Nations.

At best the whole thing had been a race against time and the
growth of Nationalism in Germany, and the Conference had
merely figured as an " also ran ". By their refusal to face facts
and reach an agreement on the question of equality with
Dr. Brüning, the statesmen of Europe had ruined what slight
chances had remained of limiting and reducing armaments, and
had opened the way for the final tragedy of the Nazi revolution.
The Conference was moribund in July, 1932, and all subsequent
attempts to resuscitate it were only the desperate attempts of
physicians to prolong existence.

[1] It was to these remarks that M. Herriot made reference in the French
Plan of November, 1932. See below, p. 77.

CHAPTER V

THE STRUGGLE FOR EQUALITY: PART I

1

When Germany issued her solemn warning to the Conference on 23rd July she did not close the door to subsequent negotiation, and an agreement was reached between Herr Nadolny and M. Herriot that at the earliest possible moment the question of equality should be taken up between the French and German Foreign Offices through the usual diplomatic channels. The German Government still had hopes that the disarmament conversations which had taken place at Lausanne would bear fruit.

M. Herriot urged especially that the question should not be raised during the month of August, in view of the fact that he had certain pressing domestic questions to deal with, but suggested an early date in September. As a prelude to this, unofficial conversations took place in Berlin in the closing days of August, when M. André Fribourg, *rapporteur* of the Foreign Affairs Committee of the Chamber, discussed the question with the Chancellor and General von Schleicher. The negotiations were, however, raised to an official status when on 29th August the German Foreign Minister, Baron von Neurath, in the presence of the *Reichswehr* Minister, handed an *aide-mémoire* to the French Ambassador in Berlin.[1] This contained three main points upon which the German Government insisted as the only conditions on which they would attend the forthcoming meeting of the Bureau of the Disarmament Conference, the general work of which was strongly criticized :—

(1) The recognition of the principle of equality in arms.
(2) The reduction of the *Reichswehr* period of service from twelve to six years.
(3) The formation of a volunteer reserve something akin to a territorial force.

[1] All documents to which reference is made in this chapter will be found in *Documents on International Affairs, 1932*, pp. 183–233. Much of the chapter is taken from a memorandum prepared by the present author for the Information Department of the Royal Institute of International Affairs.

The reasons for these three conditions, which, it will be seen, were the same as the proposals put forward by Dr. Brüning to Mr. MacDonald and Mr. Stimson on 26th April, were as follows:—

(a) The financial position alone in Germany forbade her increasing her armaments to any great extent, but the strong nationalist feeling in the country demanded the right to do so if she so desired, partly by reason of the dictates of *amour propre* and partly on account of a genuine feeling of insecurity.

(b) The twelve-year period of service in the *Reichswehr* had been condemned by military experts in many countries as impracticable, and the large number of suicides in the German army of men who were serving the last six years of their period had been put forward as a significant proof of this fact.

(c) The formation of a volunteer reserve was mainly for internal reasons. It would enable the German Government to remove the monopoly of uniformed followers from the private armies of the political parties, and it was hoped thereby to reduce greatly the number of their adherents.

The Reply of the French Government to the German *aide-mémoire* was made on 11th September. It did not reply *ad seriatim* to the points raised by the German Government, but developed along more general lines. After recapitulating the labours of France in the cause of disarmament, the Reply stated that the aim of the French Government was to arrive at a Convention which would give the nations real guarantees of peace, and, if Germany wished to co-operate with France and with other States to negotiate for and discuss such a Convention, " these discussions would make it possible to decide what the statute of Germany should be within a general statute of peace, placed under the protection of arbitration and supervision ".

Turning to the juridical aspect of the question, the French Government could not accept the argument that the Disarmament Convention must be substituted *ipso jure* for the Versailles Treaty, and that no special conditions be laid down for Germany. There was no clause either in Part V of the Treaty or in the Covenant by virtue of which a general limitation of armaments should involve the lapse of the permanent stipulations of the Treaty. As regards the content of the Convention, the French Government would regulate its progress in the direction of disarmament in proportion as it found guarantees in the general organization of peace, and the declaration made at Geneva on 22nd July was quoted on the subject of the creation of an international organization assuring security to and imposing identical obligations on all. The French proposal for an international force was still open to discussion, and suggestions were invited from other States.

The Note then dealt with the German claims as to changes in the organization of the army, including the establishment of a special militia. It was evident from the pronouncements of the German Defence Minister published in the Press, that Germany was demanding all the weapons prohibited to her by the Treaty: "there can be no doubt: rearmament is proposed." But this would at once spread to Austria, Hungary, and the other defeated States, and thus the whole problem of Central and Eastern Europe would be raised. All Europe was, therefore, strictly affected by the question put to France, who could not undertake to give an isolated answer to so vast a problem. And the whole of the naval Statute of the Powers would be involved as well.[1]

If Germany persisted in her intention, concerted action would have to be taken by all the Powers signatories of the Pact of Confidence, and the necessary negotiations would also be dominated by the Versailles Treaty, since, by Article 164, Germany undertook, after she became a member of the League, that the armaments fixed would remain in force until they were modified by the Council of the League, whose decision she undertook to observe strictly in this respect. Thus the League was the sole judge, and France was determined to remain faithful, whatever happened, to its Covenant.

Finally, it was pointed out that France could not by isolated negotiations run the risk of infringing upon the rights of the United States. The Peace Treaty signed by the U.S.A. with Germany on 25th August, 1921, gave America the benefit of the dispositions of Part V of the Treaty.

The tone of the French Note was such as to lead the German Foreign Minister to inform the French Ambassador in Berlin on 16th September that his Government, while noting with regret that the French Government took a divergent view of the problem both in its elements and in its consequences and in no essential point made any advance towards the German stand-point, was unable to promise itself any progress in the matter from a continuation of the exchange of opinion by means of Notes, but was ready to enter into any exchange of views by means of diplomatic conversations.

Two days previously, on 14th September, Baron von Neurath had also addressed a letter to Mr. Arthur Henderson, as President

[1] *Serait mis en cause.*

of the Disarmament Conference, informing him of Germany's decision not to take part in the meetings of the Bureau of the Conference which opened on 21st September. The view of the German Government, he said, was that there was only one solution to the problem of disarmament, namely,

> " That all States should be subjected to the same rules and principles in respect of disarmament, and that no discriminatory exceptional system should exist in the case of any of them. Germany cannot be expected to take part in the negotiations with regard to the measures of disarmament to be laid down in the Convention until it is established that the solutions which may be found are also to apply to Germany."

The letter continued with an official intimation to the President of the diplomatic exchanges by which the German Government had endeavoured to clear up the question of equality of rights. He was also informed that, " unfortunately, it must be stated that the German efforts have not hitherto led to any satisfactory results."

Mr. Henderson replied to the German letter on 18th September, and defended at length the Resolution of the Disarmament Conference passed on 23rd July against the criticisms of the German Government, which, he considered, prejudged the final issue. The Resolution, he said, in no way prejudiced the attitude of the Conference towards any more comprehensive measures of disarmament, or towards the political proposals submitted by various Delegations and that, therefore, the form, extent, and scope of the ultimate Convention were still undetermined, and remain to be treated at the forthcoming session of the Conference and its Committees. He concluded with an appeal to the German Government to reconsider its decision and to resume its participation at the earliest possible moment in the work of the Bureau, particularly as the prolonged absence of Germany from its deliberations might seriously affect the cause of general disarmament.

The Bureau, however, met on 21st September without German representation, and Mr. Henderson drew attention to the correspondence which had passed between himself and the German Foreign Minister. At his suggestion, discussion of this matter was postponed until a reply had been received from the German Government to Mr. Henderson's letter of 18th September. But Baron von Neurath gave it to be understood that he did not intend to make a reply, and that, in fact, Germany would not return to the Conference or its subsidiary bodies unless at the invitation of the Allied Powers and until satisfaction had been given in the matter of equality. The position remained unchanged as a result of conversations between Sir John Simon and Baron von Neurath, and between the latter and Mr. Henderson at Geneva on 25th September during the meeting of the Council, and, when all three left for their own capitals on 27th September, there was little reason to believe that progress had been made towards the resumption of German co-operation in the work of the Conference.

2

As vitally interested parties and by virtue of the Pact of Consultation of 13th July, 1932, the Italian and British Governments were kept closely informed of the progress of the Franco-German negotiations. In each case the texts of Notes were communicated before their general publication and the closest contact was maintained. In both countries it was felt incumbent upon the Government to make clear their position with regard to the Franco-German dispute, though this took a different form in each case. Signor Mussolini contributed an article which appeared in the *Börsen Courier* and the *Sunday Times* of 11th September, in which he gave a considerable measure of support to the German case. Ever since Germany became a member of the League, he asserted, there was universal recognition of her juridical equality, while Locarno also signified that Germany and France were placed on the same level. If the general standard of armaments was not lowered through the efforts of the Disarmament Conference, Germany was within her rights in increasing her own armaments. And,

"in order to avoid Germany's absence from the Conference, her right to juridical equality in the matter of armaments must inevitably be recognized."

The article concluded with an appeal to Germany to make " a moderate application of this equality of rights ".

The world, however, was anxiously awaiting the expression of opinion of His Britannic Majesty's Government, and this was defined in a statement published on 19th September. The British Note is an example of close reasoning based entirely on the legal aspects of a case. His Majesty's Government, it said, considered that it was unfortunate that a political controversy of such magnitude should arise at a moment when it was so necessary that attention and energy should not be diverted from efforts which were being undertaken, and which were so urgently needed, to restore the productive and commercial prosperity of the world. There was grave disadvantage in forcing the question of status to the front at the present moment, and, " in view of Germany's economic difficulties, the initiation of acute controversy in the political field at this moment must be considered unwise, and, in view of the concessions recently granted to Germany by her creditors, must be accounted particularly untimely."

The statement continued to the effect that no countenance or encouragement could be given to the disregard of Treaty obligations, and the British Government could not entertain as the correct legal construction of the Treaty of Versailles that Germany was legally entitled to abrogate Part V of the Treaty by any Disarmament Convention to be concluded, or by failure to conclude any Convention at all.

> " If the Preamble to Part V of the Treaty of Versailles is looked at, it will be seen that the Allied Powers, in requiring these limitations on Germany's armaments, had in mind the object or reason therein indicated. That object or reason was to render possible the initiation of a general limitation of the armaments of all nations.
> *To state what the object or aim of a stipulation is, is a very different thing from making the successful fulfilment of the object the condition of the stipulation.*[1] Still less is it possible to deduce as a matter of legal interpretation of the Treaty that the manner in which the object—the general limitation of armaments—was to be fulfilled was to be precisely the same as the manner in which Germany's armaments had been limited by Part V, for the only indication in the Treaty of the manner in which general disarmament is to be brought about is to be found in the very general words of Article 8 of the Covenant. The correct position under the Treaty of Versailles is that Part V is still binding, and can only cease to be binding by agreement."

The British Government hoped that a considerable and valuable measure of disarmament might yet be achieved at Geneva. The objects aimed at were, in the case of the more heavily-armed Powers, the largest possible reduction ; and, in the case of lightly-armed Powers, at any rate no material increase. They, therefore,

> " Conceive the object of the Conference to be to frame a Disarmament Convention upon the principle that each State adopts

---

[1] Author's italics.

for itself, in agreement with others, a limitation which is self-imposed and freely entered into as part of the mutual obligations of the signatories to one another. There will thus be, as a result of the Convention, no distinction of status ; everyone's armaments will be controlled by the same process ; and limitations which have already been prescribed by existing Treaties—such as the various Peace.Treaties and the Naval Treaties of Washington and London —will, save so far as they are modified by mutual consent, reappear in the voluntary and comprehensive compact about to be negotiated at Geneva. It will then be this last named document which is the effective obligation binding upon all."

The statement ended with a warning that a " desirable consummation cannot be obtained by peremptory challenge or by withdrawal from deliberations which are about to be resumed ; it can only be reached by patient discussion through the medium of conference between the States concerned ".

It was the purpose of the British Note to dispose finally of any legal claim on the part of Germany for unilateral abrogation of the Treaty of Versailles. At the same time it was hoped that the views of the British Government might provide the bridge between the French and German points of view. In effect, however, the Note was warmly received only in the French Press ; in Germany it acted as a " cold douche " on a public opinion which had hoped for greater sympathy, whilst in Great Britain there have been few instances in which a British statement of policy has met with so cool and critical a reception. It was felt by many that, whereas Europe had looked for a lead, she had in fact been treated to a sermon.

In the days immediately following the despatch of the French Reply to the original German aide-mémoire of 20th August M. Herriot had revived, in veiled references, the suggestion of the existence of a French dossier of German violations of Part V of the Treaty of Versailles. This, it was hinted, might be made public in the event of continued German intransigency, and M. Herriot's speech on Sunday, 25th September, was looked forward to with anxiety and expectancy on this account. When, however, the speech was made it contained no mention of the dossier, but though it differed in some small respects from previous French declarations of policy regarding disarmament, it consisted in the main of a restatement of the well-known principle that France could only disarm in proportion as her security was guaranteed, and that the guarantee France most desired was an international force controlled and operated by the League of Nations.

With regard to the German problem, M. Herriot said that the French Government noted with pleasure that they were not alone in declaring that a rearmament of Germany would be a beginning of a return to the old folly.   Rearmament was certainly at stake, and there were abundant proofs of this apart from eloquent demonstrations.   For example, the German Decree of 13th September organized the training of the young in such a way as to make them fit to bear arms, and it was one of the saddest features of the present times that the young, who should be able to profit by the terrible experience of their elders, were trained in habits contrary to moral disarmament. What hypocrisy it was to talk of moral disarmament while moulding the finest forces of life to the most sinister designs of death.   France, at least, could call the world to witness that she was free from this contagion and that her national education was directed to other ends.[1]

But, continued M. Herriot, the memories of Prussia's policy after Jena were still with them.   The recent German demands, which some might consider reasonable, coincided with the writings of military technicians who rejected the creed of Geneva and sneered at the distinction between aggressive and defensive warfare.[2]

The general impression conveyed by these writings and utterances was that Germany sought to organize a very powerful modern army capable of aggression, and France must take her stand for the present on strict respect for the Versailles Treaty and the Covenant.

M. Herriot's speech was merely an elaboration of the more curt statement made by M. Paul-Boncour on 11th September in the course of the commemoration celebrations of the victory of the Marne.   France, he said, would not allow herself to be deprived of the weapons she justly needed to defend her frontiers and to place her territory beyond the risk of devastation anew. She was not going to allow herself to be deprived of her victory, nor would she allow its meaning to be falsified.   France was determined to uphold peace, but would not suffer other nations to rearm and put her under the obligation of rearming herself.

[1] It should not be forgotten that no country has brought the military training of children and youths to a higher pitch of perfection than France under the Bill for the organization of the nation in time of war, which was sponsored through the Chamber in 1927 by the Socialist leader, M. Paul-Boncour, later M. Herriot's Minister of War.

[2] This, presumably, referred to General von Schleicher's statement that the weapons of aggression had suddenly transformed themselves into defensive weapons during the experts' conversations at Geneva.

There was a particular reason why France did not wish to incur any further military commitments, for merely by the inevitable decrease of population a substantial reduction of her military strength was being automatically brought about. France [1] would, in 1933, enter on a five-year period during which the direct effects of the comparative sterility of the war-years would make themselves evident. During 1933 the potential mothers born in 1915 would attain marriageable age at 18, and their diminished numbers would be reflected in fewer births during the coming twelve months. In 1935 the pre-destined soldiers born in 1915 would reach conscript age, but in such diminished numbers that the year was expected to reveal a drop of something like 100,000 in new effectives. It was estimated that the decrease in population directly due to " wartime sterility " during the period 1933–8 would total 1,200,000 units, giving an annual shortage of about 120,000 of each sex.

Considerations such as these contributed materially to the already formidable state of nervousness in which France found herself, and imbued French statesmen with an added zest to maintain for their country the superior position accorded her by the Treaty of Versailles. There seemed to be ample ground for agreement with General von Schleicher that " a solemn Papal Mass had been said for disarmament by the Powers, who firmly mean to persevere in the seven deadly sins of armament competition ".

The French policy and standpoint, as disclosed in these remarks of the Premier and the Minister for War, were not allowed to pass unchallenged in Germany.

On his return on 27th September from Neudeck, where he had conferred with the Reichs-President, Herr von Papen, in an interview given to the Wolff Agency, replied to M. Herriot's speech which he characterized as " unhelpful ", rendering, as it did, any understanding more difficult and confirming the completely negative interpretation of the French Note.

> " The question," said the Chancellor, " is not German disarmament, but the fulfilment of the disarmament promises of the other Powers. There is no question of German rearmament, but of German equality of status and the treatment of Germany at the Disarmament Conference on a footing of equality. . . . Our practical demands, which are very wrongly suspected of amounting to rearmament, mean nothing more than that we—naturally within the framework of the Convention—demand the same liberty to adjust our armaments to our social and national needs as is

[1] See *The Economist*, 13th August, 1932.

possessed by every other country. We demand that the same yardstick be applied to us in the matter of armament factors as to others."

The Chancellor continued that Germany had never asked to arm herself to the same extent as France and other States, but was striving for the equalization of armaments by means of a reduction of the general level. " In spite of its smallness the *Reichswehr* is to be accounted as an army of aggression, and all weapons in our hands are to be looked upon as aggressive weapons, while the mighty forces of other countries apparently serve merely the purpose of defence. We are expected to be satisfied with the formulae of legal security, while other countries keep the greater part of their enormous military armaments." The German claims, which were based not least upon Article 8 of the Covenant, demanded that its provision should apply in equal measure to all countries, and it was absolutely impossible that within the Commonwealth of the League the rights of nations should be divided into two different categories. Equality alone was the foundation of peace and of that moral disarmament of which so much was heard.

In conclusion, he said :—

" Germany is ready now as before, to accept any solution of the disarmament problem which is compatible with her honour and her security. Germany has disarmed, she waited patiently for twelve years before the Disarmament Conference at length assembled, she cannot stand by and watch the disarmament idea being falsified at that Conference by the false assessment of the disarmament factor and the application of two different yard-sticks to the individual States.

"We do not demand special rights for ourselves, but merely the same treatment as all other States. We do not demand a raising of armament level, but the disarmament of others by the same methods as are laid down for us. The pacification of Europe can never be attained if the attempt is made to degrade individual States to the position of countries of inferior status."

Herr von Papen's speech stood out in marked contrast to the blunt and unadorned pronouncements of General von Schleicher. Germany's case on moral grounds was a very strong one, but it requires only a comparison of the speeches of M. Herriot and Herr von Papen to recognize the almost unbridgeable chasm which separated the French and German points of view.

3

In an attempt to break the deadlock between France and Germany the British Government on 4th October issued

the *status quo*. The *Berliner Börsen Courier* described the British proposals as " certainly a step forward, but for the time being only a step ", but the *Vossische Zeitung* went further than this, and explained that the British plan intended to give satisfaction to the French security wishes, not by new treaties, but by a moral undertaking of the European States. " No reasonable person in Germany," it added, " intends to change untenable boundaries by the use of arms. Already, in the Treaty concluded with Poland at Locarno, the German Government has renounced any use of force. It would probably be possible to confirm this promise once again in an unmistakable manner." The *Berliner Tageblatt* regarded the new proposals as " already an essential progress because Sir John Simon did not speak merely on his own behalf, but undoubtedly made use of certain results of his conversation with Mr. Norman Davis and with the French and Italian Governments ".

On the whole, however, German opinion, though welcoming the progress made, reserved its final decision until the official statement which it was known Sir John Simon intended to make before the Bureau of the Disarmament Conference.

It was at this moment that a further contribution was made by the German Government. Beyond rejecting the July Resolution and setting forth their claim to equality in the *aide-mémoire* of 29th August, the German Government had made no further statement of its case and had never stated what they would accept in the form of a Disarmament Convention. In a number of conversations with Herr von Papen and Baron von Neurath, the present author had repeatedly urged the advisability of putting all the cards on the table and stating openly, not only what Germany required in the matter of rearmament, since it had been tacitly admitted that there was no hope of the other Powers disarming to her own level, but also what measures of disarmament she was prepared to agree to in order to facilitate the negotiation of an international convention.

In the course of these conversations a formula which would be acceptable to the German Government was finally drawn up, and this was communicated unofficially to the British Foreign Office and was later made public in a letter to the *Times* of 15th November. It was put forward as a basis for the solution of the problem of equality and comprised eight points :—

(1) The new Convention to be drawn up by the Disarmament Conference, by general agreement, to supersede Part V of the Treaty of Versailles.

(2) The period of service in the *Reichswehr* to be partially reduced.

(3) Germany to be able to create a volunteer militia not to exceed in numbers more than half the total number of the *Reichswehr* (i.e. according to present status, not to exceed 50,000 men).

(4) Germany to be accorded the means of maintaining and supplying the *Reichswehr* on a more economic scale than that provided under the Treaty of Versailles, and under the same terms as other Powers.

(5) Germany of her own free will to agree not to increase her fighting forces beyond the Treaty limit for the period of the interval between the first and second Disarmament Conferences.

(6) Germany to renounce immediately those aggressive weapons which the other nations agree to give up within a limited period of years.

(7) Germany to have the right of " token " equality in all categories of arms unlimited by the new Disarmament Convention.

(8) Germany to undertake not to increase her normal average military budget despite the reorganization outlined above.

It will be observed that the proposed concessions to Germany went no further than those put forward by Dr. Brüning in April, of which the German *aide-mémoire* of August was merely a repetition. Certain of the guarantees offered by Germany had also been proposed by Dr. Brüning, but some had been added by Herr von Papen.

This formula was certainly the most constructive offer made by Germany in the whole course of the equality negotiations, and had presumably been considered by Sir John Simon when he made at Geneva on 17th November his second statement of policy, which was accompanied by certain disarmament proposals by which it was hoped to effect a general reduction. In its turn the British Declaration went further towards meeting the German standpoint than the previous statement of 10th November.

The limitations contained in Part V of the Treaty of Versailles, said Sir John Simon, were imposed as a means of securing, in the circumstances then prevailing, the peace of Europe. It was, however, undoubtedly true that they were intended to be, and expressed to be, the precursor of the general limitation of armaments. The British Government were, therefore, as they had always been, ready and anxious to join the other Governments represented at Geneva (including Germany) in framing a Disarmament Convention which would fairly meet the latter's claim to equality. " Any hesitation which might arise in any quarter would not proceed from a desire to inflict upon Germany a permanent inferiority of status. It would spring from anxiety as to the use which might be made of the new situation, and

from fear of the resulting dangers which might threaten the
tranquillity of Europe."

In order to allay those fears the British Government proposed
that :—

" Side by side with the meeting of Germany's claim to equality
of status, all European States should join in a solemn affirmation
that they will not in any circumstances attempt to resolve any
present or future differences between them by resort to force.
The world is entitled to this specific assurance. The acknowledg-
ment by others of Germany's moral right to parity of treatment
with other nations entails upon Germany, along with others,
the acceptance of this corresponding obligation."

On this condition the British Government put forward the
following means of meeting the German claim :—

(1) The limitations on Germany's armaments should be contained
in the same Disarmament Convention as that which will define
the limitations on the armaments of others ; that is to say, the
Articles in Part V of the Treaty of Versailles which at present
limit Germany's arms and armed forces would be superseded,
and Germany's limitations would be arrived at by the same
process and expressed in the same document as those of all other
countries.

(2) The newly expressed limitations in the case of Germany
would last for the same period, and be subject to the same method
of revision as those of all other countries.

(3) Germany has declared that she has no intention of re-arming,
and that she merely desires that the principle should be acknowledged that the *kinds* of arms permitted to other countries ought
not to be prohibited to herself. If equality of status is to be
conceded, this principle must be acknowledged, and the United
Kingdom Government hereby declare their willingness, in co-
operation with other members of the Disarmament Conference,
to see it embodied in the new Convention. By what means and
by what stages this principle can be applied must be the subject
of a detailed discussion at Geneva, in which it is essential that
Germany should join. In the meantime, the United Kingdom
Government wish to emphasize two points. First, the object
of the Disarmament Conference is to bring about the maximum
of positive disarmament that can be generally agreed—not to
authorize in the name of equality the increase of armed strength.
Secondly, the full realization, in practice, of the principle of
equality cannot be achieved all at once. Confidence in the further
application of the principle will grow as it is seen that the peace
of the world has been made more secure by taking the first step.
The United Kingdom Government, therefore, conceive that
what is needed is a practical programme of stages, each subsequent
step being justified and prepared for by the proved consequence
of what has gone before."

British proposals in their final form went further towards meeting the German claim than any other declaration of policy made by any European State, and ranged Great Britain with Italy as recognizing Germany's moral right to equality of status.

4

Although Germany was still firm in her refusal to attend a " Four-Power Conference " at Geneva on equality of status, the incessant meetings of the Council and the Special Assembly, which were still wrestling with the Sino-Japanese dispute, meant in effect that Baron von Neurath was in the " forbidden city ". Unofficial conversations were being carried on in which Mr. Norman Davis, the American delegate, played a considerable part. On 3rd December, Mr. MacDonald and M. Herriot arrived in Geneva, and on 6th December the world was informed of what it already knew when a *communiqué* was issued stating that unofficial conversations were taking place and " had made useful progress ".

The matter was becoming even more urgent as the fate of the Disarmament Conference depended on an agreement, for the American delegation were tired of a conference which, in their own language, " could not deliver the goods." Mr. Davis was credited with wishing to grant equality of status immediately and unconditionally to Germany, and with closing down the Conference after adopting a resolution reaffirming the July resolutions, and creating a standing committee of all States Members of the Conference which should function until 1936, when the naval agreements would automatically lapse. This would, of course, have been the epitaph on the tombstone of disarmament.

M. Herriot opposed the immediate granting of equality of status to Germany, as he believed that it would give her the right to rearm. This proposal was subsequently dropped. Baron von Neurath returned to Geneva on 5th December and a new formula was handed to him at a private meeting of the representatives of the Great Powers on 6th December. The German delegate produced counter-proposals, among which was a claim that Germany should have the right to increase her defensive armaments, a suggestion which, of course, aroused violent opposition on the part of the French. Mr. MacDonald and M. Herriot left Geneva on the evening of 6th December, and conversations continued spasmodically in their absence.

On 8th December, Baron von Neurath, who had telegraphed to Berlin for further instructions, asked the representatives of the other Powers two questions on points which his Government felt needed elucidation :—

(1) (a) Is equality of status to receive practical effect in the future Convention " in every respect ? "

(b) Would equality be the starting-point of future discussions ?

(2) Does the term " system which provides security for all nations " include the element of security that lies in general disarmament ?

Baron von Neurath was evidently quoting from the unpublished " American Plan ".

The French provided a counter-conundrum. What did the Germans mean by " equality of status " ? Both sides promised replies.

Mr. MacDonald had returned to Geneva on the morning of 9th December, and the day was spent in an intensive attempt to reconcile the formulae put forward by the French and German delegates. Baron von Neurath moved the following resolution :—

" France states that one of the objects of the Disarmament Conference is to afford Germany, and the other Powers disarmed under the Peace Treaties, equality of rights under a regime ensuring equal security for all.

" As Germany understands equality of rights, it should be given practical effect in all its aspects in the future Convention and should be the starting point of the Conference's future discussion where it affects the States disarmed under the Treaties.

" Further, Germany takes the words " a regime ensuring equal security for all " to cover the element of security supplied, as has been recognized by the Assembly, by general disarmament."

M. Paul-Boncour, who had seen the resolution before the Session began, had telephoned it to M. Herriot in Paris, who immediately declared that it was " inacceptable "

The experts were called in in a last desperate attempt to find a formula which both Governments would accept and, contrary to expectations, they succeeded. On 11th December, Mr. MacDonald, Mr. Norman Davis, Sir John Simon, M. Paul-Boncour, Baron von Neurath, and Baron Aloisi signed the following declaration :—

(1) The Governments of the United Kingdom, France, and Italy have declared that one of the principles that should guide

the Conference on disarmament should be the grant to Germany, and to other Powers disarmed by treaty, of equality of rights in a system which would provide security for all nations, and that this principle should find itself embodied in the Convention containing the conclusions of the Disarmament Conference.

This decision implies that the respective limitations of the armaments of all States should be included in the proposed Disarmament Convention.   It is clearly understood that the methods of application of such equality of rights will be discussed by the Conference.

(2) On the basis of this declaration, Germany had signified its willingness to resume its place at the Disarmament Conference.

(3) The Governments of the United Kingdom, France, Germany, and Italy are ready to join in a solemn reaffirmation to be made by all European States that they will not in any circumstances attempt to resolve any present or future differences between the signatories by resort to force. This shall be done without prejudice to fuller discussions on the question of security.

(4) The five Governments of the United States, the United Kingdom, France, Germany, and Italy declare that they are resolved to co-operate in the Conference with the other States there represented in seeking without delay to work out a convention which shall effect a substantial reduction and limitation of armaments with provision for future revision with a view to further reduction.

The Agreement of 11th December achieved its immediate purpose of bringing back Germany to the Disarmament Conference, where her representative took his seat at the final meetings of the Bureau and the General Commission before their adjournment respectively to 24th and 31st January, 1933. But in reality very little except the principle had been conceded, and the agreed formula contained no provision for its practical application. Moreover, some of the phrases used were capable of several and opposing interpretations, interpretations which were almost immediately current in Berlin and Paris.

But at that particular moment the German Government was anxious to take what it could and was in no position to stand out for further concessions. The General Elections of July and November had shown conclusively that, whereas the German people were not yet ripe for a Nazi administration, they were united in their rejection of Herr von Papen's Government, which they were prepared to exchange for almost any other. Taking advantage of this unpopularity, General von Schleicher took the opportunity of deserting his former chief and of turning against him the machinery and influence of that very palace *camarilla* which had been operated to bring about the downfall of Dr. Brüning and the appointment of Herr von Papen.

The fact that a general strike was threatened if Herr von Papen remained in power was represented to President von Hindenburg as an overwhelming reason for the Chancellor's dismissal, and it was clearly indicated to the Marshal that his only possible successor was General von Schleicher, who accordingly became Chancellor on 4th December. The Marshal's affection for Herr von Papen, however, remained undiminished, and neither of them forgave the General for this further intrigue.

There has scarcely been a greater surprise in modern European politics than the brief Chancellorship of General von Schleicher. Those who had watched with interest, if with disapproval, his tortuous career from the *Reichswehr* to the Ministry of Defence, from the Ministry to the Cabinet, and, finally, to the Chancellorship itself, fully imagined that the General had at least the justification of a plan by which he was convinced the Reich might be regenerated.

But nothing of the sort occurred. During the seven weeks of his administration he produced no programme, and, beyond some abortive negotiations with the Trades Unions leaders, gave no indication of any policy whatever. But for the fact that the Nazi vote had in the November elections diminished by some 2,000,000 votes from that of July, and the party was consequently undergoing a period of depression and eclipse, the General would not have remained in power so long, for his enemies were as surprised at his inactivity as were his supporters. Having recovered from their astonishment, the former began to rally and to draw together. Herr von Papen began a tentative advance towards the Nazi leaders, and from that time the Schleicher Cabinet was doomed.

The Equality Agreement of 11th December, therefore, was as much as could be expected or achieved at the time. For Germany, it meant that she had passed the initiative once more, and that the next move lay with the former Allied Powers. Having captured the first line of its objective, the German Government was reconciled to a period of waiting and of consolidating its position until such time as it was strong enough to effect the practical application of the principle conceded.

Chapter VI

MACDONALD—ROOSEVELT—HITLER

1

When the Bureau of the Conference met on 23rd January, 1933, it did so under the influence of the fillip supplied by the Agreement of 11th December, 1932, which had temporarily improved the whole situation. The effect of this fillip was, however, considerably neutralized by the fact that the Sino-Japanese dispute, which had already provided the world with an example of more than a year's "undeclared" warfare, showed no signs of pacific solution as a result of the efforts of the League. Japan had remained as adamant and undeterred as ever, and was actually to give notice of her withdrawal from the League two months later (27th March). When the Conference met officially for its second session on 2nd February, Japanese troops were already moving forward to the capture of Jehol, the possession of which had been " forbidden " to them by both the Council and Assembly of the League.

The Bureau had before it the French " Constructive Plan " and the British proposals, both of which had been put forward in the previous November. Its time, however, was spent in discussing the somewhat premature question as to how supervision and control was to be exercised over the armaments of the various Powers after they had been fixed by the Convention, which it was the aim of the Conference eventually to draw up. From this academic pastime they were eventually torn by a proposal, put forward in desperation by the British Government, in the form of a " programme of work ", drawn up with a view to speeding up the work of the General Commission.

This programme, which was handed in on 27th January, and published four days later, was as follows :—

It was suggested that the Bureau should submit to the General Committee a resolution containing " directions for the ordering of the work ", and the object of the plan was to outline the form such a resolution might take.

The aim of the Bureau (in whose hands the direction of the work would be placed) should be to organize without delay practical discussion of the following topics, with the object of framing a Convention embodying them so far as they were ultimately approved :—

(1) A solemn affirmation, to be made by all European States, that they will not in any circumstances attempt to resolve any present or future differences between them by resort to force.

(2) The immediate study by the Continental European States of the possibility of reaching political arrangements defining the conditions in which each of them will be entitled to the co-operation of the other contracting States.

(3) The application of the principle that the limitations on the armaments of Germany and the other disarmed States shall be contained in the same Disarmament Convention as that which will define the limitations on the armaments of others, so that the Articles in Part V of the Treaty of Versailles, which at present limit Germany's armaments, and the corresponding provisions of the other Peace Treaties would be replaced by the Disarmament Convention as far as the disarmed States are concerned.

(4) The application of the principle that the newly expressed limitations in the case of Germany and the other disarmed States shall last for the same period and be subject to the same methods of revision as those of all other countries ; and the embodiment in the Disarmament Convention of an undertaking on the part of the signatory States to enter upon negotiations in due course before the expiry of this Convention with a view to concluding a new one for the purpose of further adjustment of armaments.

(5) The embodiment in the Convention, as regards war material, of the principle of qualitive equality, and the provision for the realization of such equality, if not immediately after its entry into force, then by specified stages. The reduction of the armies of the Continental European States to a uniform general type of organization would have to be considered in this connection.

The Political Commission should be instructed at once to study the methods for giving effect to point (1) above, while point (2) should be examined by a committee of the European Continental States set up for that purpose.

The second part of the programme was concerned with the details of disarmament in respect of effectives, land war material, the air, and the navy, in that order, and the Bureau might at once begin to compute the totals of *personnel* of the " police component " (the irreducible component) of the existing land forces of each country, both metropolitan and overseas.[1] For this purpose it should instruct the Effectives Committee to make to it within . . . days recommendations concerning the ratios to be employed in this calculation. It should also agree upon

[1] This was in accordance with the plan for the calculation of land forces contained in the proposals of President Hoover.

the percentage by which the " defence component " (the excess over the police component) of each State should be reduced, such reduction to be effected by a certain date. Finally, it should determine the stages and methods by which European Continental armies might be brought into harmony with the general type of organization adopted (see point 5, above).

And as regards land, air, and naval material the Bureau should fix maximum tonnages and numbers of tanks, maximum gun calibres, maximum weights of aeroplanes, and tonnages of naval vessels of all categories, and so on, with, in the case of the air, this further provision : that a committee of representatives of the principal air Powers should be constituted at once " to examine the possibility of the entire abolition of military and naval machines and of bombing from the air, combined with an effective international control of civil aviation ".

This programme was explained by Mr. Anthony Eden, the British Under-Secretary of State for Foreign Affairs, on 9th February at a special meeting of the Bureau called to draw up the next agenda for the General Commission. He gave it as his opinion that there was no alternative between adopting at once some such programme of a method of work, and watching the Conference flicker out in ineffective reiteration. The past year had yielded nothing except the progressive presentation of a number of plans, and this could not go on indefinitely. Sooner or later they must sort out this material, register the greatest common measure of agreement that could be realized, and classify the results into a Convention.

As for the programme itself, they had taken into full consideration the connection between disarmament and security, but had not provided, at that stage, for a study of the consultative pact, as that could best be taken in hand later. They had, however, envisaged a discussion of the arrangements for a Continental pact, and it was to be hoped that there might emerge a system which would reinforce or complete by regional understandings the measure of security already existing. The British Government regarded the part concerning the actual measures of arms reduction as of vital importance. They did not see the incompatibility between the far-reaching provisions as to effectives in both the Hoover proposals and the French plan, since the latter dealt with the qualitative aspect, but admitted that there must be quantitative reduction also.

Mr. Eden then indicated some of the questions which might come up when dealing with land and air material. Suppose, for example, they agreed that the abolition of military aircraft was the only effective method of dealing with the menace of air warfare, then they would certainly require some control of civil aviation, which he believed could be worked out. He hoped, therefore, that the Bureau would agree to appoint an air committee to work out a scheme.

In conclusion, the British Government considered that the present session should mark the entry upon a new phase—that of decisions. The various plans submitted had been dissected and discussed to the last detail, and the time had come for the Governments to shoulder their responsibilities, and to weigh the risks against the incomparably greater danger of allowing the Conference to fail.

During the discussion which followed Herr Nadolny said that he accepted the method set out in the second part of the programme ; but in the first part there were matters involving political considerations which would recur at a later stage. The practical application of equality of rights could be discussed when the programme was carried into effect ; while reserving his right to define equality at the proper time, he proposed that only the second part should be submitted to the Bureau as a practical agenda.

M. Paul-Boncour made the point that the two essentials of the French plan must be discussed first, i.e. before they proceeded to details of the reduction of sizes of ships, guns, and so on. These essentials were the proposal for mutual assistance, and, as regards effectives, the proposal to put Continental armies on a uniform basis. But he also made a reference to the agreement of 11th December, which caused some concern in Germany. When the time came, he said, France would make it clear that she could conceive equality of rights only within an organization ensuring security, and he reminded the delegates of what was perfectly true, that the December Agreement made between the Powers could not take the place of a decision of the Conference. He agreed that questions of security should be examined by the Political Committee, a course which was accordingly decided upon, and the Political Commission met for this purpose on 14th February *for the first time*.[1]

The effect made on opinion in Germany by the French Minister's statement was unfortunate. It was regarded as an attempt to destroy the Agreement of 11th December by making its validity dependent upon the conclusion of a pact ensuring

[1] It was set up in February, 1932, but had never been convened.

security which the French delegation knew quite well was never likely to be realized. Herr Nadolny was very careful, however, to say nothing which might upset the better relations which had been established by the December Agreement, and he merely remarked that he did not think it desirable to follow M. Paul-Boncour in making explanations regarding its scope. An exchange of views on that question, he felt, would only provoke a discussion on the principle of equality, but he did remind him that the December Agreement was the basis and condition of the return of Germany to the Conference.

In the end the Bureau decided to deal with the British pro- gramme in the following way : in order to avoid waste of time, the two problems of security and disarmament were to be discussed simultaneously, the former in the Political Commission and the latter in the General Commission. The consideration of the knotty problem of equality of rights (points 3–5 in the programme) was postponed. It was also arranged that the General Commission should appoint sub-committees to begin work at once and simultaneously on the three separate items of effectives, land material, and air.

Here M. Paul-Boncour reminded the Bureau of the great importance attached by France to the order of work. There should be a guarantee that the first two matters on which the States represented should give their views should be the two essential conditions of the French plan—mutual assistance and effectives, and he pointed out that he could not express his views on the reduction of material till he knew the opinion of the Conference on effectives and the unification of army types. The Bureau eventually decided that the General Commission should take the items in the British programme in the order in which they appeared there, i.e. beginning with effectives. These points having been settled, the Political Commission opened its first session on 14th February with the consideration of the British draft of a solemn affirmation by the European Governments " that they will not in any circumstances resort to force for the purpose of resolving any present or future differences between them ".

It was subsequent to the publication of the British " programme of work " that the discussion began of the French " constructive plan ". This opened on 2nd February, in the General Commission, M. Massigli being the first to speak. He described the plan as an attempt to make a synthesis of the great principles which France had already put forward, these principles being (a) that there is an indissoluble link between disarmament and security ; (b) that the reduction of arms must be adapted to the special conditions of each State in accordance with the wording of Article 8 of the Covenant ; (c) that the means of defence should be strengthened by a reduction of the forces of aggression ; (d) that the reduction by stages is based on previous experience ; and (e) that the realization of progressive reduction is incompatible with rearmament.   The French delegation attached fundamental importance to the questions of control and supervision, and to measures such as the control of international air transport and the limitation of armaments expenditure, for all of which the plan made provision.

Baron Aloisi and Herr Nadolny agreed in being unable to find, in the plan, any concrete proposal for real qualitative disarmament, or any definite provision for immediate reduction of armaments.   Of the scheme for armed contingents to be at the disposal of the League the Italian delegate said he did not think that by changing the labels of certain corps, and making them a safeguard of international equilibrium instead of a safeguard of national integrity, the Conference would in any way accomplish its task. Nor did he see how the system of sanctions would work with certain important nations outside the League. And finally, he did not like the idea of Great Britain remaining aloof from the proposed new pact.   It seemed to him, in fact, that the political, economic, and military situation of Europe, past and present, should be a warning against the idea that Great Britain should not share in the European system.

Herr Nadolny frankly refused to believe that disarmament was only possible so long as it was accompanied by a progressive organization of peace. The disarmament provided for by the Covenant was based only on the guarantees in the Covenant itself, and since then there had been Locarno and the Kellogg Treaty, not to mention other agreements such as the Convention for Financial Assistance.

He also placed his finger on one of the difficulties of organizing and using an international force when he said it would be essential to have a guarantee that this force would be used with the same certainty of success against any member of the League, and that such a guarantee could not perhaps be provided before complete equality of armaments had been secured.

More interest was aroused by the speech of the British Foreign Under-Secretary the next day, since this left the Conference in no doubt as to the decision of the British Government that the question of international security guarantees was, as far as that country was concerned, definitely closed.   Mr. Eden suggested that there was a danger, in the search for new safeguards and new formulae, of overlooking the significance of the guarantees already existing.   Those guarantees were real and substantial, and loomed large in the Government's eyes.   The security given by the Locarno Treaty was a real security, and to underrate its significance would be a mistake.   The British Government, in a spirit of realism, had abandoned the ambitious ideal of a universal effort towards mutual assistance, and sought rather to encourage a natural growth of the system of security in accordance with local and immediate needs ; Locarno had set an example which they hoped would be followed.   Whether it were followed or not, however, the Government considered that in its membership of the League and its signature of Locarno it had gone as far as it could and should in assuming definite commitments, and " I can give no hint of encouragement ", Mr. Eden continued, " that it will be possible for us to modify this attitude or to undertake new obligations, to which, I believe, the public opinion of my country is unalterably opposed."

Concluding his speech with a plea for deeds rather than words, the British delegate asked whether there was not now almost a danger that the Conference might be compelled to pass from the limitation of arms to the limitation of plans for disarmament.

M. Paul-Boncour was unable to be present in Geneva until 5th February, and the discussion was accordingly adjourned until the following Monday, 6th February, but as soon as Mr. Eden's speech had been read in Paris, and before the author of the plan had even reached Geneva to explain it, the general opinion in France was that the plan was " dead ".   The *Temps* wrote that Locarno was all very well, and indeed had " considerable importance ", but that it applied only to the West, which was not enough.   This feeling was widespread, in spite of the fact that the plan expressly excluded British participation from the proposed European regional pacts, for Mr. Eden's declaration appeared to French opinion to have reinforced Italian opposition, while, apart from this, it was at once recognized that it put an end to the proposal that British naval and air support should be at the disposal of the League.   Now that there was no more hope for the plan, feeling in Paris also hardened against the British programme of work.

Accordingly, when M. Paul-Boncour rose on 8th February to

defend his plan, interest in it was no longer more than academic, and the French statesman limited his remarks to a re-statement of motives and a refutation of some of the criticisms made during the debate. He argued that in linking disarmament with security they had only been continuing work already done, beginning with Article 8 of the Covenant and ending with the resolution of 23rd July. In any case, disarmament would have to be achieved within an organized society of nations, in which its connection with security had become apparent whenever, during the past ten years, the League had worked at the problem. No form of excommunication, whatever its moral force, could be regarded as a substitute for guarantees of mutual assistance ; and guarantees must be created superior to those already existing.

M. Paul-Boncour also defended the plan against the other criticisms which had been directed against it. He referred to the measures to be applied to naval, air, and land armaments, and said that for the last-named " a massive reduction of average daily effectives was proposed ". He also made the point that it was essential to discard the fallacy that war could be humanized ; its cruelty did not vary according to the weapons used. And as regards the proposed pact, he said that each country must have an absolute guarantee that no enemy should invade its territory with a view to its occupation. A system of financial assistance had been established ; why not, then, one of military assistance ? He made many further points in his speech in support of the French thesis :—

> It was impossible to make equitable reductions of effectives without first introducing uniformity of army types.
> Europe would have to find within her own limits her own guarantees of security, and not be driven to seek them in the four corners of the world.
> It must be clearly understood that the major excommunication which would follow a violation of the Kellogg Treaty would involve economic and financial consequences.
> Against the objections to abandoning the majority rule within the Council, the Covenant was in need of being strengthened, at least between certain European States.
> Against the difficulty of defining the aggressor, in concrete instances it was easy to ascertain who had attacked.
> And finally, as a warning, the difficulties of the plan were not as great as those which would arise from asking States to disorganize their national forces without granting them international security.

As already intimated, these considerations, important and well thought-out as they were, were presented to an assemblage which had already made up its mind that the French plan could not form the basis of the Convention for which the Conference had met. The British declaration played a large part in this, and the opposition of Italy and Germany also had its influence, but another development was equally effective in dealing the plan its *coup-de-grace*. This was the statement made by Mr. Hugh Gibson on 7th February, in which he made it clear that the U.S. Government meant to stand aloof from the discussion of the details of the plan. The first task under the plan was, as M. Massigli himself had pointed out, to reach agreement between the Continental States of Europe. It was only when this had been done that other States would have to determine whether it was worth their while to undertake the agreements outlined in order to bring about general agreement. Inasmuch as the plan was designed to settle a Continental European problem, the U.S. delegation did not feel called upon to express an opinion as to how far it would fulfil its purpose. The European aspect of the plan must be disposed of, he said, before they could discuss other aspects, and it would be hypothetical rather than real to offer any comment on that part of it which concerned non-European States or non-members of the League. As for what America might be disposed to do, this would be largely determined by the measure of actual reduction which the Conference might achieve.

This declaration made it very clear that no support could be expected from America for the French thesis of security and disarmament, in that order, and the French Government has been much preoccupied with the almost universal nature of the opposition to its plan. As against the American attitude, however, there was one other point. Speaking at the Bureau meeting on 10th February, Senor de Madariaga (Spain) presented what amounted to the reverse aspect of the attitude shown in Mr. Gibson's statement when he said that the countries of the European Continent could not undertake further special engagements before they knew what the non-European nations would do. The general pact contemplated in the first part of the French plan was the necessary framework of the Continental pact, and the countries which would be parties to the wider instrument should first declare their attitude in order that the two parts might be brought into line.

Such differences of point of view produced a deadlock which was not removed when Mr. Eden, reverting to the actual disarmament proposals contained in the French Plan, suggested that a drafting committee of twelve should draw up the terms of reference under which the question of effectives would be sent to the Effectives Committee. This course was adopted, but it did little more than cause a suspension of the argument between the two opposing points of view.

The French proposals aimed at securing the standardization of armies on the basis of short service and a limited number of effectives, on the ground that an army of conscripts called up for short terms of training—8 to 9 months was suggested—was fitted only for defence. In the French view a combination of the militia system and the professional army would be the worst possible solution of the effectives question, as it would produce armies capable of offence, whereas the adoption of the short-service system would make it possible to bring about a general reduction of effectives, both by a decrease in the number called up, and by a reduction in the period of service.

During the discussion of details, however, other points of difference appeared. Assuming that all Continental armies were unified, or " standardized ", was this to apply to overseas forces, and if so, to all of these ? Again, was pre-military training to be included in the period of training conscripts ? This second question was dropped by general consent, after Herr Nadolny had attempted to get a negative answer accepted, as it was obvious that agreement could not be hoped for ; and as to the first, the discussion soon made it clear that France did not for a moment contemplate that the short-term system—so desirable in her eyes in the case of Continental armies—should apply to colonial forces. Mr. Eden also made it clear that, in practice, short-service could not apply to all British oversea forces, and the German delegate, no doubt realizing Great Britain's position and responsibilities in India, was ready to admit that this was the case, but he evidently did not feel the same about France and North Africa. He argued (and in this he was supported by the Italian delegate) that standardization should certainly apply to those colonial forces which were stationed near the home country, and said that no less than half of the French army consisted of oversea troops on a long-service basis, of which about two-thirds were normally stationed near, or even in, France. But M. Cot, while admitting that colonial forces might be limited, was firmly resolved that the short-service system for them was impossible.

It is not surprising that no agreement was reached. In the end a resolution submitted by M. Cot on 17th February was adopted by the General Commission on 22nd February, but

the voting was 21 to 5, with no less than 31 abstentions.   And
the resolution did no more than provide that the Commission
should note that only a military status of a defensive character
was compatible with a regime of security, and that in Continental
Europe a short-term army with limited effectives was the type
representing the most defensive character, the adoption of which
would make it possible to bring about a general reduction
of effectives and progressively render them comparable.

In the discussions in the Air Commission and the Political
Commission differences of an equally serious character appeared.
The former could not make up its mind which to take first,
the question of the entire abolition of naval and military aircraft, or that of the control or internationalization of civil
aircraft.   When, eventually, on 20th February it decided to
discuss the question of internationalization the voting for it
was 7 to 6, with 6 abstentions, including the U.S.A.—a difference
of opinion which augured ill for the chances of any useful decisions.
Here again the divergences of points of view were deep-rooted.
The French Government believed in the principle of internationalization and the establishment of an international police
force ;   the German in the necessity of the abolition of military
aircraft as the preliminary to all other measures.   M. Cot's
reply to this was that, even if military aircraft disappeared, civil
machines could easily be transformed into military weapons,
and this view was shared by a number of countries, including
Belgium, Czechoslovakia, and Yugo-Slavia.   Both the German
and Italian delegates, however, flatly refused to discuss the
question of internationalization until that of the entire abolition
of fighting aircraft had been decided, with the result that the
discussions ended in deadlock.[1] On 2nd March the usual procedure
was adopted of appointing a sub-committee to study the question
of internationalization, and on 7th March a second similar body
was set up to study that of forming an international air police.

In the Political Commission it was the British proposal for
a solemn affirmation against the use of force which caused most
discussion.   Though the text of this was simple enough a number
of delegates wished to submit amendments, and on 15th February
yet another sub-committee, of thirteen States, was set up to consider the draft.   The Soviet delegate, no doubt with Japan and the

---

[1] As illustrative of the atmosphere in which the discussions were conducted, the contention that it was impossible to effect any air disarmament
except by stages was met by the German statement that Germany had in
one year abolished 15,700 aircraft and 27,000 air engines.

U.S.A. in mind, urged that it should be widened to include non-European nations, though Mr. Eden had pointed out that it was a predominantly European problem, because they were, at that stage, discussing how they could help to meet the French plan of security in so far as it affected Europe. At a later stage, he said, when they came to consider the consultative pact, they could more appropriately undertake the examination of problems which affected non-European countries.

In spite of this there was a desire to make the text more precise than the British draft had done, and it was felt to be a distinct achievement that on 28th February the sub-committee succeeded in drafting a formula which was acceptable to both the French and German delegates. This provided that the signatories should state in the preamble to the " no force " declaration that they desired to prohibit resort to force in the same conditions as those in which the Kellogg Treaty prohibited it ; while in the declaration itself they would state that they would in no circumstances have resort to force as an instrument of national policy. When, however, on 2nd March this formula was accepted by the Political Commission, the value of this action was discounted by the fact that 14 representatives abstained, while the Soviet delegate made a reservation that its application should be universal.

The next stumbling-block was presented by the French draft pact of mutual assistance, discussed for the first time by the Political Commission on 4th March. An attempt was made to get a text prepared by a drafting committee set up for the purpose, but both Italy and the U.S.S.R. refused to take part, while Germany and Hungary said they could only send observers. And this was after a resolution asking the Political Commission to accept the principle of a Continental pact of mutual assistance had been adopted, but the voting was 14 to 5, and the 5 adverse votes included Germany, Italy, Austria, and Hungary, while Belgium abstained.

Everything possible to present the plan in a favourable light had been done by M. Paul-Boncour. He pointed out that mutual assistance was no new idea ; it was to be found in the Covenant, and the time had now come to apply it in detail. The undertaking not to resort to force was the logical basis of the scheme, but as force might still be used it was necessary to go further and make provision against aggression. And a few days later M. Massigli brought the subject into the discussion of the question of limiting land war material. A vote against the scheme for

mutual assistance would, he said, inevitably entail the failure
of any extensive plan of disarmament, for the extent of the
reductions of material contemplated would depend on the
guarantees obtained in regard to effectives and security. Here
he was voicing the same opinion as had been expressed in the
discussions on effectives, and the effect was to bring Herr Nadolny
to his feet again with the argument that a reduction in arms
must come first.   He was sure that world opinion was on
Germany's side in demanding such a reduction by the power-
fully armed States, and not the creation of new guarantees of
security against countries which were already disarmed.

It was obvious that discussions on these lines would lead
nowhere, and the debate ended, on 9th March, without any agreement, after M. Massigli had again said that, so long as it was not
known whether States would be called upon to face an attack
with their own resources alone, and so long as it was not known
whether equality of rights would correspond with equality of
obligations, a number of delegations, others as well as the French,
would be unable to state whether they would be prepared to
forego many of their weapons. This was tantamount to saying
that France could not consider a reduction of her strength in
weapons to the level of other Continental countries unless she
could count upon assistance from other Powers under some
scheme of mutual assistance going beyond that which already
exists in the Locarno Treaties.

2

But whilst these wranglings were in process at Geneva, events
were taking place in Germany which were to change the history
of the world.

With the New Year it had become evident that the position
of General von Schleicher's Government was growing more and
more precarious. With a peculiarly perverse genius the Chancellor
had followed in his predecessor's footsteps and had alienated
even the small amount of support remaining to him. With the
exception of the eleven votes of the industrialist People's Party
he had no support in the Reichstag whatever. The Social
Democrats and Communists, though rivals for power, were
united in their opposition to a dictatorial government ; the
Centre held aloof from any " compromise government " ; the
Nazis, with whom the Chancellor had once hoped to form a
coalition, refused to share power, and when one of their leaders,

Gregor Strasser, entered into negotiations with General von Schleicher, his hint of insubordination was instantly quelled by Herr Hitler, who " disciplined " him severely and stripped him of his Party offices, though he had been one of the oldest members of the Nazi movement.

There remained the Nationalists to whom the Chancellor might have .turned for support, but these also he antagonized. He was persuaded of the soundness of Dr. Brüning's policy of expropriating, in return for compensation, the huge bankrupt estates of East Prussia, which were kept alive by the funds poured into them by the Government by means of the *Osthilfe*, and which there was no hope of ever regaining.   But at the mention of expropriation the Junkers bridled and countered with that bogey formula " *Agrarbolschevismus* ", which had played so prominent a part in the fall of Dr. Brüning. The same influences were now employed against the General, and the already existing dislike of the President for his Chancellor was fanned to white-heat.

General von Schleicher's reply to these hostile forces was to threaten publication of the scandals of the *Osthilfe* loans, the stench of which reeked to heaven and whose mud splashed even to the steps of the Presidential Palace itself. Here indeed was a Pandora's box which, being opened, poured forth a flood of loathly, crawling things.   There stood disclosed land-owners, bankrupt through their own ineptitude, whose estates had been " reconstructed " three times, and, after a fourth breakdown, had been ceded, under the *Osthilfe*, to a daughter who was still a minor. There were absentee landlords too, who, with the money loaned to them by the Government to reconstruct their estates, had bought motor-cars and driven to the Riviera, whilst banks and tradesmen who had trustfully given them credit remained unpaid. There were those, also, in the inexorable report of the Government investigator, who squandered the public money on " wine and women ", yet nevertheless received more public money since their names had been for centuries coupled with their estates.

The *Osthilfe* had been advertised as the means of saving the peasants. But it came to light that nine-tenths of the " peasants " were estate-owners, and that only the smallest percentage of the money reached those whom it was intended to benefit. The scandal affected not only the average land-owner, it struck at the titled leaders of the powerful *Landbund* ; none were spared. The National Donation to President von Hindenburg of the

Manor of Neudeck was itself not exempt from criticism, for it was alleged that no donation tax had been paid on it, and that succession tax had been evaded by the simple device of making out the deed of gift in the name of Colonel Oskar von Hindenburg, the President's son.

By means of these disclosures the Chancellor hoped to cow the Junkers and bring them to heel ; he thought to spin one of his usual intrigues and did not realize that he was sawing off the branch upon which he himself was sitting. At one stroke he had destroyed the only two sources from which he might have received support. For 200 years the Army and the Junkers had been identical, inseparable, an alliance cemented by bonds of common interest. General von Schleicher had broken the bond. In entering upon his struggle with the Junkers, he was ignorant of the strength of the economic and political interests which he was attacking, and he was too superficial to sense the power of tradition which hundreds of years had centred in one caste. Moreover, he had grievously annoyed the President, and, by connecting the name of Colonel von Hindenburg with the *Osthilfe* disclosures, had broken up the triumvirate—of himself, the Colonel, and Dr. Meissner, the President's Secretary of State— through which he had influenced the Marshal's policy.

As one man the thirteen thousand Junker families rallied to the defence of their caste. They surrounded the President and clamoured for the Chancellor's dismissal ; the Palace teemed like an ant-heap which has been stirred with a stick. It was at this moment that Herr von Papen sought to play the *deus ex machinâ*.

The motives which actuated Herr von Papen in these January days will doubtless always remain obscure. Certainly his colossal vanity, which made his continued disappearance from the public eye intolerable to him, played an important part, for the itch of ambition had been greatly excited during his six months as Chancellor. Certainly, too, there was the lust to revenge himself upon General von Schleicher, who had ousted him from the Chancellorship by intrigue and plotting. And, in all fairness, it must be believed that he was not yet undeceived as to his own capacity to make a captive of Herr Hitler, to harness the Nazis to his own chariot, and to unite them in a great alliance with the Junkers and heavy industry.

Nor was this dream entirely impossible of realization. The November elections had cost the Nazis 2,000,000 votes and 35 seats in the Reichstag. They were bankrupt in every sense of the word, having not even enough money to pay the salaries of the *Führer's* own body-guard. Money they must have, and if he could supply the funds Herr von Papen had a right to make his own terms. Thus he who, when he had been Chancellor, had threatened the industrialists for subsidizing the Nazis, now put forward every effort to bring them together. A greater politician might have succeeded ; as it was, Herr von Papen, far from harnessing the Nazis, was riveting upon his own wrists the fetters which should bind him captive to their chariot wheels.

The first conference between Herr von Papen and the Nazi Leader took place at Cologne on 8th January at the house of the great banker von Schroeder, who represented the interests of heavy industry, and here a draft treaty of alliance was concluded. Three weeks later the seat of negotiations was removed to Berlin, Herr von Papen going to the Palace, Herr Hitler to his own headquarters at the Kaiserhof Hotel, across the Wilhelmplatz.[1] The date was 28th January. For three days the negotiations were prolonged, with General von Schleicher still scheming desperately at the *Reichskanzlei*, a stone's throw from either camp.

In desperation the Chancellor summoned Leippert, the Trades Union leader, and proposed to him a general strike, supported by the Army. But though this plan found many supporters among the young officers of the *Reichswehr*, who dreamed of re-establishing the old Prussian Warrior-state on the foundation of the labouring class, the Trades Unions would have none of it, and the Chancellor, having asked for, and been refused, a dissolution of the Reichstag, disappeared into obscurity.[2]

But still the negotiations between the two camps remained inconclusive. Now the Palace would make a concession, now the Kaiserhof. On the Saturday night it seemed as if no agreement could be reached. The air was heavy with presage of evil ; rumour followed rumour. The city spent a restless night ; armed police patrolled the streets and guarded the public buildings. On the Sunday morning the Palace made a final offer. Herr Hitler should receive the Chancellorship for himself, and the Reich and Prussian Ministries of Interior for

---

[1] National Socialist accounts of these negotiations may be found in General Göring's *Germany Reborn* (Elkin Matthews, 1934), pp. 111–18 ; and Dr. Goebbels' *Vom Kaiserhof zum Reichkanzlei* (Zentralverlag der N.S.D.A.P., München, 1934).

[2] General von Schleicher and his wife were murdered by the Secret Police on 30th June, 1934, in the course of the " clean-up " of the opponents and critics of the National-Socialist regime.

his party ; in return Herr von Papen should be Vice-Chancellor and *Reichskommissar* for Prussia, and Herr Hugenberg, for the Junkers and heavy industrialists, should unite in his own hand the Reich and Prussian Ministries of Economic Affairs and Agriculture ; whilst the Ministries or Foreign Affairs, Finance, and Defence should remain in the hands of Baron von Neurath, Count Schwerin von Krosigk and General Baron von Blomberg respectively.

Whilst the Nazi leaders in the Kaiserhof were considering these terms, which gave them control of the whole police force of Prussia but necessitated their agreement with Herr Hugenberg's economic theories of *Autarchie*, the news came from Herr Werner von Alvensleben, a member of the *Herrenklub* and an emissary in the negotiations, that General von Schleicher was marching on Berlin, with the troops of the Potsdam garrison, to arrest Herr Hitler, Herr von Papen, and Colonel von Hindenburg for high-treason. How true this news was remains obscure, but it had the effect of stampeding both camps into agreement and union in face of a common danger. The Nazis agreed to Herr von Papen's terms provided that Captain Göring, who was to be Prussian Minister of Interior, should also become Minister without portfolio in the Reich Cabinet, giving them three votes instead of two. This amendment the Palace accepted,[1] in three hours the pact was sealed, and on 30th January Herr Hitler entered the *Reichskanzlei* with power to dissolve the Reichstag.

On the evening of 30th January, when the great torch-light procession, with which the Nazis had celebrated their advent to power, had passed cheering through the Brandenburger Tor into the night, there was no prouder man in Germany than Herr von Papen. How splendidly it had all come out in the end and how well his plans had carried. Von Schleicher had paid the penalty for his treachery at last, and Hitler, at last, too, was a hostage in the camp of the Nationalists. The *Osthilfe* scandals had been suppressed and the 13,000 Junker families saved once more, and all at the cost of three portfolios. Why, with himself governing Prussia, with Hugenberg and the Nationalists and heavy industrialists, with Seldte and the *Stahlhelm* all in the Government, the position was as safe as could be. " We can always out-vote them in Cabinet " he

---

[1] " How wonderfully had the aged Field-Marshal been used as an instrument in the hand of God "(!), wrote General Göring at a later date. (See *Germany Reborn*, p. 115.)

gaily next morning assured an acquaintance who had the curiosity to question the safety of his position.

Alas for his vanity, his complacency, and his dreams. In a few weeks, when the elections of 5th March had given the Nazis, materially aided by the Reichstag fire, a vote of seventeen million, or 49 per cent of the electorate, Herr von Papen found himself deprived of the government of Prussia, which passed— *vae victis*—to Captain Göring. A new Reich portfolio of Propaganda with Dr. Goebbles at its head appeared in the Cabinet. Hugenberg was obstructed at every turn ; Seldte cringed to the crack of the Nazi whip and the *Stahlhelm* mounted the swastika. Hitler, who had at first been contented to be received by the President in the presence of the Vice-Chancellor, now intimated his intention of going alone to the Palace. Moreover, Herr von Papen's better instincts and natural good nature were revolted by the bestialities of the Brown Terror, Germany for months after the elections cast a pall of fear over which and sent a shudder of horror throughout the civilized world.

Too late did he awake to a realization of the true state of things which he had created, to find himself playing the role of hostage for which he had cast the Chancellor.[1]

3

The deadlock at Geneva and the Nazi Revolution in Berlin convinced the British Government that they must abandon the policy of having no policy, which they had pursued during the past twelve months at the Disarmament Conference, and must make some definite contribution to the discussions which should, if possible, force an issue one way or another. The War Office, the Admiralty, the Air Ministry, and the Foreign Office were, therefore, set to work to produce a draft Convention which should combine provision both for security and disarmament

[1] Appalled by the degree to which the German mind had been imprisoned as a result of the National Socialist Revolution, Herr von Papen, in the course of a now historic speech at the University of Marburg on 17th June, 1934, made an appeal for moderation and the toleration of constructive criticism. To a great degree this speech precipitated the crisis of 30th June, and in the course of the " clean-up " on that day nearly the whole of the Vice-Chancellor's staff were either shot or arrested, while he himself only escaped detention through the personal intervention of the President. He was finally " relieved " of the Vice-Chancellorship, to become Minister to Vienna after the assassination of Dr. Dollfuss on 25th July.

and which could be regarded as a concrete basis for a final
agreement.

At the same time Mr. Eden was recalled to report, and at
a meeting of the Cabinet on 4th March gave a detailed and
complete account of the position arising out of the sessions of
the Bureau and the General Commission. It was a story which
confirmed the Ministers in their previous conviction that something must be done and done quickly. Had only this most
laudable desire for action and contribution found earlier expression, the history of the Disarmament Conference might have
been very different. The policy of the British Government
throughout the spring and summer of 1933 was so admirable that
it throws into still darker shadow the lamentable periods of inaction
which preceded and followed.

On 9th March Mr. Ramsay MacDonald and Sir John Simon left
for Geneva, having a short interview with M. Daladier on their
way through Paris. Immediately on their arrival the British
Ministers began a series of conversations with the chief representatives of the United States, France, Germany, and Italy, while
the Press enlivened their despatches with suggestions of a
conference between Mr. MacDonald, Signor Mussolini, Herr
Hitler, and an American delegate, to be held somewhere in
Italy. These rumours were put to an end to by the publication
on 15th March of an official announcement that Mr. MacDonald
and Sir John Simon had received a cordial invitation from
the Head of the Italian Government to visit him in Rome, an
invitation which they had been happy to accept.

In the early days of the London Foundling Hospital, founded
in 1739 by Captain Coram, a retired sea captain, unwanted
children were placed in a basket hung outside the gates, the
depositor rang the bell and left hastily. Mr. Ramsay MacDonald
treated the new British Disarmament plan in much the same way.
He addressed the General Commission of the Conference on
16th March, the Convention was circulated immediately after
his speech, and he left for Rome the next day. Hardly had he
returned when he left again, this time for the United States,
to discuss world problems with President Roosevelt.[1]

Mr. MacDonald began his speech by explaining why his
Government had felt called upon to intervene in order to speed
up the business of the Conference. It was time to enter the

---

[1] The inveterate peripateticism of the British Prime Minister caused
a London newspaper, on his return, to carry a headline, " Mr. MacDonald
visits England ! "

last phase, and he asked, was any conference ever faced with issues which raised more sharply the questions of life and death of great States ? The fabric of civilization could almost be heard creaking about their ears. The compartmental method of surveying the problems of disarmament had yielded its maximum usefulness, and it was time for somebody to produce a complete scheme.

In preparing a scheme they had to consider whether this scheme should not meet two requirements ; that of disarmament, and the fact that every nation asked to have its responsibilities and its gifts related to actual existing circumstances. An old friend of his, and a great servant of international peace, had recently said, " Either Germany is given justice and freedom or Europe will risk destruction." Those were words which every delegation must ponder over and over again. Justice and peace would have to be based on contributions from both sides—from the armed and the disarmed.

Mr. MacDonald went on to explain the twofold meaning of the Five-Power Declaration—the grant of equality, a military concession, and the undertaking never to use force for the attainment of political ends. " Revision certainly," he remarked, " revision, however, not at the point of the bayonet, but at the point of reason expressed and exchanged across a table."

He then read out the two germane clauses of the Declaration. These meant : security (no resort to force on account of superior potential position given by a declaration of equality), and the reaching of equality by stages. Speaking as the chairman of the Five-Power Conference he said that that declaration, which was made for its psychological effect, was inexplicably tied up and made part of the declaration that they were all in favour of equality.

The problem of peace was psychological. Confidence had been disturbed by recent events, but an adjournment would be the most heartbreaking confession of failure that the Conference could indulge in. The British delegation therefore offered a business document covering the whole field of disarmament. It was less a British Government proposal than a service to the Conference.

The plan assumed a transitional period, but it was to be fixed for five years. He knew it would satisfy nobody ; it was not a shop-window affair or a message from Mars. It had five characteristics :—(1) It was not indefinite, but for five years. (2) It was not a rearmament convention. (3) It provided for control. (4) It set up bodies like the Disarmament Commission to study further disarmament and the solution of future political problems. (5) It gave opportunity to restore confidence so that the fears they had had to contend against during the past few weeks should be removed before the next Conference.

They had been impressed by the French Plan for the standardization of armies and by the Hoover proposals, and had suggested figures for the Continental countries. He then gave some details of the plan, and concluded by reminding them that, while there might be risks in the plan, as in any plan, it would be worse if there were no plan. If they failed, the stream of events would lead to catastrophe.

The Convention would replace those provisions of the Treaties of Versailles, St. Germain, Neuilly, and Trianon which still limited the arms and armed forces of Austria, Bulgaria, Germany, and Hungary.

In describing the British plan, Mr. MacDonald said, " We begin in our draft proposals with articles dealing with the organization of peace. And there we lay down quite plainly that no nation which has signed the agreement of this Conference, which I hope is going to be signed, can be indifferent to a breach of the Kellogg Pact by any other nation. We couple that with the provision relating to supervision which will give some security that whatever obligations have been undertaken are being actually carried out. In that, on the matter of neutrality, we use the idea expressed at such a timely moment, and so clearly and emphatically by Mr. Stimson, the late Secretary of State to the U.S. Government."

The Convention was then distributed.[1] It opened with four articles to be concluded by all the parties to the Kellogg Treaty. By these it was declared that any war undertaken in breach of that Treaty was a matter of interest to all, and should be regarded as a breach of obligations assumed towards each one of them. The contracting parties then agreed to limit their armaments as provided in the Convention.

In the event of a breach or threat of a breach of the Treaty, there should be a conference between the parties, if any five of them, including one at least of the Great Powers, so requested. Any conclusions reached at the conference would have to be concurred in by the representatives of all the Great

[1] For text of the British Draft Convention, see below, p. 267, Appendix II.

Powers and by a majority of the other Governments participating.

Under disarmament, the question of effectives was dealt with first, and the Convention stated that the principle of computing them by the average of the number of days' duty performed had secured universal acceptance as the fairest method of taking account of armies with differing periods of service. It was thought advisable to put the whole of the land forces of the Continent on a comparable basis, and with a view to limiting the power of aggression to reduce them to a militia basis by fixing eight months as the maximum period of service.

Working on the principle of average daily effectives, the longer the period of service the smaller would be the number of men trained each year. Provision was also made for a fixed ratio of long service personnel to conscription in all Continental armies. A table showed the averages of daily effectives not to be exceeded in these under two heads—stationed at home and overseas. The figures for the principal Powers were :— Germany, at home 200,000, overseas nil ; France, 200,000 and 200,000 respectively ; Italy, 200,000 and 50,000 ; Poland, 200,000 and nil ; Belgium, 60,000 and 15,000 ; Rumania, 150,000 and nil ; Czechoslovakia, 100,000 and nil ; Yugoslavia, 100,000 and nil ; and Russia, 500,000 and nil. Hungary would be allowed 60,000, but Austria was not shown.

As regards material, the maximum calibre for land guns should be 105 mm. (4·5 ins.) but existing guns of up to 155 mm. (6 ins.) might be retained. For coast defence guns the limit would be 405 mm. (16 ins.). The maximum tonnage of tanks would be 16 tons. All prohibited material would be destroyed by stages.

As regards naval reductions, the object was to extend the Treaty of London to include France and Italy, and further to stabilise the remaining naval forces of other Powers at the figures reproduced in the Armaments Year Book, 1932, i.e. to hold the situation created by the Naval Treaties until the conference due in 1935.

The truce in capital ship-building would be extended to all, except that Italy might lay down one vessel, (France having laid down *Dunkerque*.)

There would be no construction of 8 in. gun cruisers, except as already provided for. All other construction would be purely for replacement and conform to the qualitative limitations already in force. Germany would be free from the Versailles limitations, but her naval position would be stabilized up to the end of 1936 at its existing condition. She would conform to the truce in capital ship building and limit her other vessels to replacement, the qualitative limitations of Versailles being removed.

A Permanent Disarmament Commission was to be set up, to take immediate steps to prepare for the Conference of 1935.

Bombing from the air would be prohibited, except for police purposes in certain outlying regions, and military and naval aircraft abolished. This would be dependent upon the effective supervision of civil aviation, to prevent its misuse. The number of machines capable of use in war allowed to the principal air Powers would be reduced to 500 (i.e. for France, Japan, Italy, U.S.A., U.S.S.R., and the United Kingdom) with lower totals for the others (i.e. Poland, 200 ; Czechoslovakia, 200 ; Spain, 200 ; Yugoslavia, 200 ; Rumania, 150, and Belgium, 150).

No aircraft, except troop-carriers and flying boats, should exceed three tons in unladen weight. No dirigibles should be built or acquired. Aeroplanes exceeding the limits allowed would all be disposed of by the end of the period of the Convention. Civil aviation would be dealt with on the lines proposed by the British delegation on 30th June, 1932.

Finally, the use of chemical, incendiary, and bacterial weapons, against any State and in any war, should be prohibited. The right to retaliate against a violator of this prohibition would, however, remain.

The draft Convention was a genuinely honest attempt to translate into practical terms the Agreement of 11th December, both in regard to German equality and also to French security. For that reason it made a number of concessions to the different view-points concerned. It adopted the principle of the French proposals for the standardization of armies for the Continental European States on the lines of conscript militia, but offered an alternative to the security proposals contained in the French Plan.

The British security proposals comprised the first five articles of the draft Convention and provided in effect for a new pact of consultation, in which it was hoped to secure the co-operation of the United States :—

   Article 1. The following articles (2–5) are concluded between those of the parties to the present Convention who are parties to the Pact of Paris.
   Article 2. It is hereby declared that any war undertaken in

breach of that Pact is a matter of interest to all the High Contracting Parties, and shall be regarded as a breach of the obligations assumed towards each one of them.

Article 3. In the event of a breach or threat of breach of the Pact of Paris, a conference between the High Contracting Parties shall at once meet at the request of any five of them, provided that at least one of the Governments mentioned by name in Article 4 joins in that request. Such request may be addressed to the Secretary-General of the League of Nations, whose duty it will then be to make arrangements for the Conference and to notify the High Contracting Parties accordingly. The meeting shall take place at Geneva, unless any other meeting-place is agreed upon.

Article 4. Any conclusions reached at such meeting shall, to be valid, require the concurrence of the representatives of the Governments of the United States of America, the United Kingdom of Great Britain and Northern Ireland, France, Germany, Italy, Japan, and the Union of Soviet Socialist Republics, and of a majority of the representatives of the other Governments participating in the Conference, exclusive in each case of the Parties to the dispute.

Article 5. It shall be the object of the said Conference, if called in view of a threat of breach of the Pact, to agree upon the steps which could be taken in respect of such threat, and, in the event of a breach of the Pact of Paris being found to have occurred, to determine which party or parties to the dispute are to be held responsible.

When the Commission adjourned for the Easter Recess on 27th March, it was agreed that the delegations which wished to submit amendments and make statements regarding the text of Part 1 of the Convention should do so before 20th April. The first two delegations to take such action were those of Poland and Italy, but the latter merely sent a communication to state that it reserved its right to propose amendments to any additions, modifications, or reservations which might be submitted by other delegations. Poland's attitude was more critical towards the text of these five Articles, and her delegation wished to amend Nos. 1, 2, and 3. The main object of the changes suggested was understood to be the filling of a gap, " which no doubt was not intended," as the British draft would only be open to the signature of those States parties to the Convention which were also signatories of the Kellogg Treaty. The Polish amendment, accordingly, allowed the States which are bound by the League Covenant, but have not signed the Kellogg Treaty, to join in the undertakings.

The Polish amendment was the first to be submitted to the Commission at the opening of the session on 25th April, and it was followed by that of China. This proposed that in Article

2 the words " war undertaken in breach of that Pact " should be replaced by " resort to war or to force for the purpose of resolving international differences ". The delegation also suggested alterations in Articles 3 and 4 and the addition of a new Article, while the Soviet delegation was asking that a conference should be called at the request of any three of the High Contracting Parties, instead of any five, as provided in Article 3.   After conversations with the Polish and Chinese delegates, Mr. Eden offered to take out Article 1, and to this the Commission agreed.

A new position, however, arose on 26th April when Mr. Norman Davis demonstrated the attitude of the United States towards the proposals contained in Part I.   It was, he said, both the practice and policy of the United States to confer where questions affecting peace were concerned ; Part I, however, introduced a new element in the codification of the principle of consultation and its incorporation in a disarmament convention. The American Government appreciated the importance of harmonizing the situation of the United States with any constructive methods to meet the special needs, particularly on the European Continent, for adequate organization of machinery for preserving peace, but he suggested that, before reaching a final decision on Part I, the Commission should pass on to other sections of the draft Convention, especially Article 94, dealing with the duration of the Treaty, which affected each and every decision arrived at.

The Bureau thereupon decided on 27th April that discussions on Part I by the General Commission should be adjourned and that they should proceed at once to the consideration of Part II, which dealt with the problem of effectives.   Here, however, the new developments in Germany made themselves very clearly apparent, and the proceedings of the Disarmament Conference became inextricably merged with the situation as a whole, which in its turn was dominated by the alarm produced by Nazi Foreign Policy.

4

When Herr Hitler's Coalition Government came into power in the last days of January, 1933, the world at large experienced a feeling of apprehension as to what foreign policy this new Germany would pursue.   The reception accorded by the Nazi Party to the Lausanne Agreement,[1] and the very definite pro-

[1] This had been one of unqualified repudiation. Dr. Goebbels had stated that the Nazi Party did not consider itself bound by the Agreement, since Herr von Papen had not had their authority to sign it.

nouncements made on Treaty Revision, taken in conjunction with a perusal of the Chancellor's autobiographical work *Mein Kampf*, did not give reason to expect that this policy would be altogether a peaceful one.

Immediate fears were somewhat allayed by Herr Hitler's election pronouncement at Cologne on 2nd February to the effect that

> " The Government is conscious of the duty of this free and equal people to work for the maintenance and strengthening of peace, which the world needs as never before. Great though our love is for our Army, as the bearer of our weapons and the symbol of our great past, we should nevertheless be happy if the world, by limiting its armaments, made an increase in our own unnecessary ".

But the tone of the Government's policy underwent a drastic change after the Reichstag fire of 27th February, and the consequent overwhelming victory at the polls on 5th March. The ruthless savagery with which the Government dealt with its political opponents, the medieval brutality of Jew baiting, and the wholesale suppression of pacifists, not excepting a distinguished Prussian Major-General with a gallant war record, shocked public opinion throughout the world, and Herr Hitler's statement at the inauguration of the new Ministry for Propaganda shortly after the elections that " I will fight against and extirpate the philosophy of Marxism and also the idea of peace ", came as a confirmation of Europe's worst fears.

So overwhelming had been the victory of the Nazi and Nationalist Parties in capturing Germany for the new regime and in sweeping away the last remnants of *Das System*, that for the moment the whole Administration gave the appearance of being drunk with power and victory. As a result, events took place in Germany which succeeded in antagonizing her former friends and in consolidating the opposition of those States which had previously been opposed to the Nationalist policy. In England, Italy, and Austria there had been for some time an increasing volume of sentiment favourable to Germany and to her case for Treaty Revision. This sentiment changed overnight, and in England, at any rate, both public and official opinion towards Germany returned to its war-time antagonism. In Italy there was considerable resentment against the imitation of Fascist policy and the bringing of it, thereby, into disrepute, and it was made clear from the first that Germany would receive no support from Rome for any attempt to incorporate Austria

in a Nazi State, but rather that every assistance would be
rendered to Austria in opposing such a measure. In Austria,
itself, all the old longing for union with Germany diminished
with the reorganization of the Reich into a series of Federal
Provinces each controlled by *Statthälter* nominated by the
Government. To enter a Germanic Federation maintaining
her own autonomous Government was for Austria one thing ;
to become a Nazi Province, something very different.

On the other hand, the natural opponents of Germany, notably
France and Poland, regarded with the utmost scepticism Herr
Hitler's statement to the Reichstag that his Government stood
for " a long-term consolidation of peace by the really great
national Powers, in order to restore the mutual confidence of
the peoples ", and compared this with the action of his Government
in erecting in West Prussia a Memorial looking out towards
the Corridor and bearing the inscription " Never forget, Germans,
of what blind hatred robbed you. Bide the hour which will
expiate the shame of this bleeding frontier ".

Even States which had hitherto maintained a neutral attitude
towards Germany were not immune from Nazi propaganda
and Nazi threats. The Danish Government was forced to prohibit
the sections of the Nazi Party formed on Danish territory,
as a result of demonstrations in South Jutland demanding
the return to Germany of Northern Schleswig, which had been
ceded to Denmark under the Treaty of Versailles after a plebiscite
held in February, 1920.

A series of " goodwill " missions did little to improve the
situation.   In Rome, Captain Göring, the Prussian Premier,
as there is good reason to believe, received no slight admonition
both from the Duce and from the Holy Father. In Scandinavia,
Herr Boggs attempted to justify in the most callous manner
the thrashing of a woman Socialist in Berlin by saying that,
if it had happened, no doubt she richly deserved it. In London,
Dr. Rosenberg was left under no illusion as to the feelings of
the British public and of British statesmen as to the manner
in which the German Government had suppressed the liberty
of the subject and had maltreated the Jewish population. But
perhaps the most signal failure was the mission of certain
Nazi Ministers to Austria. In this country the Chancellor,
Dr. Dollfuss,[1] having made himself Dictator with the

---

[1] By reason of his small stature and of the vigorous character of his
policy, Dr. Dollfuss had become popularly known in Vienna as the " Milli
Metternich "

assistance of the Heimwehr, displayed unexpected courage and vigour. In spite of considerable opposition and even a certain amount of dissension within the ranks of his own supporters, he prohibited the wearing of Nazi uniforms and refused to accord to the visiting German Ministers the right to speak publicly or to address themselves to their Austrian political sympathizers in any public manner. Finally, the Bavarian Minister of Justice, Dr. Frank, was courteously but firmly escorted across the frontier.

But it was at the Disarmament Conference at Geneva that the new German policy was most marked. The Draft Convention presented by Mr. MacDonald to the Conference on 16th March had adopted in Part II the French proposals for the standardization of armies for the Continental European Powers on the lines of conscript militias, a scheme aiming at the abolition of professional armies of the type of the *Reichswehr*. The German Delegate, Herr Nadolny, had, during the discussion on Part II, which began on 27th April, refused to consider this proposal and was opposed even to the acceptance of the British Plan as a basis for a future Convention. He also refused point-blank to admit of the incorporation of the semi-military organizations such as the Storm Troops and the *Stahlhelm* in the total of Germany's effectives, and demanded for Germany that the question of standardization be left over for discussion by a future Permanent Commission after the Convention had been signed, claiming that in the meantime Germany could retain both the *Reichswehr* and the semi-military organizations, in addition to repeating the claim for equality in offensive as well as defensive weapons. In effect, he proposed to tear out the whole of the chapter on standardization from the Draft Convention, a suggestion which was tantamount to wrecking the British Plan.

The German Delegation maintained an attitude of complete intransigency in these views, and refused to put forward any constructive counter-proposition. The position reached on 8th May was one of complete deadlock, and the situation assumed an appearance of extreme tension.

In the meantime, private influences from several quarters had been urging Herr Hitler to make a public statement regarding his foreign policy, and especially with regard to peace, particularly after the occasion of a debate in the House of Commons on 13th April, when the most definite opinions were expressed from all Parties in the House as to the British attitude towards Germany. Led by Sir Austen Chamberlain, the House expressed itself as being unable to regard the moment as opportune for discussion of Treaty Revision, in view of the manifestation of the new spirit of German nationalism, which appeared to be the worst type of Prussianism with added savagery and racial pride.

The first reaction to this debate in Germany was one of intense indignation, and the *Chargé d'Affaires* in London was instructed to deliver to the British Foreign Office a protest against the sentiments expressed.   More sober consideration, however, demonstrated to Herr Hitler the necessity of improving the state of public opinion in England towards Germany, and in a speech delivered at Munich on 23rd April he began a series of statements on the pacific policy of Germany which led up to his final dramatic declaration on 17th May. He had already stated, before the Reichstag on 23rd March, that it was the sincere wish of his Government to refrain from any increase in armaments if foreign countries were at least disposed to carry out their obligations radically to disarm. He now went further and gave his Munich audience

> " A clear affirmation of the policy of peace, which Germany needs and wishes to maintain ; Germany, however, cannot further be branded as a second-class nation, but must be recognized in the world as a factor of equal rights ".

Two days later, on 27th April, the Wolff Agency published a statement by the Vice-Chancellor, Herr von Papen, emphasizing the repeated avowals by Herr Hitler in favour of peace, and declaring that Germany needed peace more than any other nation, because the war and the Treaty of Versailles had dealt her the worst wounds. It had been hoped that the Chancellor would include a similar statement in his great declaration of policy to German Labour on 1st May, but, apart from the bare words " we want peace ", there was no mention of foreign policy, save for a curious exhibition of inferiority complex in the statement that the world was persecuting Germany, had turned against her, and would not recognize the right of Germans to protect their homeland.

More practical, however, was Herr Hitler's next step. In an endeavour to alleviate tension on Germany's Eastern frontier, he received the Polish Ambassador in Berlin on 4th May, to whom he declared that it was the intention of the Government to determine its standpoint and action towards Poland strictly within the framework of the existing Treaties, and expressed the hope that the two countries should examine their common interests in an objective manner. This statement, which was equivalent to a re-affirmation of Germany's Eastern obligations under the Treaty of Locarno, was an important step and one calculated to ease the tension in Warsaw.

The value of all these advances, however, was completely nullified by the state of affairs at Geneva, already described. It was useless for Herr Hitler to avow a peaceful policy when his representative at the Disarmament Conference was blandly refusing, not only to accept the British proposals, but even to put forward any counter suggestion of his own. Throughout Europe there was the feeling of a portent of disaster, and there began to circulate rumours of the danger of a preventive war waged by Poland and France against Germany before that country had the time to rearm.

The obduracy of Herr Nadolny at Geneva was given added point when an article appeared in the *Leipziger Illustrierte Zeitung* of 11th May by the German Foreign Minister, Baron von Neurath, announcing Germany's intention, whatever the result of the Disarmament Conference, to rearm in military and naval aircraft, heavy artillery, and man power. He declared that :—

"Equality of status has been formally acknowledged through the Five-Power Declaration of December 11th last. No agreement about general limitation and reduction of armaments will be acceptable by Germany which does not bring practical realization of this equality of status. Germany's standpoint is morally and legally beyond criticism. What is right for others is right for Germany. Such weapons and armaments as the others hold to be necessary for their security can no longer be dispensed with for Germany's security. If no agreement about general disarmament is reached and the full sovereignty of the States in armaments is thus declared as a principle, it will have to hold good in the same manner for Germany. The right to live and the freedom of the German nation cannot be determined by a different measure from that used for other nations."

Elsewhere in the article he declared that Germany would be compelled to provide herself with large calibre artillery, and that the same applied to effectives.

The effect of this article, coupled with Herr Nadolny's attitude at Geneva, had the worst possible effect on the situation, and provided the occasion, in the course of a debate on foreign policy in the House of Lords on the same day, for a declaration by Lord Hailsham, the Minister for War, that any attempt on the part of

Germany to rearm in contravention of the Treaty of Versailles would be a breach of the Treaty and " would bring into operation the sanctions which that Treaty provides ". [1]

The situation was very seriously complicated by a reply which the German Vice-Chancellor, Herr von Papen, made to Lord Hailsham in the course of a speech at Münster on the following day, 12th May, in which he described the War Minister's statement as "hypocrisy". But it was not this item in Herr von Papen's speech which had so grave an effect. It was what followed which sent a shudder through those who read it outside Germany. For the Vice-Chancellor went on in the vein of the most extreme war-time Prussianism, declaring that Germany on 30th January, 1933, had " struck out the word pacifism from its vocabulary ".

> " Pacifist war literature made out that he who fell on the field of honour died an unnatural death. It had no understanding for the old military song ' There is in the world no better death than to be slain by the foe '. It could not understand the ancient German aversion to death on a mattress . . . What the battlefield was for man motherhood was for woman . . . a philosopher had said that he was no man who was not a father ; it was even more true that she was not a woman who was not a mother.[2] The maintenance of eternal life demanded the sacrifice of the individual. Mothers must exhaust themselves in order to give life to children. Fathers must fight on the battlefield in order to secure a future for their sons."

Though the German reading public had learned not to attach too great an importance to Herr von Papen's authority as a statesman and, therefore, the effect of his speech in Germany was to a large extent discounted, it was impossible for Europe as a whole not to be deeply concerned by such remarks from a man who had

---

[1] It is not clear to what sanctions Lord Hailsham referred, and there has been no little discussion amongst experts on international affairs and international law in most of the capitals of Europe as to what steps could be taken in the event of a deliberate infraction by Germany of the military clauses of the Treaty of Versailles. The provision for armed sanctions such as the re-occupation of the Rhineland is to be found only in that section of the Treaty which deals with reparations. The only provision for action in the military section of the Treaty is to be found in Article 213, whereby " Germany undertakes to give every facility for any investigation which the Council of the League of Nations, acting if need be by a majority vote, may consider necessary ". No provision is made for any action in the event of such investigation by the League establishing a breach of the Treaty.

[2] " So much for Jeanne d'Arc," was Mr. Garvin's comment in the *Observer*.

held the office of Chancellor, and was, in fact, Vice-Chancellor. The speech may probably be explained by the fact that it was an attempt on the part of Herr von Papen to maintain his already very difficult position with the Party which he had so gratuitously placed in power, and that he was already reaping the whirlwind he had sown.

The week which opened on 14th May was one of the most momentous in the post-war history of Europe. The deadlock at Geneva ; the declared intention of Germany to rearm at whatever cost ; the threat of sanctions by Lord Hailsham and the wholly deplorable reply to this by Herr von Papen had combined to create an atmosphere highly charged with mistrust and suspicion. It is no exaggeration to say that the danger of war seemed to have been brought within measurable distance, and it was not an unfortunate chance that allowed Dr. Rosenberg to acquaint himself at first hand with the deep-seated disapproval expressed by all sections of official and public opinion in England towards the direction which German foreign policy had taken.

The gravity of the situation was fully realized by Herr Hitler. Now or never was the time to make before the world his declaration of a policy of peace. The importance of the occasion alone demanded a statement which only the Chancellor himself must make. No deputy must tell Germany and the world what Herr Hitler himself intended to do. With an appreciation of the fact that his word must be spoken to the German people as a whole, the Chancellor chose as his medium the tribune of the Reichstag rather than the private microphone, and he, therefore, summoned Parliament in special session on 17th May.

The world awaited Herr Hitler's pronouncement with a degree of anxious expectancy which has been accorded to the words of no other German statesman. Would he choose the path of peace and compromise or would he, like the Roman envoy before the Carthaginian Senate, shake out the fold of war from his toga ? So great was the fear that the latter course might be pursued that President Roosevelt took the opportunity of indicating to the nations of the world, and to Germany in particular, the only line of policy upon which America could co-operate for the peace of the world.

On 16th May, that is to say the day before the Reichstag session, President Roosevelt addressed to the Emperors, Kings and Presidents of the fifty-four States participant in the Disarmament and Economic Conferences a Message on political and economic peace, in which he called upon them to take four steps in which the United States would co-operate :—

(1) To accept and act upon the British Disarmament Plan.

(2) To agree upon the time and procedure for taking the steps which were to follow.

(3) To agree that while the first and following steps were being taken no nation should increase its existing armaments over and above the limitations of Treaty obligations.

(4) That all nations should enter into a solemn and definite Pact of Non-Aggression ; that they should solemnly re-affirm the obligations they had assumed to limit and reduce their armaments, and, provided that these obligations were faithfully executed by all signatory Powers, individually agree that they would send no armed force of whatsoever nature across their frontiers.

The concluding words of President Roosevelt's Message struck a warning note to any potential peace-breaker. " If," said he, " any strong nation refuses to join with genuine sincerity in these concerted efforts for political and economic peace . . . the civilized world will know where the responsibility for failure lies." [1]

There is little doubt that the Roosevelt Message, and the report which Dr. Rosenberg made to him on his return from London on 15th May, seriously influenced Herr Hitler in the composition of his speech. He must have learned, which the German people had not, what an amazing revulsion of feeling there had been both in England and America towards Germany. He must have realized that the revolutionary Nazi foreign policy had succeeded in encircling Germany with suspicion and enmity. He had good reason to be alarmed at the fruits of his policy, and had received a strong warning from the Minister of Defence, General von Blomberg, that with the present state of German armaments he could not be responsible for the results of this policy if it were pursued much further. At least common prudence, if not conviction, may have brought about a statesmanlike moderation in his language.

Before a crowded Reichstag the Chancellor delivered a speech which could scarcely have been equalled by Stresemann or Brüning. After ascribing most of the world's ills to the Treaty of Versailles which, though it provided no solution for the world's problems, no German Government would of its own

[1] Important though the President's message was, it scarcely warranted its description by Mr. Ramsay MacDonald at the Pilgrims' Banquet on the night of the 16th, that " America has boldly, openly, cut her moorings on the quays of the New World and has launched herself under full sail, with high courage and with fine determination, on to new waters ".

accord break without being able first to supplant it by a better
one, Herr Hitler passed on to make some concrete proposals.
" No fresh European war," he declared, " was capable of putting
something better in the place of the unsatisfactory conditions
which to-day exist . . . the outbreak of such a madness without
end would lead to the collapse of the existing social order in
Europe." He then repeated the basis of Germany's claim for
equality, but added : " Germany is at any time ready to assume
further international security obligations if all nations are
prepared to do so and Germany benefits thereby. Germany
is also ready without further ado to dissolve her entire military
forces and destroy the weapons left to her if other nations will
do the same. If, however, they are not willing to carry out
the disarmament stipulations of the Treaty of Versailles, then
Germany must at least maintain her claim to equality."

Herr Hitler declared that his Government would accept the
British Plan as a starting point for the solution of the disarmament problem on two conditions. First, destruction of the
existing German defence system must not be imposed without
the concession of qualitative equality ; and, secondly, the
transformation of the present system, which was not desired
by but was forced upon Germany, must proceed in proportion
as the other States actually disarmed. Germany was ready
to renounce instruments of aggression if, during the five years
of transition, other nations made the same renunciation. She
was ready to accept the five-year transitional period for the
restoration of her national security in the expectation that after
that period a real equality would have been achieved with other
nations. Further, she was prepared to accept a general international control of armaments, and would include in that control
organizations the non-military character of which could thus
be established clearly before the world. In return Germany
insisted that the French Colonial troops must be reckoned as
part of the French Army, as they could be used at once on the
mainland of France.

Referring to the Roosevelt Message, the Chancellor welcomed
it warmly and was ready to accept it as a method of relieving
the international crisis. Germany was ready to join any non-
aggression pact, for she was not thinking of any attack but only of
her own equality, and he welcomed the possibility suggested in
President Roosevelt's proposal of bringing the United States
into European relations as a guarantor of peace. The German
Government wished nothing better than to settle all difficult

questions with other countries by peaceful methods. Germany would tread no other path than that laid down by the Treaty, and would discuss all political and economic questions only within the framework of and through the Treaties.

As a rider to these guarantees of the new Germany's pacific intentions, Herr Hitler added a warning note to the effect that, as a permanently defamed people, it would be impossible for Germany to continue to belong to the League of Nations.

The effect of this speech was greatly to ease the tension of the situation. The pronouncement had gone very far towards meeting the British proposals at Geneva and had shown a real anxiety on the part of the Chancellor to express what he had to say in the philosophy of a good European. Some hesitation was evinced in certain quarters as to the genuineness of the sentiments expressed, but these fears were somewhat allayed when, on 19th May at Geneva, Herr Nadolny publicly stated that the German Government accepted the British Draft " not only, as hitherto, as a basis of discussion but as a basis for the future Convention itself ", and that any modification which would be proposed would be "in conformity with this new idea ". Three days later, on 22nd May, he formally withdrew the German amendment deleting the chapter on standardization from the British Draft.

Further efforts to give rapid effect to the sentiments expressed in Herr Hitler's speech were made when Capt. Göring, the Prussian Prime Minister, left suddenly for a week-end visit to Rome, as a result of which it was announced that he and Signor Mussolini, together with the British and French Ambassadors, had reached a tentative agreement with regard to the Four-Power Pact.[1]

The effect of Herr Hitler's speech had been not only to clear the air, but also to achieve a diplomatic and tactical victory. Germany had been placed in the position of being responsible for the breakdown of the Conference. Herr Hitler's offer and its immediate putting into force had removed this impression, and had replaced the onus of a potential breakdown upon France. With a subtlety that few had expected of him, Herr Hitler had achieved in one day a very great deal. The tone of the British Press immediately became more friendly, particularly that of the Sunday papers, and the focal point of the crisis was changed from German obduracy to the value of the American offer made by Mr. Davis on behalf of the President, on 22nd May.

[1] See below, p. 140.

For the moment the crisis at Geneva had been averted, and Germany had to some extent rehabilitated herself in the eyes of the world.

5

The statement which Mr. Norman Davis made to the General Commission on 22nd May seemed as if it removed one of the gravest obstacles to the conclusion of a world security pact— the uncertainty of the attitude of the United States. The search after the formula for a pact of consultation which would include American co-operation had long occupied experts in international affairs, but the progress had been very slow.

Mr. Stimson had hinted at the possibility of such an agreement in complement to the Kellogg Pact as early as 1929, and the willingness of the United States to co-operate with the League in the early days of the Sino-Japanese dispute of 1931 gave very considerable encouragement.[1]   A further step seemed to have been taken when Mr. Stimson, in his address before the Council on Foreign Relations on 8th August, 1932, committed himself to the statement that the Kellogg Pact had rendered neutrality illegal.[2]   The statement had been eagerly seized upon in Europe and had found its place both in the French Plan and the British Draft Convention, while Mr. MacDonald had made specific references to it in his speech of 16th March.   During his visit to the United States in April the British Prime Minister had discussed the situation with Mr. Roosevelt and had found him refreshingly sympathetic.   The President's Message to the rulers of the world on 16th May had been regarded as an advance, but it contained no definite commitment and the world waited anxiously for this.   Six days later it came, when Mr. Davis addressed the General Committee.

Explaining what his Government was prepared to do Mr. Davis said—" We are willing to consult with other States in case of a threat to peace with a view to avoiding a conflict. Further than that, in the event of the States in conference determining that a State has been guilty of a violation of its international obligations and taking measures against the violator, then, if we concur in the judgment rendered as to the responsible and guilty party, we will refrain from any action tending to defeat such collective efforts which the States may thus make to restore peace." Mr. Davis went on to express his approval

[1] See *Disarmament and Security*, pp. 268–280.
[2] See above, p. 63.

of the British Plan and to promise full support for its adoption.
He suggested that armaments should be reduced to the levels
laid down in the Peace Treaties, and added that the United States
were also prepared to assist in formulating and taking part in
a system of adequate supervision to ensure the effective carrying
out of any measures of disarmament.

The other delegates immediately recognized the immense
importance of Mr. Davis's statement, and the immense implications which it carried. With the assurance of American co-
operation in dealing with an aggressor State, whose guilt of
aggression American representatives would have shared in
determining, the operation of Article 16 of the Covenant itself
became a possibility, for it banished at least the bogey of
American men-of-war convoying American merchantmen through
a League blockade. Dreams which had not been cherished
since the definite refusal of the United States in 1920 to enter
the League began once more to shape themselves. No American
succour or assistance for a State at war in defiance of her obligations, meant, as a corollary, that every succour and assistance
would be given by America to those States who were enforcing
the obligations and reducing the recalcitrant signatory to a state
of proper submission. For immediate purposes the American
declaration removed the objections which Mr. Davis himself
had raised on 26th April to the discussion of Part I of the British
Draft Convention.

Sir John Simon at once proposed that Part I of the Convention
should now be examined Article by Article, and on 24th May
submitted to the General Commission three new Articles to take
the place of Articles 2–5 of the original Part I of the British
Draft. The new Articles read :—(1) In the event of a breach
or threat of breach of the Pact of Paris, either the Council or
Assembly of the League of Nations, or one of the parties to the
present Convention who are not members of the League of
Nations, may propose immediate consultation between the
Council or Assembly and any of the said parties to the said
Convention ; (2) It shall be the object of such consultation
(a) in the event of a threat of a breach of the Pact to exchange
views for the purpose of preserving the peace and averting
conflict ; (b) in the event of a breach of the Pact to use good
offices for the restoration of peace ; and (c) in the event that
it proves impossible thus to restore the peace, then to determine
which party, or parties, to the dispute are to be held responsible ;
(3) The provisions of the above Articles do not in any way

prejudice the rights and obligations of the Members of the League nor conflict with nor limit the powers and duties of the Assembly and the Council under the Covenant.

Sir John Simon explained that Article I had been drafted so as to make provision for a proposal or invitation addressed from within the League to non-Members, or by a non-Member to those within the League, to join in a consultation. " I think we may assume that in appropriate cases that invitation might well be accepted and we should thus have provided for that method of consultation to which Mr. Norman Davis referred." Article II declared what would be the object of the consultation, and they had in mind the explanation given by Mr. Davis, in which there was "manifestly an effort . . . eventually to modify the strict regard for the law of neutrality . . ." Article III was new ; it applied only to Members of the League and made it clear that nothing proposed in Part I in the least qualified their obligations under the Covenant. Part I in its new form provided a suitable foundation for any subsequent co-operation between League Members and non-Members.

Mr. Davis replied that he had the impression that the new Articles were in harmony with his Declaration, and M. Paul-Boncour thanked the British and United States delegates for their " extremely important " statements of policy. He suggested that as these statements had so clarified the situation it would be better if the General Commission were to consider Part II of the British Draft (Material) while the Europeans discussed Part I amongst themselves.

The Bureau decided that Parts I and II should be discussed alternately. It was, however, impossible to get the two subjects distinct, as the Turkish delegate suddenly raised the question of the freedom of the Straits. M. Paul-Boncour at once pointed out that this meant the revision of Treaties. After this interlude the General Commission debated, turn and turn about, the calibre of guns and security and qualitative disarmament. But the further the discussion was continued the more clear became the difficulties to reach agreement. An old controversy was revived in a fresh attempt, sponsored by the delegation of the U.S.S.R., to define the aggressor. Japan demanded the deletion of Article 23 (dealing with naval armaments) as she had only accepted the Treaty of London on condition that her navy should not be limited to the figures laid down beyond 1935. This started the usual wrangle over capital ships, cruisers, submarines, etc.

Finally on 31st May the Bureau decided—(1) that the General Commission should go on to the decisive second reading of the British Draft, but should adjourn as soon as the non-committal first reading had been conducted. (2) That the Bureau should then spend three weeks, 5th–25th June, at work on the draft, preparing for the second reading. (3) That the General Commission should meet subsequently, probably on 3rd July, to begin the second reading, and take decisions on the draft.

In the course of a debate on the Disarmament Conference in the House of Commons on 26th May, Sir John Simon traced at great length the definitions of neutrality which had existed at different periods, as an introduction to pointing out the great change which had come out in the attitude of the United States. Mr. Davis's declaration in Geneva had altered the whole situation. After saying that he welcomed the better turn of Herr Hitler's statement of policy, Sir John Simon summed up the Government's policy under five heads :—(1) to welcome and respond to President Roosevelt's Message ; (2) to make it clear that Great Britain could not proceed further on the lines of unilateral disarmament, whereupon it had already gone so far, but to point out through the British proposals how much further disarmament by agreement could go ; (3) to recognize the validity of other countries' concern for security : Part I of the draft, together with the United States' declaration, had done much to meet it ; (4) not to undertake liabilities other than already assumed under the Covenant and the Locarno treaties, but to join in the proposed consultation pact which would complete the concentric rings of arrangements designed to promote security by bringing into these arrangements the U.S.A. ; (5) to maintain that international disarmament must depend on policy, and therefore to be permanent and effective must depend upon securing better relations between European States.

Unfortunately, at this moment, almost at the very time when Sir John Simon was addressing the House, the world was accorded one further example of the great difficulties attendant upon the putting of trust in American diplomacy, and indeed in entering into any negotiations with the United States at all. Undoubtedly, Mr. Davis had spoken on 22nd May with the knowledge, consent, and approval of the President and his Administration. There yet remained the Senate.

Isolationist sentiment in the United States had been seriously concerned by the gradual drift, first of Mr. Hoover and later of

Mr. Roosevelt, to an increased degree of co-operation in European organizations. Despite the change in the administration, the isolationists were still strong in Congress, and especially on the Senate Committee on Foreign Relations, that all-powerful body through which every treaty negotiated by the United States must pass before it can be ratified or implemented. The Committee had before it a resolution, which had been officially backed by President Hoover, authorizing the President to declare an embargo on the export of arms to an aggressor nation. The adoption of such a resolution by Congress would have given substantial backing and confirmation to Mr. Davis's statement at Geneva, and would have demonstrated to the Disarmament Conference that the United States was prepared to support her promises by action.

Alarmed, however, at the growing talk of the abandonment of neutrality by the United States, the Committee on Foreign Relations determined to do all in their power to make this step impossible. An amendment was put forward to the resolution by Senators Johnson and Vandenberg, though its true author was John Bassett Moore, the great authority on international law, and formerly a judge of the Permanent Court of International Justice, so altering it that the President could only declare a simultaneous embargo on all shipment to *all parties* involved in the dispute. The effect would be to make action by the President in support of international action against an aggressor impossible and would retain full independence of judgment in any case to Congress.

Despite efforts at persuasion and compromise by Mr. Hull, the Secretary of State, the Committee remained adamant and the resolution in its amended form was adopted on 27th May, the isolationists openly congratulating themselves that their efforts had " retained the status of neutrality for this nation ".[1]

Thus .the American gesture, from which so much had been hoped, was negatived before it was a week old, and the Disarmament Conference returned to its eternal wranglings and dissensions, which continued without effect throughout the month of June. Their deliberations, however, were relieved by one incident not altogether lacking in humour.

On the 24th of June the entire German Press published a report that foreign aeroplanes had flown over Berlin the previous evening and had dropped leaflets " insulting the Government

[1] The Senate adopted the amended text without debate or roll-call on 28th February, 1934, despite the opposition of the White House.

in an incredible manner ''. Not even the most energetic and inquisitive of the foreign journalists in Berlin had seen the aircraft referred to, nor could they find anyone else who had done so. Yet the aerial invaders must have flown very low and have acquired considerable precision of aim, for, by a curious coincidence, the only leaflets which were found had been picked up in the Wilhelmstrasse between the Foreign Office and the Ministry of Propaganda !

At once Captain Göring, Reichsminister for Air, placed an order for the construction of two fast police planes, whose duty would be to '' pursue and establish the identity of invading foreign air-raiders such as visited Germany yesterday ''. At once the *gleichgeschalltet* Press began to clamour that this '' attack '' must compel Germany finally and definitely to demand equality in the air, as well as on sea and land, and on 26th June the Secretariat of the Disarmament Conference received more than seventy protests from municipal authorities, associations, and private persons in Germany against the flight over Berlin of aeroplanes '' which have not yet been identified ''.

Apart from this incident, however, the second session of the Conference pursued its weary way without arriving at any definite result. The public had lost interest in it and were far more concerned with the prospects of the World Economic Conference which opened in London on 12th June, and with the all-important question of whether Germany was rearming or not. All confidence in the Conference had vanished, together with any hope of its ever attaining even a partial success, and the adjournment on 30th June passed almost unnoticed.

Despite the opposition of Herr Nadolny, and the abstention of the Hungarian delegate from voting, the General Commission agreed with the proposal of the Bureau that the public meetings of the Conference should be adjourned *sine die* and that the President of the Conference should proceed to conduct private negotiations with the various Governments on all the points outstanding. And, thus, having most satisfactorily, from their own point of view, '' passed the buck,'' the delegates dispersed to their own countries.

CHAPTER VII

ROMAN INTERLUDE

1

But, while these discussions at Geneva were becoming more and more atrophied, there was in progress, first in Rome and later in other European capitals, a parallel series of diplomatic manoeuvres which on 15th July concluded in the signing of the Four-Power Pact between Italy, Great Britain, France, and Germany.

The genesis of the Four-Power Pact is to be found in the foreign policy pursued by Signor Mussolini for many years. He had always believed that the first, and indeed the essential, condition for the peace of Europe was a good understanding between Italy, Great Britain, France, and Germany. His disappointment that the Locarno Treaty failed to bring about this desired result is reflected in the speeches which he made during the years following that agreement. "The label on the bottle remains," he said on one occasion, "but the contents have evaporated."

When addressing a monster demonstration of Fascists at Turin during the celebrations of the Tenth Anniversary of the March on Rome, Signor Mussolini made a series of important announcements on foreign affairs. He began by proclaiming Italy's desire for peace and the sincerity with which she had put forward her disarmament proposals. He declared that she had no intention of leaving the League of Nations at the very moment when that body found itself in difficulties. He referred to Germany's "just claim" for equality of status: "it must be recognized, and the sooner the better. At the same time, as long as the Disarmament Conference is at work, Germany cannot ask for any measure of disarmament, but should the Conference not reach an agreement, then Germany could not remain in the League of Nations unless this inequality is wiped out." He then outlined very clearly the thought which was to take form in the Four-Power Pact.

[1] All relevant documents quoted in this chapter will be found in *Documents on International Affairs, 1933*, edited by J. W. Wheeler-Bennett. Oxford University Press, 1934, pp. 236–276.

" There have been efforts to free Europe from this organization, which is too universal in its scope. But I think that if, to-morrow, on a basis of justice and of the recognition of our incontrovertible rights, won by the blood of so many generations of young Italians, there could be created the necessary and sufficient premises for a collaboration of the four great Western Powers, Europe could find peace in the political sphere and soon the economic crisis which is torturing her would come to an end."

The original draft of the Four-Power Pact was dated "*Rocca delle Camminate*, 4 *Marzo XI*".[1] Signor Mussolini, as he said subsequently, had been thinking about it for a long time, and during one of his rare holidays in his native Romagna he wrote the first draft of the Pact. It was based in the first instance on the Locarno Treaty and in the second on the so-called " No Resort to Force " Pact which had been proposed in Geneva in 1932, but Signor Mussolini wished to implement the vague clauses of the latter by a clear and permanent understanding between Italy, Great Britain, France, and Germany. The original text read as follows :—

(1) The four Western Powers, Germany, France, Great Britain, and Italy, undertake to realize among themselves an effective policy of co-operation with a view to maintaining peace in accordance with the Kellogg and Anti-War Pacts. They also undertake to act in the sphere of European relations in such a manner that this peace policy will be adopted in case of necessity by other Powers as well.

(2) The four Powers confirm the principle of the revision of treaties in accordance with the clauses of the Covenant of the League of Nations in cases in which there is a possibility that they will lead to conflict among the States. They declare at the same time that the principle of revision cannot be applied except within the framework of the League and in a spirit of mutual understanding and solidarity of reciprocal interests.

(3) France, Great Britain, and Italy declare that in case the Disarmament Conference attains only partial results the equality of rights recognized for Germany shall have an effective meaning, and Germany undertakes to realize this equality of rights by stages which will be determined by successive agreements among the four Powers through the usual diplomatic channels.

The four Powers undertake to reach similar agreements with regard to Austria, Hungary, and Bulgaria.

(4) In all political and non-political European and extra-European questions, as well as in the colonial sphere, the four Powers undertake to adopt as far as possible a common line of action.

(5) This political agreement of understanding and co-operation, which will be submitted if necessary for Parliamentary approval

[1] *Il Patto Mussolini*, Senatore F. Salata, Mondadori, Milano, 1934.

within three months, will have a life of ten years, and will be automatically extended for another ten years unless it is denounced by one of the contracting parties one year before its expiration.

(6) The present Pact will be submitted to the Secretariat of the League of Nations.

This first article contained in Signor Mussolini's opinion the essence of the whole matter, and, after many revisions and amendments, it remains the guiding principle of the final form of the Pact. In the course of many speeches delivered in the last few years Signor Mussolini has reiterated his belief that peace can only be secured in Europe by a revision of certain provisions in the Peace Treaties. He has also made it clear that such revisions must be made through the machinery of the League of Nations, i.e. in conformity with Article 19 of the Covenant which states :—

" The Assembly may from time to time advise the consideration by Members of the League of treaties which have become inapplicable and the consideration of international conditions whose continuance might endanger the peace of the world."

2

Before leaving Geneva Mr. MacDonald, on 17th March, told the journalists that he wished to discuss with Signor Mussolini the distracted state of Europe and to see whether it were not possible to restore peace and confidence by organizing a group of Powers all desirous of the maintenance of good relations among themselves. It was at this meeting with the journalists that Mr. Ramsay MacDonald coined the phrase " The Peace Club ", with which the European Press made much play during the succeeding weeks. M. Daladier was informed on the telephone of the plan and, either on his own initiative or at Mr. MacDonald's suggestion—the French Press could not decide which version of the story was correct—hurried to Geneva to see his British colleague before he left. Mr. MacDonald subsequently announced that he carried with him M. Daladier's warm wishes for a successful outcome of his visit.

While the British Ministers were being flown from Geneva to Ostia in a seaplane piloted by General Balbo, Signor Mussolini was receiving the British, French, and German Ambassadors at the Palazzo Venezia and handing to each a copy of his draft of the proposed plan. When Mr. MacDonald and Sir John Simon landed at Ostia they were met by the head of the Italian Government and the British Ambassador, Sir Ronald Graham, who

immediately gave them the draft scheme. They read it in the
motor car in which they were being driven to Rome by Signor
Mussolini. [1]

The British statesmen received the warmest welcome from the
Roman public and from the Italian Press, and their conferences
were punctuated by a round of entertaining and sightseeing.
On the morning of 19th March an official *communiqué* was
published announcing that " after a full and exhaustive exchange
of ideas on the general situation, the Ministers examined in
their conversations a project for an understanding on the larger
political questions put forward by the head of the Italian
Government with the object of securing the collaboration of
the Four Western Powers in an effort to promote, in the spirit
of the Kellogg Pact and the ' No Force ' declaration, a long
period of peace for Europe and the world ". At a reception
given to the Press at the British Embassy, Mr. MacDonald told
the journalists not to read anything more in the *communiqué*
than it actually contained. It was a vain plea, for the floodgates
of comment, insinuation, and criticism, based on supposition,
were immediately let loose all over Europe.

Indeed the concatination of circumstances, Mr. MacDonald's
presence at Geneva, his readiness to visit Rome, the presentation
of a new British Convention, the existence of Signor Mussolini's
draft project, meant that a scheme, which might have been
elaborated more easily through ordinary diplomatic channels,
had to be announced to the world. " Secret diplomacy " may
have its faults, " open diplomacy " its drawbacks, but diplomacy
conducted to the deafening chorus of newspaper clamour over
most of a Continent is almost impossible.

On his way back from Rome Mr. MacDonald stopped in Paris
for conversations with the French Government, which he subsequently described as " very friendly ". By this time the French
Press had become definitely hostile ; it discovered a sudden
enthusiasm for the League, it denounced what it described
as a " European directory ", and declared that an effort was
being made to settle vital matters affecting the smaller States
without consultation. The *Figaro* enlivened the proceedings
by describing Mr. MacDonald as " *un pacifiste sanguinaire* ".
The Press of the Little Entente and Poland needed no encouragement to fling itself into the fray.

---

[1] Those who have had experience of the Duce's driving may conclude
that the British Ministers were not able to derive a very complete knowledge of the Italian proposals from this preliminary perusal !

Mr. MacDonald communicated to the French Government the modifications to the original draft which had been made during his conversations in Rome, which had been forwarded from Rome to Berlin. In conversations with the Italian Ambassador, Herr Hitler, Baron von Neurath, and Herr von Bülow had already given a warm welcome to Signor Mussolini's proposals. They considered that " revision " was still made to depend too exclusively on the provisions of the Covenant and that the rearmament of Germany should not be postponed for so long a period as ten years. But on receipt of the first revised version they again expressed their readiness to take part in the discussions, though they preferred the original scheme.

3

On 23rd March Mr. MacDonald, in what Signor Mussolini described as an " eloquent and courageous speech ", took the first opportunity of informing the House of Commons " regarding what happened whilst the Foreign Secretary and myself were in Geneva and Rome ". Unfortunately, Mr. MacDonald's hearers did not share Signor Mussolini's sentiments, as the feeling in the House and the country was that " Dr. Parker made that darker which was dark enough before ". Mr. MacDonald began with some observations on the new British proposals which, he said, had been rendered necessary by the deadlock that had occurred at Geneva. " There were," he said, " two essentials in that plan of ours. First of all it contained for the first time figures regarding various arms ... Until figures had been produced there could be no progress, because the thing that every nation wanted to avoid was the production of figures. Yet, curiously enough, delegate after delegate in the course of interviews begged me to have the courage to produce figures for them . . . There is another point. We are pledged to give equality to Germany. The time has gone by when by a combination of any Powers any European people can be kept down by obligations which it regards as being inconsistent with its self-respect and its honour, and now we have made it perfectly clear that the obligations that are to be placed upon the nations of Europe are to be obligations of honour and moral responsibility, obligations which will be all the more serious for them since they have taken them upon themselves in a voluntary way. But, as again I said at Geneva, events have happened that have enormously increased the risk of taking a big step like that at the present moment, and our plan presupposes quite clearly a transition stage. During that stage of progress towards equality, equality itself will not be carried out, but during it there shall be no rearmament and no question of rearmament. . . ."

Mr. MacDonald then went on to deal with the negotiations in Rome, describing what he believed to have been in Signor Mussolini's mind and emphasizing the need for Treaty Revision under Article 19 of the Covenant. The original plan was, he declared, really a basis for discussion. " We were not asked to approve or disapprove." He tried to soothe the fears of the smaller States by saying that they had a right to be consulted whenever their special interests were concerned, and that nothing would be done except within the framework of the League. He said that the Government welcomed Signor Mussolini's idea and referred in general terms to the dangers that threatened Europe if two of the greater Powers were driven by circumstances to opposing views. " This project, if made to work, if we can get the idea accepted and carried out, will prevent all that. If we fail in courage and be afraid to remember that we all signed Article 19 of the Covenant of the League of Nations, we shall not evade the difficulties which its provisions sought to avert . . ." Mr. MacDonald did not give any detailed account of the proposal but contented himself by saying " the conversations at Rome amounted to this—that now, when it is perfectly plain to everybody that national life is being revitalized in Europe, the four Powers should meet, before they may be driven apart, to try to remove by negotiation the dangers that will have to be met in any event . . . The British Government is now working at a plan, trying to fit it for its purpose, and to devise a means of handling what is admittedly a problem of the greatest delicacy. The reconsideration of treaties, however, is not enough. The other nations have to make a contribution of their own, and that contribution must be a substantial one. It must be such a contribution, in such form, and of such importance, as will place beyond the shadow of doubt that when these changes are made they are not to pursue in Europe anything but a co-operative and friendly policy. If the Four Powers come together, if a way can be devised for joining with their views those of the smaller nationalities concerned, and for examining the causes of fear leading now to an unwillingness to disarm, who would dare to deny but that the most effective work for peace which has been done since the War will have been accomplished? That may well have been begun by the Italian plan.

" In any event . . . we pay a hearty tribute to the humanity
of the intentions embodied in the project of the Italian Prime
Minister and Governments, and hope that the means of co-
operation for which they are in search will be found . . . Let
it be co-operation in a form and a spirit which may well draw
to it the sympathy and the aid of one Power, our friend beyond
the Atlantic."

The House received from Mr. Grenfell, who was leading
the Opposition attack in the absence of Mr. Lansbury through
the illness of his wife, the details which the Prime Minister
had abstained from giving. Quoting from an alleged interview
with M. Daladier in the *Temps*, Mr. Grenfell read a practically
full version of Signor Mussolini's original draft, but, in the absence
of official information, members were not prepared to accept
this as sufficiently authoritative to serve as the basis for debate.

Except for a pungent attack by Mr. Winston Churchill on
the whole disarmament policy of the Government and the
regulation party attack of the Opposition, the debate was, on
the whole, friendly, though many members complained of the
lack of information on the exact terms of the new proposal.

4

On the same day Herr Hitler addressed the Reichstag. Referring
to the plan of the Italian Government, he said : " The far-reaching
plan of the Head of the Italian Government to re-unite the
European Powers in a real policy of peace is warmly welcomed
by the German Government, which attaches the greatest importance to this proposal. The German Government is ready to
collaborate loyally in this plan for the peaceful co-operation
of the Four Great European Powers."

The soothing words of Mr. MacDonald did nothing to allay
the alarm and indignation of the Little Entente and Poland ;
the Press of the various countries was described in Italy as being
in a " state of hysteria ". On 25th March the Permanent Council
of the Little Entente, meeting in Geneva, issued a statement
declaring that it was of opinion that all collaboration between
States which made its goal the establishment of friendly relations
between them was desirable and salutary, but it could not
admit that the cause of good relations between the various
countries was helped by arrangements which had for their
aim the disposal of rights belonging to other States, whether
such agreements obliged their signatories to take concrete
decisions, or whether the purpose was that the signatories

should exert pressure on countries which were not parties to
the agreements. It was impossible to dispose, either directly or
indirectly, of the property of others, and the States of the
Little Entente "formulate at once the most explicit reserve
towards the eventual conclusion of such agreements in all that
might concern their rights and property".

Meanwhile the Paris Press had been continuing the campaign
against the proposed Pact and naturally welcomed the declaration
of the Little Entente with enthusiasm. Opinion amongst politicians, and even among members of the Cabinet, was divided.
M. Daladier was supposed to be in favour, M. Paul-Boncour
doubtful, while attacks in the Chamber came from both the
Right and Left. Hot foot on the heels of the official announcement came M. Titulescu to Paris to urge the views of France's
"satellite" nations. M. de Jouvenel, whose ambassadorship
in Rome had done much to improve Italo-French relations,
arrived to explain and, as it subsequently appeared, to defend
the Pact. The French Government was in a difficult position ;
distracted on one side by what it regarded as the new threat
to security from a Nazi Germany, on another by the protests
of its Allies, on another by the attacks on any policy which
would mean an entente with Italy—attacks fanned as usual
by the *Fuorusciti* [1]—it hesitated to take a line which would
alienate the sympathy of the British Prime Minister, the
enthusiastic god-father of the infant. Opposition might bring
about the very result that it feared, the isolation of France
from the other three great Occidental Powers and the odium
of having torpedoed a proposal for the pacification of Europe.
Any subsequent failure of the Disarmament Conference would
also inevitably have led to the accusation that it was the result
of French action.

On 30th March the usual leakage occurred in Paris and the
text of the original draft was published in the French Press.
As the substance had long been known in Paris it aroused little
excitement, but gave fuel to the attacks. But as the *République*,
which was credited with expressing the views of M. Daladier,
inquired, "if France continues to say 'no', what is to
happen next?"

What was actually happening was a series of interviews
between M. Paul-Boncour, the British Ambassador, M. de
Jouvenel, and the agitated M. Titulescu, while the Quai d'Orsay

---

[1] Anti-Fascist *émigrés* in foreign countries.

worked feverishly to produce their own modifications of the British modifications of the original. When Mr. Norman Davis was on the point of starting for Europe the President was asked by a journalist if the American representative was going to join the " Peace Club ? " " What is that ? " replied Mr. Roosevelt, and, when the journalist had explained the allusion, " What is the subscription to this Peace Club ? " enquired the President. The proposal was discussed with Mr. Norman Davis on his arrival in Paris at the beginning of April, and before he left for Berlin Mr. Davis was reported to have said that though it was not a matter which directly interested America, the United States welcomed any suggestion which would improve the European political situation.

Amended versions and documents dealing with the Pact became as thick as leaves in Vallombrosa. On 24th March the British Government had circulated their first ideas on the question, on 2nd April the Belgian Government addressed an *aide-mémoire* to the French Government in which it warmly supported the proposed agreement, so long as it was in conformity with the Covenant of the League and provided that Belgium was always consulted when its special interests were concerned.

On 3rd April, after a sitting of three hours, the French Cabinet issued a *communiqué* to say that it had considered the Italo-British proposals and had decided to reply. M. Titulescu, meanwhile, left Paris for London to continue his campaign against the Pact and was received by the Prime Minister and Sir John Simon. In order to state the views of the Little Entente, Colonel Beck, the Polish Foreign Minister, had gone to Bucharest and Belgrade to concert further measures against the proposal.

On 5th April a " summary " of the French plan was published in Berlin and aroused immediately a chorus of protest in the German Press. It was believed that the original draft was being so watered down in London and Paris as to be entirely valueless to Germany, who desired to see a practical agreement which would lead to the revision of frontiers. That country had no interest in another vague and general agreement on the blessings of peace. There was also great indignation over the idea that the French Government had proposed that the Little Entente should be brought into the Pact.

5

At last on April 10th, after many alarums and excursions, the French text and its accompanying memorandum were agreed upon and dispatched. The memorandum was unexpectedly friendly in tone ; it was chiefly concerned with the necessity of a strict observance of all previous agreements and particularly the Covenant of the League. It made a special point of safe-guarding the interests of other States ; any action was to be taken through the regular organs of the League ; "no arbitrary choice was to be made among the Articles of the Covenant ; while a reference in general terms of revision of treaties could only cause alarm—which, however unjustifiable, would only be an obstacle to a *rapprochement* between nations." The French Government was glad to see that "equality of status" for Germany was only to be achieved by stages and that rearmament was excluded. They declared their support for the British Disarmament Plan, which gave a definite basis for discussion in the Conference with necessary amendments.

Finally, the French Government did not wish to see co-operation restricted to questions of which the League of Nations was already seized.

The following is the text of the French draft :—

(1) The High Contracting Parties will consult one another on all questions which directly concern them, and will endeavour mutually to practise, within the framework of the League Covenant, an effective policy of co-operation for the maintenance of peace.

(2) The High Contracting Parties, in view of any application which may be necessary in Europe of Articles 10, 16, and 19, decide to examine among themselves, without prejudice to decisions which can be taken only by the regular institutions of the League, all proposals which may tend to give full effect to the methods of procedure laid down in these Articles.

(3) Renewing, in so far as they are concerned, their common decision of December 11th, 1932, the High Contracting Parties decide to make the British Draft Convention a practical basis of discussion which will enable the Disarmament Conference to work out as quickly as possible a convention to ensure a substantial reduction and limitation of armaments. The convention will provide for its later revision in view of any further reductions. Germany, for her part, recognizes that equality of rights within a system which provides for the security of all nations can be attained only by stages in conformity with Article 7 of the Covenant and by virtue of the agreements which will be concluded to this end.

(4) The High Contracting Parties affirm, in a general way, their intention to act in concert in all questions of common interest for Europe (especially those concerning the restoration of the European economy), of which the settlement is not provided for by any existing procedure of the League of Nations, but

might usefully be sought within the limits of the Committee of Inquiry for European Union.

(5) The present agreement is concluded for a period of 10 years from the exchange of ratifications. If, before the end of the eighth year, none of the contracting parties has notified to the others its intention to end the agreement, it will be considered as renewed and remain in force indefinitely. Each contracting party will then have the right to terminate it by denunciation with two years' notice.

(6) The present agreement will be ratified and the ratifications exchanged as soon as possible. It will be registered at the League Secretariat in conformity with the provisions of the Covenant.

It will be noted that all the direct reference to " revision of the Peace Treaties " which had appeared in Signor Mussolini's Draft, (and which had been reproduced in the British Draft of 24th March), had now been discreetly veiled under a reference to Articles 10, 16, and 19 of the Covenant. The inclusion of Article 16 arose from the French clinging to the enforcement of sanctions, while security once again appeared in the proposed modification to Article 3 of the draft. The economic restoration of Europe was substituted for the original suggestion of collaboration in colonial questions.

In the debate on the Adjournment in the House of Commons on 13th April, the Four-Power Pact again came under fire, the speech of the day being made by Sir Austen Chamberlain, who was supported by Labour, Liberal, and Independent members. The feeling in the House was animated by the indignation felt in the country over the internal policy of Germany and the bellicose speeches of certain Nazi leaders. Sir Austen, to the surprise and disappointment of his Italian friends, made a reasoned attack on the Four-Power Pact. He complained of the lack of information and the unrest and confusion which ignorance and rumours had produced. " All that we know about the Pact . . . is that it contains two ideals, renewed assurances on the part of the four great Powers that they will not have recourse to force for the settlement of international disputes, and some proposal for the revision of the Peace Treaties . . . I do not wish by any words of mine to feed the jealousy which does exist among the smaller Powers at the co-operation and agreement among the great Powers." He believed that such co-operation was essential but that it did not need a Pact to make it workable. Revision he thought a very dangerous word ; it should not appear in the mouth of any statesman or the policy of any Government until they were prepared to define very closely the limits within which they think revision should take place. "What is passing in Germany seems to me to render this a singularly inopportune moment to talk about the revision of treaties, and I must say that I think it is of little good talking so loudly about the revision of treaties whilst the originators of the conversations repudiate, each on its own behalf, every idea that concessions are to come from them."

Sir John Simon came to the defence of the proposed Pact. He told the story once again of what had happened in Rome, dealing first with co-operation between the four Powers and then with Treaty Revision. "The conception of co-operation or collaboration between the four great Powers is no doubt capable of more than one meaning. The meaning that we have attached to it throughout, and the meaning that, so far as we know, has been attached by the others concerned, is that we should endeavour by consultation, co-operation and communications to secure that there shall not be the formation of two opposing blocks in which one or other of these great Powers shall find themselves opposed to the other. In the whole of this debate I have heard much that is very wise as to some of the dangers of this proposal ! I have heard nothing said of another danger—what is the alternative to there being a common co-operative view entertained by these four Powers ? The alternative is that they should go different ways." Sir John Simon went on to describe how he thought revision should be approached, not by the discussion of this or that position, but by a co-operative effort to provide suitable machinery for revision, in fact to implement Article 19 of the Covenant. "The whole point from beginning to end is a question of machinery." It was better to try and think out a method " as a means of securing that irregular and violent methods are not employed ". He tried once again to reassure the smaller Powers that the great Powers had no intention of establishing a directory.

Public opinion in Great Britain was at the time more concerned with the treatment of the Jews and pacifists in Germany than with anything else, and those portions of the various speeches which dealt with the Four-Power Pact aroused but little interest.

The German amendments to the Pact are dated 24th April and follow the lines which might be expected—a strengthening of the Article dealing with revision. In the event of a failure of the Disarmament Conference, "equality of status" was to be immediately effected ; if the Conference succeeded, "equality" was to be achieved by stages over a period of five years.

The next statesman to intervene in the European debate was

Dr. Beneš, who made a speech lasting for several hours to a plenary session of the two Houses of the Czechoslovakian Parliament.[1] In the course of it he surveyed the whole field of international affairs since the war ; it was in fact from another angle a reproduction of Signor Mussolini's famous speech in the Senate in 1928.[2] Dr. Beneš began with a reference to the signing of the Pact of the Little Entente " which means for Europe the formation of a new international community, the organization of a section of Central Europe into a solid block, and the ultimate *rapprochement* of the Little Entente and Poland ". He did not, however, explain why it should be proper and desirable for the Little Entente to bind itself to pursue an identic foreign policy on all occasions, and when the Great Powers proposed to sign a treaty of consultation, such an action immediately became black treason to Europe and the League. Dr. Beneš devoted a good deal of attention to Italian foreign policy and declared that the proposed Four-Power Pact was the synthesis of the policy of the last ten years. " It visualizes giving to Italy and Germany a status of equality among the Four Great Powers, and to underline the exceptional position of those Powers in regard to other States, particularly those of Central Europe. It seeks to establish a new European equilibrium, and will weaken the military forces of France and her allies by the military strengthening of the defeated nations. By the revision of the Treaties it will create a new balance of power which will weaken the position of the Little Entente and Poland. It will ensure the satisfaction of Italy's colonial ambitions."

Dr. Beneš, after an unsympathetic review of the Italian desire for Treaty Revision and a statement of the past and present attitude and actions and policy of Czechoslovakia, declared that, were revision undertaken except by a unanimous vote of the Assembly under Article 19, the countries concerned would leave the League.[3] He then laid down the conditions under which he was prepared to consider Treaty Revision. Slight adjustments of the frontiers might be possible if there were :—(1) no external

---

[1] For the complete text of the speech, see *Sources et Documents Tchécoslovaques*, No. 21. *La Question du Directoire Européen et la Révision des Frontières*, " Orbis," Prague, Fockova, 62.

[2] For complete text of Signor Mussolini's speech, see *Italian Foreign Policy*, 1918–1931, Muriel Currey. Nicholson and Watson.

[3] Dr. Beneš' exact words were : " *Vouloir écarter cette condition par l'intervention d'une nouvelle procédure, par un vote à la majorité ou par un vote en dehors des interessés, c'est un vain désir, car les Etats ainsi touchés préféreraient quitter la Société des Nations plutôt que de laisser d'autres qu'eux décider souverainement sur cette question.*"

pressure ; (2) mutual agreement among the States concerned after a period of peaceful co-operation without threats or pressure ; (3) adequate compensation to satisfy the interests of both parties, their Parliaments, and public opinion.

After many criticisms and objections, Dr. Beneš suddenly retraced his steps and declared " that the Government of Czechoslovakia considered the idea of collaboration between the Great Powers to be both wise and just. He thought Signor Mussolini's invitation would prove extremely useful if the final result were acceptable to all. It sincerely wished success to the plan. The Great Powers could deal with a whole series of questions which did not affect the rights of other States. For example, they could come to a definite agreement with Austria about the Austrian problem, eliminating all jealousies—what a comfort this would be for Central Europe ! "

Dr. Beneš then explained the terms on which Italy could enjoy the friendship of Czechoslovakia, and said that the point of view of the Little Entente had been clearly stated in Paris and London.

6

Reference has been made in the previous chapter to the change in the European atmosphere brought about by Herr Hitler's speech, but Signor Mussolini was not at the end of his difficulties in reconciling the French and the German points of view of the Four-Power Pact. Captain Göring flew to Rome and spent 19th and 20th May in discussing the question with Signor Mussolini. After consultation with the British and French Ambassadors, new texts were drafted on 20th and 21st May. Mr. MacDonald and Signor Grandi were both the guests during the week-end of Sir Robert Vansittart, the Permanent Under-Secretary of the British Foreign Office, and were working equally hard to support both in Paris and Berlin the efforts of Signor Mussolini.

The discussions turned on the text of Article 3. On this point, that of equality of status, Germany declared that she was unable to accept the proposals of the other Powers. She agreed that they made a declaration which was of great value to Germany, but feared that it was merely general and did not bind them to any definite action. On the other hand, Germany had to undertake not to seek equality for the duration of the Pact— i.e. for ten years. As a result the attainment of equality depended on the arbitrary decision of each of these three Powers : whether the British Plan was accepted at Geneva or no, whether other countries reduced their armaments or not, Germany would have renounced all liberty of action for ten years.

The Italian Government argued that it was necessary to deal with the existing political situation, not with what might or might not be the situation five years hence. Nobody could foresee what would happen during that period, or expect that, as a result of the Pact, Germany could renounce liberty of action for ten years. The German Government appreciated the " realism " of this argument, but refused to accept it. In view of all post-war experience, Germany was not prepared to assume a formal undertaking in the hope that it would be modified by future events.

As a result of Signor Mussolini's personal intervention, the Wilhelmstrasse produced a new draft of the disputed article in an effort to " equalize " the obligations of all the Powers concerned. If this were not accepted, the German Government would return to its original proposal to restrict the duration of the Pact to five years. On the other hand, the German Government was properly nervous of the effect that would be produced if it appeared that they were endeavouring to reduce the period during which they undertook to " keep the peace ".

The knowledge of these difficulties encouraged the opposition in France, and particularly M. Herriot, to renew their attacks. In a heated debate in the Chamber on 22nd May, M. Marin declared that they would destroy the Daladier government if it dared to sign the Pact. M. Daladier refused to be browbeaten, and replied " I shall sign the Four-Power Pact if it is satisfactory ". The Foreign Affairs Commission of the Chamber opposed it at its meeting on 24th May, but reserved judgment until after the return of M. Paul-Boncour from Geneva, whither he had been sent to calm the fears of the Little Entente and to take part in the discussions of the Conference on the British Draft Plan.

On 30th May, M. Daladier faced a fractious and turbulent Chamber ; he was violently attacked by both the Right and the Left, but he stuck to the Pact and declared his intention to initial a draft which he considered satisfactory. On the same day the Permanent Council of the Little Entente met in Prague and graciously stated that they had no objection to the proposed Pact, as they had received the text from the French Government which was in conformity with the French memorandum of 10th April, i.e. it established the principle that it could only apply to questions which exclusively concerned its signatories ; that the competence of the League would not be in any way infringed, and that unanimity would be essential on application of Article 19.

The Little Entente had received from the French Government guarantees against any attempt at a revision of the Peace Treaties. In spite of these French protestations Poland announced that her attitude remained " decidedly negative ".

At this moment, what was to have been the final version was being prepared at the Palazzo Chigi, and it was officially believed that the initialling would take place in Rome on 1st June, but a fresh hitch, at once annoying and ridiculous, occurred. The villain of the piece on this occasion was the telephone. The Quai D'Orsay, it subsequently appeared, was working on the previous text, not on that which had been accepted in Rome, London, and Berlin, and which M. de Jouvenel had thought was the basis of agreement of his Foreign Office. In view of the obvious need for haste, much of the negotiations had been conducted by long-distance telephone calls, and a misunderstanding had occurred somewhere. It is a sign of the extremely friendly relations which existed between M. de Jouvenel and the Italian Foreign Office that he immediately declared—" If anyone is to blame, I am." The whole trouble had again arisen over Article 3. " Suppress it altogether," said Paris. " No," chorused London, Rome, and Berlin, and the tedious work of finding an agreed formula began once more. Whitsuntide intervened, and the statesmen of Paris, London, and Berlin punctually went away for their holidays; only Signor Mussolini remained at work. On 6th June M. de Jouvenel received authorization to sign, but Herr Hitler was still missing and no action could be taken in Berlin until he returned at last, at 6 p.m. on 7th June. Herr von Hassell was informed that the new version of Article 3 had been approved, and the " all clear " was given. On the evening of 8th June the Pact was initialled at the Palazzo Chigi by Signor Mussolini, Sir Ronald Graham, British Ambassador, M. de Jouvenel, French Ambassador, and Herr von Hassell, German Ambassador. The desire of the British and Italian Governments to see it concluded before the opening of the World Economic Conference on 12th June had been achieved, but with only four days to spare.

The final text ran as follows :—

FINAL DRAFT
June, 1933
AGREEMENT OF UNDERSTANDING AND CO-OPERATION.
PREAMBLE

The President of the German Reich, the President of the French Republic, His Majesty the King of Great Britain, Ireland,

and the British Dominions beyond the Seas, Emperor of India, and His Majesty the King of Italy ;

Conscious of the special responsibilities incumbent on them as possessing permanent representation on the Council of the League of Nations, where the League itself and its members are concerned, and of the responsibilities resulting from the common signature of the Locarno agreements ;

Convinced that the state of disquiet which obtains throughout the world can only be dissipated by reinforcing their solidarity in such a way as to strengthen confidence in peace in Europe ;

Faithful to the obligations which they have assumed in virtue of the Covenant of the League of Nations, the Locarno Treaties, and the Briand-Kellogg Pact, and taking into account the declaration of the renunciation of force, the principle of which was proclaimed in the declaration signed at Geneva on December 11th, 1932, by their delegates at the Disarmament Conference and adopted on March 2nd, 1933, by the Political Commission of that Conference ;

Anxious to give full effect to all the provisions of the Covenant of the League of Nations, while conforming to the methods and procedure laid down therein, from which they have no intention of departing ;

Mindful of the rights of every State, which cannot be affected without the consent of the interested party ;

Have resolved to conclude an agreement with these objects, and have appointed as their plenipotentiaries :—

Who, having exchanged their full powers, found in good and due form, have agreed as follows :—

(1) The High Contracting Parties will consult together as regards all questions which appertain to them. They undertake to make every effort to pursue, within the framework of the League of Nations, a policy of effective co-operation between all Powers with a view to the maintenance of peace.

(2) In respect of the Covenant of the League of Nations, and particularly Articles 10, 16, and 19, the High Contracting Parties decide to examine between themselves, and without prejudice to decisions which can only be taken by the regular organs of the League of Nations, all proposals relating to methods and procedure calculated to give due effect to these articles.

(3) The High Contracting Parties undertake to make every effort to ensure the success of the Disarmament Conference and, should questions which particularly concern them remain in suspense on the conclusion of that Conference, they reserve the right to re-examine these questions between themselves under the present agreement with a view to ensuring their solution through the appropriate channels.

(4) The High Contracting Parties affirm their desire to consult together as regards all economic questions which have a common interest for Europe, and particularly for its economic restoration, with a view to seeking a settlement within the framework of the League of Nations.

(5) The present agreement is concluded for a period of 10 years from the date of its entry into force.

If before the end of the eighth year none of the High Contracting Parties shall have notified to the others its intention to terminate the agreement, it shall be regarded as renewed and will remain in force indefinitely, each of the High Contracting Parties possessing in that event the right to terminate it by a declaration to that effect on giving two years' notice.

(6) The present agreement, drawn up in English, French, German, and Italian, of which the French text prevails in case of divergence, shall be ratified and the ratifications shall be deposited at Rome as soon as possible. The Government of the Kingdom of Italy will deliver to each of the High Contracting Parties a certified copy of the *procès-verbaux* of deposit.

The present agreement will enter into force as soon as all the ratifications have been deposited.

It shall be registered at the League of Nations in conformity with the Covenant of the League.

Done, at Rome, the ——————— in a single copy, which will remain deposited in the archives of the Government of the Kingdom of Italy ; certified copies will be delivered to each of the High Contracting Parties. In faith whereof the above-mentioned plenipotentiaries have signed the present agreement.

8

On 7th June the French Government had addressed practically identical notes to the Governments of the Little Entente and Poland. After declaring that there was nothing in the Pact which would affect the treaties already in existence between these countries and the French Republic, the notes went on to call the particular attention of the Governments to Article 2. This, it was declared, " precludes the examination of the principle of revision and of specific cases of revision, but makes possible the examination of suggestions for proper method and procedure to implement the Articles of the Covenant of the League of Nations, particularly with regard to Article 19. On the one hand, no question of revision can be raised except in accordance with Article 19. On the other, in the event of an examination of procedure, if one or more States should wish to raise a territorial question decided by the treaties and propose to do so by discussion in the Assembly on the basis of Article 19, the French Government will not accept any proposal that would tend to modify the conditions under which the Assembly can invite States Members of the League to undertake a new examination of treaties which have become inapplicable and the maintenance of which might endanger the peace of the world. The unanimous vote of Members present, including the nations concerned, is necessary for the application of the general principles of the Covenant and must continue to govern the conduct of the Assembly in such a case."

It will be noted that the French Government did not invite the adhesion of the other signatories to these definitions of the scope of the Four-Power Pact. and from the point of view of international law and diplomatic procedure it is very questionable how far one party to an agreement has the right to attempt such a definition. Certainly the other signatories are in no way bound by the declarations of the French Government.

Signor Mussolini had stated that the Pact embodied a political conception in a political form, and this was the note of his speech in the Senate on the evening of 7th June. He began by a review of the past and present state of Europe, and declared that the Pact was the logical and inevitable consequence of the situation created by the Treaty of Locarno, and passed on to a brief review of the negotiations. None of the modifications which had been made affected the fundamental purpose of the agreement which was embodied in Article 1. " Much of the opposition to the Pact," he said, " was more the result of sentimental reactions than of clear reasoning. We were not endeavouring to create and stabilize a definite and unalterable hierarchy of States. Such a hierarchy with regard to the Western States of Europe exists objectively and historically ; but that hierarchy does not mean supremacy, or a directory which imposes its will on others. In the League of Nations itself, an organization which was inspired by orthodox democratic conceptions of equality, a hierarchy was established by the Covenant, which laid down that certain States should have permanent seats on the Council, that others should have semi-permanent seats, while other States are elected in turn. The States with permanent seats are precisely the four Western States, England, France, Germany, and Italy. These States have, therefore, according to the Covenant, the power of constant directive action, and they have greater responsibility both to each other and the world. On the condition, more or less normal and friendly, of their relations with each other depend the tranquillity and peaceful development of the other nations."

Signor Mussolini went on to discuss the two other " political articles ", 2 and 3 ; Article 19 of the Covenant had only been " admitted " when it was agreed that Articles 10 and 16 should also be mentioned. This question of Treaty Revision had caused the greatest difficulty during the opening of the negotiations, the question of disarmament during the later stages. He referred to the very important speech made by Dr. Beneš in the Chamber in Prague during April, and welcomed the statement of that Minister that he was not an anti-revisionist " *sub specie æternitatis* ".

Dr. Beneš had said that revision could only take place in a peaceful atmosphere, and it was precisely to create such an atmosphere that the Four-Power Pact had been proposed.   His review of the difficulties over Article 3 pointed to the contrasts of the French and German attitudes.

In describing the attitudes of the various Governments, he paid warm tributes to the spirit of friendliness and conciliation shown by all parties to the Pact.   Italy and Great Britain occupied a very special position, as they were the joint guarantors of the Locarno Treaty.   His references to France were particularly cordial and in line with the policy of an Italo-French entente, which Signor Mussolini, in the face of much discouragement and difficulty, had pursued ever since he assumed office.   He believed and hoped that as a result of the Pact " the outstanding questions between France and Italy . . . would assume an entirely different aspect . . . and that they would be easily settled ". He was fully " convinced that the German Government was sincerely desirous of peace ", and quoted the " solemn affirmations " of Herr Hitler and Captain Göring.

As ever, he warned his hearers against undue optimism.   " It must not be imagined that there will be no more disagreements or that disagreements will be settled as if by magic. . . . The Pact has been created in order that there may be the possibility of settling such questions as arise. . . . As for the League of Nations, it will find itself strengthened and not weakened by this method of collaboration between the Permanent Members of the Council."

The importance of the Pact lay not so much in the letter as in the spirit.   " It is the spirit which will write ' finis ' to the chapter of European history since the war and will begin another chapter.   It is the spirit which will guarantee ten years of peace to Europe during which the dangerous and complex problems of internal and international peace can be solved.   In every country the negotiations of the Four Powers have been followed with the deepest interest, and at some moments with the gravest anxiety. Its signature will give rise to more or less interesting discussions in the circles of professional politicians, but it will be welcomed with real satisfaction by the peoples who, unaffected by such sophistries and nearer to real life, feel intuitively the moral value of such historical events."

The French Government had to face a stormy debate in the Chamber on 10th June when the Pact was discussed, but eventually carried the day with a substantial majority.

M. Daladier responded to Signor Mussolini merely by saying : " The Italian Government believes that in addition to the actual words of the Pact there is behind them a desire of the Italians and the French to settle the questions between the two countries with loyalty on both sides, and by a simultaneous effort to overcome the difficulties of these days." These phrases did not hold out much hope that a more conciliatory spirit would be shown in Paris.

The despatch from the British Government to the Ambassador authorizing him to initial the Pact added nothing to what was already known of the history of the negotiations and the views of the Government. But little mention was made of the new agreement during a rambling debate in the House of Commons on 5th July, though Sir John Simon, in winding up his debate, made one interesting and important observation. There was at the time great anxiety in Europe over the possibility of a Nazi attempt forcibly to absorb Austria into the Reich. Sir John Simon said : " I have been asked a number of questions to-day on the very difficult situation in Austria. I say without hesitation that the whole sympathies of this country are with Austria in her effort to preserve her position. It is most fortunate that the Four-Power Pact should be negotiated and initialled, because it does give an opportunity, which I hope will be used, to assist that country and Dr. Dollfuss to maintain her undoubted rights in the face of very grave circumstances."

The Pact was signed in Rome on 15th July, and on 18th July M. de Jouvenel left Italy at the conclusion of his six months' term as French Ambassador. The warmest tributes were paid by the Italians to his efforts to establish better relations, and there is no doubt that it was largely due to his advocacy that the French Government supported the Pact. He displayed a courageous and self-sacrificing spirit, for a French politician who shows himself to be a friend of Italy courts the most violent attacks from both the Right and the Left in his own country.

No treaty of modern days has been the subject of more controversy than the Four-Power Pact. Its critics and opponents have attacked it from two entirely opposite and contradictory standpoints. On the one hand, it was assailed as being a danger to peace because it proposed to establish a " Directory " of Great Powers to enforce Treaty Revision, and on the other it was denounced as being so vague and general in its terms as to be entirely useless. At the same time there are those who complain that Signor Mussolini's original proposal had been so much modified in order to secure acceptance by France and Germany that it cannot lead to those very objects for which they believe it was suggested. This is not the view of Signor Mussolini himself, as is proved by his speech in the Senate.   He insisted that what was vital had remained untouched—i.e. the pursuit of a policy of effective co-operation between all Powers with a view to the maintenance of peace.   These doubters also ignore one likelihood which was present in the minds of the British and French Governments, the danger of Europe becoming divided into two blocks of Powers. Were Italy, Germany, Austria, Hungary, and Bulgaria ranged against France, Belgium, Poland, and the Little Entente, with Great Britain oscillating nervously in the centre, it would indeed spell disaster to Europe.

Whether the Pact itself has a future usefulness it is not yet possible to say, nor how its effect may be nullified by the Franco-Soviet proposals put forward during the following summer.[1] But it is certain that the situation in the early summer of 1933 was considerably relieved as a result of Signor Mussolini's initiative and his personal efforts to bring about a better under standing.   The negotiations gave the Disarmament Conference a fresh lease of life, and the existence of such an agreement among the nations who hold the future of Europe in their hands may yet prove of use in the settlement of disputes.

" As to the Four-Power Pact," said Signor Mussolini in his speech to the Council of Corporations on 13th November, 1933, " it has of late been enveloped in silence.   Nobody talks about it, but everyone is thinking about it.   And for this very reason we do not intend to take any initiative or to accelerate the development of a situation which must logically and inevitably mature by itself."

[1] See below, p. 229.

CHAPTER VIII

M. LITVINOFF'S TRIUMPH

1

The Union of Socialist Soviet Republics has, in its seventeen years of existence, been more fortunate in its diplomats than any other revolutionary Government of modern times. Unlike revolutionary France, Italy, and Germany, it has drawn very little upon former diplomatists of the previous regime and has been represented abroad almost entirely by servants of the Revolution, drawn in most cases from the humblest origins. Without doubt there were mistakes and setbacks, due to lack of experience and too great revolutionary zeal, but notwithstanding these and the many other drawbacks under which a revolutionary regime has at first to labour, the fact remains that the Government of the Soviet Union has a better record of diplomatic successes than any other in Europe, save perhaps that of Italy.

Three brilliant foreign ministers, Trotsky, Chicherin, and Litvinoff, and a galaxy of distinguished ambassadors, as, for example, Krassin, Karakhan and Krestinsky, not only demonstrated to the world the strength of the new regime but also, to a great extent, made it palatable to the nations of the East and West, or at least did much to improve the general atmosphere of horror and revulsion caused by the Red Terror and the embarrassing activities of the Comintern. It is no little diplomatic achievement that in seventeen years the Soviet Union has attained and surpassed the position held in European politics by the Russian Empire.

Of the three Commissars for Foreign Affairs, it was reserved to Trotsky to negotiate the Peace of Brest-Litovsk and to win thereby the very necessary breathing-space which was needed to consolidate the revolution. Then, when the crash and thunder of the Civil War and the Allied Expeditions of Intervention had subsided, Chicherin, the only one of the three who had noble blood or previous diplomatic experience, appeared, a star upon the international horizon. A series of peace agreements with frontier States ; the diplomatic *coup* with Germany at Rapallo ; the steady march of events towards the great year of 1924 when

149

the Great Powers recognized and resumed relations with the Soviet Union ; and the initiation in 1925 of the policy of neutrality and non-aggression, marked his period at the Narkomendel as one of great achievement and success, during which the Soviet Union had resumed her place as a world Power, though with some reservations.   Worn out with illness and overwork, M. Chicherin, in 1927, at a moment when Soviet diplomatic fortunes were suffering something of an eclipse, due to the rupture with Great Britain arising out of the Arcos Raid, resigned and handed over the direction of foreign policy to his brilliant lieutenant.

M. Litvinoff, who may yet be known in history as the greatest of the three, bided his time, remained undisheartened by rebuffs and reverses, and finally entirely restored Soviet diplomatic prestige by his masterful handling of the position created by the Kellogg Pact in 1928 and in his successful negotiations for the resumption of diplomatic relations with Great Britain in the following year.   Thus rehabilitated, Soviet diplomacy entered upon a period of unshadowed success which reached its apogee in the year 1933 with the London Agreements and recognition by the United States of America.   Few countries have been as fortunate in their foreign minister as the Soviet Union, few statesmen have deserved more of their country than M. Litvinoff.

2

It would seem now almost to have become an axiom that an unsuccessful Economic Conference should be the occasion for a diplomatic victory on the part of the U.S.S.R.   Just as the only concrete development of the Genoa Conference of 1922 was the Treaty of Rapallo, which marked the return of the Soviet Union to Europe, so the London Conference of 1933 will be remembered by the fact that it was in the course of its deliberations that M. Litvinoff negotiated his Conventions for the Definition of the Aggressor, and thereby took a step of very great importance in European diplomatic history, both directly and indirectly.

This new development has for its point of departure the Litvinoff Protocol of February, 1929, whereby the Soviet Foreign Commissar provided a piquant counterpart to the Pact of Paris concluded in the previous August.   At that moment the Soviet Union had treaties of neutrality and non-aggression with Persia and Afghanistan,[1] on the one hand, and with Germany and

---

[1] Similar treaties also existed between Turkey and Persia, and Persia and Afghanistan.

Lithuania on the other, and, in addition, had similar treaties somewhat despondently under negotiation with other of the Baltic States and with Poland.

This system of bi-lateral treaties, which had originally been devised as a counterblast to the Locarno Agreements, was based upon the understanding that, in the event of either of the contracting parties being the victim of unprovoked aggression, the other would remain neutral, and conversely that both parties agreed not to attack one another nor to participate in any alliance or political agreement with a third party directed against either of them.[1]

The negotiations preceding the Litvinoff Protocol were remarkable not only for the reply which the Protocol made to the Kellogg Pact, but also for the checkmating by M. Litvinoff of an attempt by the Polish Ambassador in Moscow, M. Patek, to bring the Baltic States to the signature of the Protocol under the auspices of Poland. So great was the success of M. Litvinoff that within the space of a few months every limitrophe State to the western and southern frontiers of the Soviet Union from Finland to Afghanistan, with the remarkable inclusion of Rumania and the uninvited accession of the Free City of Danzig, had either signed or adhered to the Protocol of Moscow.[2]

Satisfied temporarily with this success, M. Litvinoff rested on his laurels ; time was on his side and events inevitably played into his hands. The appearance of the Nazis as the second largest party in the Reichstag after the German elections of September, 1930, gave Europe a shock which had its immediate repercussions upon Soviet foreign relations, and the rapid march of events in Germany caused many European States to look w.th a more friendly eye upon the Soviet Union.

Poland and the Eastern European States looked apprehensively at the ever-growing power of the Nazi Party in Germany, and became more and more inclined to secure their Eastern frontiers by a *rapprochement* with Moscow and thereby leave their hands free to deal with this new phenomenon in Central Europe. France, too, anxious alike as to the menace on her own frontier and on those of her Polish and Czechoslovakian allies, whom she was bound by the Locarno Pact to support against aggression, brought her influence to bear in advising them to improve their relations with the U.S.S.R.

[1] For a full *exposé* of the Soviet system of treaties of neutrality and non-aggression, see *Disarmament and Security*, pp. 312–332.
[2] For details of the Litvinoff Protocol, see ibid., pp. 249–255.

The result of this new development was a further crop of treaties of neutrality and non-aggression concluded in 1931 and 1932 with France, Finland, Poland, Esthonia, and Latvia.[1] Rumania still stood aloof, hampered to a certain extent by internal dynastic troubles, but the increasingly earnest tone of the representations made by the Polish Minister at Bucharest were beginning to have their effect.   It will be remembered that the French Government had at the outset made the final conclusion of a Franco-Soviet Pact conditional upon the signature of similar treaties by both Poland and Rumania.   The Soviet-Rumanian Treaty was, therefore, the missing link in the chain. Negotiations were conducted intermittently and agreement was reached upon the general lines of a pact, but the question of Bessarabia remained an obstacle in the way of final agreement.[2]

But the new situation in Germany outran the steps taken to counteract it, and with the advent of Herr Hitler and the Nazis to power in January, 1933, there was a further manifestation of a desire on the part of Europe to reach fundamental understanding with the Soviet Union which would ensure the neutrality of that Power in the event of an infraction of peace.

By this time, however, there had entered into the scheme of things a new factor and one which made the desire for an understanding between Europe and the Soviet as keen in Moscow as in the Western capitals.   The establishment of the Japanese in Manchukuo, with its consequent international complications and potential hostilities, made the U.S.S.R. as keen to secure her

---

[1] These treaties were concluded on the following dates : With France on 29th November, 1932 ; with Finland on 21st January, 1932 ; with Poland on 23rd November, 1932 ;   with Esthonia on 4th May, 1932 ; with Latvia on 5th February, 1932.

[2] Rumania required a specific reference to Bessarabia which would signify Soviet recognition of her sovereignty and of the Dniester as the frontier, and would include the Province in the non-aggression undertaking. The Soviet Government, on the other hand, could not agree to this as it would amount to tacit acquiescence in the Rumanian " occupation ". M. Litvinoff was, however, prepared to add a second paragraph to the first article (renouncing the use of force), laying down that any attempt to solve by force any existing territorial or other disputes would be a violation of the pact.   Direct negotiations having failed, M. Herriot obtained from the Soviet Ambassador, on the occasion of the signature of the Franco-Soviet Treaty on 29th November, 1932, a reaffirmation of " its pacific intentions towards Rumania " and of its willingness to leave the possibility of signature open to Rumania for a period of four months. At the same time the Soviet Government declared its fidelity to a " policy of non-recourse to violence for the solution of litigious questions, as also to its obligations under the Pact of Paris of 27th August, 1928 ".   The Rumanian Government, however, insisted on its condition, and the negotiations were allowed to drop.

European frontier and to turn her full attention towards the East as were the Eastern European States to ensure the stability of their borders, and this concatentation of circumstances resulted in a series of developments which reached their climax with the signature in July of the Conventions to Define the Aggressor.

In every scheme of non-aggression which has so far been evolved the main difficulty had always been the definition of the aggressor. The Geneva Protocol of 1924 had decreed that the party which refused to submit its disputes to pacific settlement should be so branded. But the Protocol was abortive. The Locarno Agreements had defined the aggressor as that Power which first moved troops into the demilitarized Rhineland zone. But the Locarno Agreements were but local. The search for an adequate definition became acute in the latter stages of the second session of the Disarmament Conference, and a Sub-Committee on Security was appointed to endeavour to find a solution. The agile brain of M. Politis produced a Resolution, which was subsequently adopted by the Committee on 24th May, 1933, which provided that the State should be recognized as the aggressor which should first commit one of the following actions :—

(1) Declaration of war on another State.
(2) Invasion by armed forces of the territory of another State, even without declaration of war.
(3) An attack by its land, sea, or air forces, even without declaration of war, upon the territory, vessels, or flying machines of another State.
(4) A naval blockade of the coasts or ports of another State.
(5) Support accorded to armed bands, which, organized on its territory, shall have invaded the territory of another State or refused, in spite of the demand of the invaded State, to take on its own territory all the steps in its power to deprive the bandits aforesaid of all aid or protection.

M. Litvinoff, upon whose proposals for non-aggression submitted on 6th February, 1933, to the Disarmament Conference the Politis Resolution had largely been based, at once adopted the revised formula as an instrument of Soviet foreign policy, and, taking advantage of the perturbation occasioned in Europe by Nazi foreign policy, seized the opportunity of the gathering of foreign statesmen at the London Economic Conference to propose to the States parties to the Moscow Protocol that, without waiting for the final conclusion of the Disarmament Convention, they should adopt amongst themselves the Politis Definition of Aggression in the form of a Multi-lateral Convention. This proposal was accepted by all with the exception of Finland and

Lithuania, and a Convention was signed on 3rd July between Afghanistan, Esthonia, Latvia, Persia, Poland, Rumania, Turkey, and the U.S.S.R., accepting the Politis Definition of Aggression with the additional undertaking that no consideration of a political, military, economic, or any other character should serve as an excuse, or a justification, for aggression.   An annex to the Convention gave further indications whereby an aggressor might be determined.   Thus it was recorded that no act of aggression should be deemed to be justified, *inter alia*, by any of the following circumstances :—

(*a*) The internal condition of a State as, for example, its political, economic, or social structure, the alleged defects of its administration, disturbances arising from strikes, revolutions, counter-revolutions, or civil war.

(*b*) The international conduct of a State, as, for example, the violation or the danger of violation of the rights or interests, material or moral, of a foreign State, or of its nationals, the rupture of diplomatic or economic relations, measures of economic or financial boycott, differences relative to economic, financial, or other obligations to foreign States, and frontier incidents not falling under one of the cases of aggression indicated in the Politis formula itself.

Furthermore, it was agreed by the parties concerned that recognition of this formula " must never serve to legalize the violations of international law which might be implied in the circumstances enumerated above ".

A separate Convention was signed between the U.S.S.R. and Lithuania on 5th July, thereby bringing one of the defaulters into line, but in the meantime, on 4th July, a further step had been taken in that the Little Entente,[1] together with Turkey, had signed a further Convention identical with the other two, but containing an additional article extending to other countries the right of adherence to it.[2]   Finland, which had not signed the first Convention, adhered to the second on 23rd July, and the Soviet Ambassadors in London, Paris, and Rome approached the respective Foreign Ministers with the suggestion that Great Britain, France, and Italy should also adhere.   The desire of Moscow to obtain as wide a sphere of adherence as possible was made clear

[1] It is understood that a private understanding was arrived at between M. Litvinoff and M. Titulescu that, in all future relations between Rumania and the Soviet Union, discussion of the Bessarabian problem should be omitted.

[2] This same article provided that notification of adherence should be communicated either to Moscow or Angora.   It is interesting to note that the Turkish Government had given active and valuable assistance to M. Litvinoff in the negotiations.

by the statement to the Press by M. Litvinoff that " it goes without saying that the Soviet Union is ready to sign similar conventions with any other States irrespective of their geographical
position and existing relations with itself ''

3

It is difficult to emphasize the importance of this new development in Soviet foreign policy and the effect thereof upon the
European situation as a whole.   Primarily, of course, the chief
result was that of improved Soviet-Polish relations, and this had
been in progress over a period of some three to four years.   Ever
since the result of the German elections of 1930, Marshal Pilsudski
had realized the danger to Poland of the inevitable accession to
power of the Nazi Party and the consequent demand of an
awakened Germany for an active revision of the Treaty of
Versailles.   In the two years ensuing he had, therefore, directed
his policy towards a *rapprochement* with the Soviet Union, a
policy which bore fruit in the summer of 1933.   At the same time
he took steps to obtain from Herr Hitler a definite statement of
German policy towards Poland.   This was achieved on 4th May,
when identic statements were made by the *Reichskanzler* in Berlin
and the German Ambassador in Warsaw to the Polish Ambassador
and Foreign Minister respectively, to the effect that it was the
intention of the German Government to determine its standpoint
and action towards Poland strictly within the framework of the
existing Treaty, and expressing the hope that the two countries
should examine their common interests in an objective manner.
Though this statement was equivalent to a reaffirmation by
Germany of her Eastern obligations under the Treaty of Locarno
and was thus calculated to ease the tension in Warsaw, Marshal
Pilsudski was considerably more relieved to receive a few days
later an indication of the success of his policy towards the Soviet
Union.   This was derived from a series of articles by M. Radek in
the *Izvestia*,[1] declaring it to be the policy of Moscow to oppose
Treaty Revision.

" The way to revision of the predatory Versailles Peace "—
wrote Radek—" leads through a new world-war.   Discussion
of revision is the smoke-screen behind which Imperialism prepares
the most terrible and ruthless war that the human brain can
conceive, a war by comparison with which all the horrors of the
Imperialistic War of 1914–1918 will pale. . . . The mere fact
that revision of the Versailles Treaty is linked up with the victory

[1] Appearing between 12th and 24th May, 1933.

of Fascism shows how much this revision could reckon with the interests of the masses of nations which are regarded by the *Fascisti* as ' lower '."

This new orientation of Soviet Foreign Policy had the most important potential implications. An assurance of Soviet neutrality would make a very substantial contribution to Poland's chances of victory in the event of a clash with Germany in a " preventive " or any other war, and it should be remembered that uncertainty about Moscow's attitude played an important part in restraining Poland from aggressive moves at the time of the French occupation of the Ruhr in 1924.

Some few weeks after the publication of the *Izvestia* articles, M. Radek paid a visit to Warsaw in the course of which, at his own request, he spent five days in the Polish Corridor making something of a study on the spot of one of the principal problems of Treaty Revision in Eastern Europe.

The *rapprochement* between the two countries was carried a stage further when a high official of the Soviet Commissariat of Education visited Warsaw with the object of presenting to the Polish Government a file of the prison records referring to Marshal Pilsudski from 1890 to 1905, during which time the Marshal spent an aggregate period of four years in Siberia. In exchange for this the Polish Government, not to be outdone, presented to the Lenin Institute in Moscow all the papers and belongings which Lenin had left at Cracow in 1914 after his hurried departure at the outbreak of the war.

This " cultural " exchange of historic relics was but the prelude to a visit of a more important nature. The Chiefs of the Air Staffs of the Ukraine and of Soviet White Russia, that is to say the two territories of the Soviet Union bordering on Poland, came to Warsaw and were taken on a tour of factories and air bases. A return visit of Polish Air Chiefs took place in the autumn.

Propaganda was to play its part in the cementing of this new Polish-Soviet friendship, and in September a party of some twenty journalists from Moscow visited Poland, while a corresponding number of Polish journalists returned this visit in November. To crown all, in February, 1934, Colonel Beck, the Polish Minister for Foreign Affairs, went in his official capacity to Moscow, thus returning the visit of M. Chicherin in 1926.

Before this event, however, Polish diplomacy had scored a further remarkable success in the negotiation of the Non-aggression Declaration with Germany on 26th January, 1934.[1] By

[1] See below, p. 197.

this means Marshal Pilsudski had secured his western frontier for
a period of ten years, yet Colonel Beck, in the course of his visit
to Moscow, was enabled satisfactorily to explain that this new
agreement in no way invalidated the Polish-Soviet *rapprochement*.

The Soviet Union, therefore, having checkmated the Nazi
policy, advocated by Herr Alfred Rosenberg, that Poland might
be compensated for the loss of the Corridor by the annexation of
territory in the Ukraine, could turn her attention to her Eastern
problems with an easy mind as regards affairs in the West.

4

But it was in the East that the key to the present development
of Soviet Foreign Policy was to be found.   Protected by a screen
of non-aggression agreements on its Western and Southern
frontiers, the Soviet Union could at last concentrate upon the
new situation created by the establishment of Manchukuo and
the advance of Japanese power in the East.

This story begins in 1925, when on 21st January
M. Yoshizawa signed with M. Karakhan a treaty providing for
the resumption of diplomatic relations, the settlement of certain
outstanding differences, and the granting to Japan of important
mining concessions in Soviet territory.   It was rumoured at the
time that attached to the treaty was a secret agreement, what pur-
ported to be the text of which was published by a Russian
newspaper in Shanghai.   By this, in return for long-term credits
from Japan, the Soviet Government promised further mining
concessions and recognition of Japan's "positive policy" in
Manchuria.   The existence of this secret agreement was officially
denied, but the remarkably long-suffering attitude of the Soviet
Government towards recent developments in Manchuria, though
clearly also dictated by a desire to avoid a conflict, might seem to
argue some such pledge to Japan.

However this may be, and for whichever, or both, of these good
reasons, the Soviet Government have repeatedly expressed their
willingness to conclude a pact of neutrality and non-aggression
with Japan.   On December 31st, 1931, the presence of
M. Yoshizawa in Moscow, on his return to Japan from the Paris
Embassy to assume the post of Foreign Minister, was seized upon
by M. Litvinoff to make a proposal.   The Japanese Government
did not, however, appreciate the value of such an agreement,
holding that signature of the Pact of Paris provided a sufficient
guarantee of non-aggression, while Japanese military opinion was
definitely opposed to an undertaking of non-aggression which did

not extend to economic relations and Communist propaganda. Consideration of the suggestion was, however, promised, and there the matter was allowed to rest until October, 1932.

By that time Manchukuo had been established and had been recognized by Japan in a Protocol signed on 15th September, which in effect amounted to a military alliance. The Lytton Report had also been published, and, in anticipation of the discussion imminent at Geneva, it was considered by Soviet officials that the time was opportune to renew the suggestions of a pact, and press for Japanese acceptance. The Japanese Foreign Office, on the other hand, were anxious to strengthen Japan's position at Geneva, and recognition of Manchukuo by the U.S.S.R. as a condition of signing the proposed pact might be a valuable diplomatic asset. Preliminary discussions on an agreement took place in Tokyo towards the end of October between the Foreign Minister of Manchukuo, M. Hsieh Chieh-shih, the Japanese Ambassador in Moscow, M. Hirota, and the Soviet Ambassador in Japan, M. Troyanovsky. It was reported at the same time that large Japanese orders for petroleum were being placed in Moscow. The negotiations, however, remained of an explanatory character and were eventually abandoned, the Soviet Foreign Office holding to its view that signature of a non-aggression pact should be preliminary to any discussions and to a decision on the recognition of Manchukuo, the Japanese Foreign Office being equally determined that the pact, if signed, should form part of a series of agreements, including recognition of Manchukuo, the settlement of its boundaries and those of Mongolia, of the future of the Chinese Eastern Railway, and of certain questions outstanding in Manchuria. While desiring a settlement on its own terms, neither party was prepared to make concessions to the other's views. M. Matsuoka, however, visited M. Litvinoff in Moscow, on his way to present the Japanese case at the special League Assembly, and discussed the question with him, and later the suggestion of a non-aggression pact between the Soviet Union and Manchukuo was put forward in the Japanese Press. The Soviet Union was not to be put off, and insisted that no agreement could be concluded with Manchukuo unless a pact were signed simultaneously with Japan.

On 13th December, 1932, a *note verbale* was handed to the Soviet Ambassador in Tokyo containing the official reply of the Japanese Government to the proposal made by M. Litvinoff to M. Yoshizawa in the previous December, stating that Japan was not yet prepared to conclude an agreement, but suggesting the formation of a Japano-Soviet-Manchukuo frontier commission to deal with any incidents which might threaten to disturb normal relations. This suggestion the Soviet Union agreed to consider in its reply of 4th January, 1933. It repeated its conviction that the conclusion of a non-aggression pact was a preliminary stage to any agreement for the settlement of incidents, in that it would constitute a fundamental guarantee of a non-aggressive policy, the strict pursuance of which would remove the danger of such incidents. The correspondence was published on 16th January by the unilateral action of the Soviet Foreign Office.

This action in effect served to emphasize the stalemate reached between Soviet Russia and Japan. That the advantage of position remained with Japan may be surmised from the fact that the Soviet offer of a pact still remained, as it were, on the table, and it was one of " the principal tasks " of the new Soviet Ambassador, as M. Yureneff stated on his arrival in Japan in March, to reopen negotiations for the inclusion of a pact of non-aggression with " *la puissante nation d'Extreme-Orient qu'est le Japon* ".

Point has been given to the Soviet anxiety to conclude such an agreement by recent developments in the matter of the Chinese-Eastern Railway—that perennial source of friction. The recent dispute between Manchukuo and the Soviet Union regarding the withdrawal of rolling-stock, claimed to belong to the railway, was merely the culmination of a long series of incidents all concerned with the railway. But the rolling-stock dispute was, it would seem, to judge by the lengths to which the authorities were prepared to go—the blocking of the line at the frontier, the stoppage of through traffic from Vladivostok, and the delivery of an ultimatum to the Soviet Union—utilized by Manchukuo, supported by Japan, to force the issue. That the Soviet Government realized the dangers of the situation was clear from the proposal for the sale of the railway to Japan, which came from M.Litvinoff shortly afterwards. That this was one of the questions which the Soviet Government was unwilling to discuss until after the signature of a non-aggression pact is significant. Negotiations regarding the sale opened in Tokyo on 15th June, 1933, between Soviet and Manchukuo representatives, under the auspices of Japan, who had preferred to recommend to Manchukuo the purchase of the railway. So far, however, they have yielded little result, the time having been occupied by long discussions regarding the purchase price and the Soviet's title to sell the remainder of the lease.

There the situation in the Far East must be left, with the passing comment that the tension between the Soviet Union and

Japan was seized upon by China as a suitable opportunity to renew diplomatic relations with the U.S.S.R. in December, 1932. But there is an important background to the whole of Soviet foreign policy in its latest aspect—the steady development of Western Siberia, with an ever-increasing transfer of the main centre of industry into the Urals. It is important that since the Revolution there has been a general swing towards the East. It will be remembered that Lenin's doctrine was that the Communist seed should be sown in the East. The vigorous pursuance of that policy must inevitably, sooner or later, bring the Soviet Union into conflict with Japan, avowedly anti-Communist, and never more so than under the influence of the military urge, both internal and external. With this in mind the significance of the Soviet non-aggression policy in the West, and Soviet efforts to extend the *cordon sanitaire* to the East, is obvious.

5

What, then, was the effect on Europe as a whole of this new development of Soviet foreign policy ? Primarily the effect was twofold : the isolation of Germany and the provision of a counter-blast to the Four-Power Pact signed on 15th July. Though it might be argued that Germany had no cause to object to the policy of pacification pursued by the Soviet Union, inasmuch as the Treaty of Rapallo and the recent extension of the Berlin Agreement of 1926 served the same ends as the new Convention, this was something of a fallacious argument. The fact remained that the Soviet Union had come down on the side of " No Revision ", and by so doing had greatly eased the minds of those anti-revisionist States whose policy up till then had been restricted by the uncertainty of the attitude of Moscow. The *Reichswehr* General Staff could till that moment confidently rely, in the case of hostilities in Eastern Europe, on the fact that a considerable part of the Polish forces, and consequently—by reason of the Treaty of Alliance of 1926—of the Rumanian forces, would be retained on the Soviet frontier, but the Polish-Soviet *rapprochement* and the participation of Rumania in the Conventions of 3rd and 4th July had greatly minimized this likelihood.

The Four-Power Pact had created an oligarchy of the Western Powers to which Germany was admitted. The new development in Soviet policy had created for the U.S.S.R. a position in Eastern Europe without peer or rival, and had definitely put her " on the map " as a leading Power in the diplomatic world.

The effect upon France and Italy was, by the very reason of things, contrary. The isolation of Germany was part of French policy, and the fact that a rejoinder had been made to the Four-Power Pact, which had never been popular in Paris, was not unwelcome to the Quai d'Orsay. Conversely, Signor Mussolini, whose child the Four-Power Pact was, may well have regarded with a certain dismay the appearance of a new factor running counter to his policy. For the Four-Power Pact had threatened to destroy the French capacity to mobilize the League vote on any particular subject, more particularly that of Treaty Revision, and the possible support of the Soviet Union for an anti-revisionist policy strengthened the hands of France as it weakened those of Italy.

As a result both Italy and France paid court to the Soviet Union. Signor Mussolini took advantage of M. Litvinoff's visit to Rome to sign with him a Pact of Non-aggression on 2nd September, 1933, similar to that already negotiated with France in 1932, and on the occasion of the Foreign Commissar's second Italian visit, on his return from the United States in December, the Duce made every effort to remove from his mind the impression that the Four-Power Pact was in any way directed against the Soviet Union. Indeed, the support of that country was sought most earnestly both in extending the influence and scope of the Pact and also in the reorganization of the League of Nations.

The attitude of France was more positive. Fear makes strange bedfellows, and. for France the threat of a rearmed Germany represented a reason for restoring the *entente* with the Great Power in Eastern Europe. For the first time since the Revolution of 1917 there was an exchange of military *attachés* between Paris and Moscow during the summer of 1933. M. Herriot toured the Soviet Union and re-established that personal contact between the Third Republic and Revolutionary Russia which M. Albert Thomas had made with M. Kerensky. M. Pierre Cot, the Air Minister, with a high officer of the French Air Staff, paid an official visit to Moscow ; and, perhaps most important of all, French officers began to fill the places left vacant by the withdrawal, or dismissal, of the German military experts with the Red Army. In return, the Soviet Union agreed to reopen discussions on the settlement of the problem of the debts owed to France by the Imperial and Republican Russian Governments.

As the year drew on and the European situation became more acute, after the withdrawal of Germany from the Disarmament

Conference and the League, the Franco-Soviet *rapprochement* grew stronger.   Uncertain as to the eventual attitude of Great Britain in the event of German rearmament, and gravely anxious concerning the increasing degree of agreement between Germany and Poland, French diplomacy, urged on by the French General Staff, began to incline more and more to the forging of a tangible link in the chain of Franco-Soviet friendship.   A military alliance, similar to that of 1895 with Imperial Russia, was openly advocated in December, and a draft agreement was even declared to be in existence in Paris.   M. Paul-Boncour was warmly urged to continue his journey to Moscow after his visit to Warsaw in the New Year.

Even after the storm of the Stavisky scandals and the tragedy of 6th February had swept M. Paul-Boncour into obscurity, his successor, M. Louis Barthou, a man of very different calibre, did not abandon the policy of friendship with the Soviet Union, though when he visited Warsaw in April, 1934, time and the pressure of events in Western Europe would not allow of his going on to Moscow.[1]

6

Enough has been said to show the important results which this development had on both Asiatic and European policy, and it remains only to consider the position of the U.S.S.R. itself.   Undoubtedly the internal situation of the Soviet Union had its influence on their diplomatic policy, and, owing to economic difficulties, the need to avoid foreign complications was greater than ever.   This has now been achieved at the double price of Bessarabia and the final jettisoning of the Trotsky policy of continuous revolution.   Herein lies the true inwardness of this new Soviet policy.   The hope of world revolution has been, at least temporarily, abandoned, and correspondingly there has been a tacit acceptance of the political *status quo* by the Soviet Union.

But what has been gained ?   Not only the guarantee of peace in the West, but also the corollary of the abandonment of world revolution, that is to say, the recognition by the world of the U.S.S.R. in its true position as a political force.   For, with the recognition of the Moscow Government by Spain on 27th July, and by the United States on 17th November, and with Great Britain, having composed the difference occasioned by the Metro-Vickers trial, negotiating a new trade agreement, the diplomatic

[1] For M. Barthou's subsequent policy regarding the Soviet Union, see below, p. 229.

fortunes of the Soviet Union stood higher at the close of the year than at any time subsequent to 1924, that halcyon year of Recognition.

Not the least interesting aspect of the situation was the apparent return of the Soviet Union to the former Tzarist policy of being the dominant factor in Eastern Europe, and of expansion of influence in the Far East. It is not impossible that there may be a resumption of that same attitude towards China which Borodin and General Galen made famous in the years 1924 to 1926, and in Europe a revival of the Pan-Slav policy and of the *entente* with France, with Poland as an ally instead of an integral part of Russia, and with France, as the sponsor of Yugoslavia, figuring in the role of an accessory before the fact. Well might M. Litvinoff in Moscow, in reviewing the year 1933, experience a feeling of satisfaction, a sense of something attempted, something done.

Chapter IX

THE STRUGGLE FOR EQUALITY. PART II.

1

But if the World Economic Conference had been a scene of triumph for M. Litvinoff, it had certainly been the reverse for Mr. Arthur Henderson when he arrived to carry out the mandate of private negotiation which had been given him by the General Commission before its adjournment on 30th June. Not without reason Mr. Henderson had thought that, with the statesmen of the world gathered together in London, he would have ample opportunities in the intervals of the Economic Conference to discuss with them the problems which were holding up the sessions at Geneva. He was grievously deceived.

Long years of political association with Mr. MacDonald as a colleague might have taught Mr. Henderson that there was no room for two kings in Brentford or two Conference Presidents in London, and for all the contacts he was able to make he might just as well have stayed in Geneva. Indeed there have been few more pathetic pictures than that of Mr. Henderson sitting alone on one of the lounges in the delegates' *foyer* and gazing enviously at the milling groups of representatives who surged up and down the floor and cast not a glance at the lonely, rubicund, kindly figure in the corner. On the outskirts of these scrimmages hung, like a half-back, Mr. Henderson's faithful Achates, M. Aghnides, Director of the Disarmament Section of the League Secretariat, who spared no effort to " collar " delegates as they broke away from their groups and to transform the picture of Mr. Henderson from " Solitaire " into " Conversation Piece ". But even when M. Aghnides' efforts were crowned with success, his prey would vanish from his clutches into another group before they had crossed the brief distance to Mr. Henderson's sofa.

This state of things continued for upwards of a week, and by the middle of July Mr. Henderson realized that the delegates to the Economic Conference were " too busy " to discuss disarmament. He, therefore, left London to pursue his negotiations in the Continental capitals, and for the next few weeks he journeyed through Europe like Diogenes looking for an honest man.

Mr. Henderson went first to Rome, arriving on 14th July, and discussed the situation with Signor Mussolini and the Italian delegates to the Disarmament Conference. The Duce urged him to emphasize in his future discussions with French and German statesmen the importance of using the new spirit created by the Four-Power Pact as a basis for fresh negotiations [1]—but unfortunately neither Paris nor Berlin attached the same importance as Signor Mussolini to this latest international instrument. On the technical side the Italians were emphatic that any disarmament convention which the Conference might adopt must include an effective system of control and supervision.

From Rome Mr. Henderson went to Berlin and was received with every courtesy, though in himself he combined almost all the elements most anathema to the Nazi State. He was a pronounced pacifist, a species of which the German variety was rapidly becoming a *rara avis* confined in concentration camps ; he had been Secretary of the British Labour Party, whose German colleagues, the Social-Democrats, had been suppressed, with the Trades Unions, and their funds confiscated ; more than this, he had been president of the loathed Second International which had so loudly acclaimed the Weimar System in Germany. Despite these discrepancies of view, however, the Ministry of Propaganda in its daily orders to the Press gave instructions that Mr. Henderson was not to be mocked or railed at, and that the same should apply to the Disarmament Conference.

Mr. Henderson had conversations with Baron von Neurath, General von Blomberg, and Herr Nadolny in Berlin, and later in Munich with the Chancellor. These talks, during which he urged that the signature of the Four-Power Pact should be followed up by establishing general contact between Herr Hitler and M. Daladier, led him to announce that he was confident that the divergence on a number of important points "had been narrowed ". To which Baron von Neurath replied that it was not the *German* standpoint that was obstructing the progress of the Disarmament Conference, and added guardedly that " diplomatic preparations would be necessary " before any such meeting of the Chancellor and M. Daladier, as Mr. Henderson had proposed. The suggestion was received with equal reserve in Paris, where Mr. Henderson finished his tour on 22nd July.

Strangely enough the President of the Disarmament Conference did not appear much discouraged as a result of his European

---

[1] The Pact was formally signed on 15th July, during Mr. Henderson's visit to Rome.

visits. He was in fact definitely optimistic, and it appeared to him that considerable progress had been made, in which the questions at issue fell of themselves into two categories ; those upon which agreement seemed relatively easy and those on which agreement was more distant. In the first of these classes Mr. Henderson included non-recourse to war on a universal basis ; definition of an aggressor ; control and supervision ; standard-ization of Continental European armies (including trained reserves, effectives, and colonial forces) ; control of budgetary publicity ; bombing from the air ; the early setting-up of the Permanent Disarmament Commission ; and naval questions.

There was a number of subjects in this list which a man less confident and optimistic than Mr. Henderson might have included in the second category of problems more difficult, but even as it was this latter list was formidable enough. Therein Mr. Henderson numbered the period of duration of the first Dis-armament Convention ; the size of tanks and artillery ; the reduction of land material either by destruction or otherwise ; the manufacture of and trade in arms ; military and naval aviation ; penalties against violation of the Disarmament Con-vention ; and the application of the principle of equality.

The difficulty in finding agreement on the last point alone might have been sufficient to damp Mr. Henderson's optimism, for the period of his visits in the Continental capitals corresponded with the beginning of that tension in Europe which eventually rendered it impossible for France to declare her ability to grant the measure of equality in arms which Germany demanded.

2

In the Europe which Mr. Henderson traversed in July, 1933, the spell of Herr Hitler's avowal of peace was already beginning to wear thin, in Germany and elsewhere, and this process con-tinued until the final rupture of 14th October. To be sure, the Chancellor continued his protestations of peace, proclaimed the end of the period of active revolution, and emphasized that the two and a half million S.A., S.S., and *Stalhelm* were but the spear-head of Europe's battle-front against Bolshevism ; yet the announcements of his lieutenants and the actions of his followers belied these sentiments. Captain Röhm announced that the whole German nation must pass through the education of arms either in the *Arbeitslage* or in one or other of the semi-military organizations, showing that a " nation in arms " was aimed at.

A recrudescence of assaults on foreigners who did not salute passing Nazi detachments called forth protests from a number of diplomatic representatives in Berlin. The murder of the well-known pacifist, Dr. Lessing, by Nazis at Marienbad in Czechoslovakia, the kidnapping of German refugees from over the Swiss frontier and the border of the Saar Territory, and the arrest and expulsion of the *Daily Telegraph* correspondent, because he described the martial bearing and equipment of a parade of S.A. and S.S. in Munich, produced a state of mind in Europe anything but credulous of the pacific intention of Germany, and well-nigh convinced of the reverse.

And above all there was the case of Austria. " Herr Hitler," said a Nazi acquaintance to the author, " will compromise on nearly every question save two—the Jews and Austria." With the German Chancellor's anti-Hebraic complexes this is no place to deal, but the latter obsession, that of Austria, plays an important part in the story.

The desire for an Austro-German *Anschluss* dated, of course, from considerably before the Nazi Revolution. It was in fact a product of the Revolution of 1918, and an article of the original draft of the Weimar Constitution provided for the union of the two countries. This article was deleted at the behest of the Allied Powers, who took every means possible to prevent such a step. Article 80 of the Treaty of Versailles and Article 88 of the Treaty of St. Germain forbade Germany and Austria respectively to unite without the consent of the League of Nations, but even this precaution was not strong enough to allay the fears of newly created European States, and the bogey of the *Anschluss* was an important factor in the foundation of the Little Entente.

In both countries there was manifested a genuine desire for union, though in the Reich certain elements in Prussia looked askance at this political strengthening of the Catholic South, and in Austria there were many who dreaded the cold influence of Prussia. The nearest that these dreams of union had attained was in 1931, when the Austro-German *Zollunion* startled Europe and brought its own Nemesis in its wake.

Any desire on the part of Austria for amalgamation was, however, distinctly damped by the arrival in power of the Nazi Party in Germany with its threatened re-organization of the Reich into a series of provinces. To enter a Federal State as a component part having sovereign rights was for Austria one thing, to be *gleichgeschalltet* into a " region " of the *Dritte Reich* and governed by a *Stadthalter* appointed from Berlin quite another.

But Herr Hitler, an Austrian himself,[1] was determined that his mother-country should be incorporated in that new Germany which he had forged, as the southern bastion of that great empire of which he dreamed, stretching from the Strasburger Kirche to the Riga Dom and from South Jutland to the Adriatic. He bitterly resented both opposition to his schemes in Austria itself and disapproval in Europe as a whole, and gave orders that this wayward sister should be " contained " willy-nilly.

The early attacks of the Nazis after the elections of March were successfully rebuffed by the Government of the *Bundeskanzler*, Dr. Dollfuss, and after the Reichstag Speech of 17th May aggressive action was suspended as an earnest of Germany's pacific intentions.

This truce, however, lasted only until 27th May, when the Reich Government suddenly raised the *visa* fee for Austria to the prohibitive figure of a thousand Reichsmarks (£50 at par), thereby striking at the tourist traffic, which was one of the most important factors in the economic life of the country. To this the only effective reply the Dollfuss Government could make was to negotiate trade agreements with France, Poland, and Yugoslavia, and raid the headquarters of the Austrian Nazi Party in the principal towns in the country. Thus began a campaign of mutual recrimination and reprisal which disturbed the peace of Europe throughout the summer.

Dr. Dollfuss appealed to the Powers interested in the maintenance of an independent Austria, and in the course of a visit to Signor Mussolini on 4th June he received an assurance from the Duce that " independent Austria has a warm friend in Italy ". The *Bundeskanzler* next visited London to attend the World Economic Conference and received an ovation which was unequalled during the whole course of that body's deliberations. His speech, in which he quoted Schiller's lines that " the best man cannot live in peace if his wicked neighbours do not leave him in peace ", was loudly cheered.

The absence of the Austrian Chancellor, however, was the signal for an outbreak of political terrorism in Vienna and the country at large, which caused him to spend a good deal of time on the telephone. He arrived back in his capital on 17th June and decreed at once the disbandment of the S.A. and S.S. detach-

[1] Adolf Hitler was born at Braunau in Austria in 1889 ; he did not become a German citizen until February, 1932, when he took the oath of allegiance to the Reich and announced himself a candidate for the Presidential election.

ments throughout the country and the prohibition of the wearing of Nazi badges.[1]

Their hopes of intimidating the Dollfuss Government by direct terrorist means having been frustrated, the Nazi authorities of the Reich proceeded to use other methods, to which retaliation was less easy.   Night after night wireless broadcasts from Munich of a particularly invidious character openly invited the population of Austria to overthrow their Government and to declare themselves a Nazi State on the model of Germany, and these were followed by " air-raids " over Austrian territory during which leaflets were dropped containing similar appeals.

The world reacted in admiration to the courageous stand which Dr. Dollfuss was making against this amazing example of " moral " aggression, and the phrase " brave little Austria " began to circulate in the same manner in which " brave little Belgium " had been used in 1914.   German diplomacy had perpetrated another of its periodic colossal blunders, and had once again picked on a little State to bully.

Conversations between the Powers during the first week of August as to whether joint action should be taken in making a protest to Berlin disclosed the fact that there existed a diversion of opinion.   Great Britain and France were for a stiff tripartite protest, Italy " did not think that it would be either prudent or necessary to join in a _démarche_ just now ".   Accordingly, the Italian Ambassador made " friendly representations " to the German Foreign Office on 6th August and received an assurance that the Government would "do its best " to prevent propaganda air-raids and broadcasts ; but when next day the French Ambassador and the British _Chargé d'Affaires_ formally invoked the Four-Power Pact, and stated that in the view of their Governments " certain recent incidents of German propaganda in Austria were inconsistent with existing treaty obligations ", they were informed that the German Government did not consider the invocation of the Four-Power Pact as proper, that there had been no treaty infractions of any kind on the German side, and that interference in the Austro-German dispute was, therefore, " inadmissible."   No such reply had been made by a German Government to an Allied representative since the Armistice, and the whole affair marked a definite change in the tone of diplomatic exchanges between Germany and other European Powers.

---

[1] The Nazi Party itself was not suppressed, since under the Austrian Constitutional Law a Party is not a tangible thing ; only a political creed, not a political organization.

Great Britain and France, however, were not prepared to carry the affair further and were, therefore, forced to swallow the rebuff.

Throughout the month of August the Nazi campaign against the Dollfuss Government became intensified. The broadcasts continued relentlessly, the acts of terror were multiplied: Every method of subversion was brought into play. The diplomatic bag of the German Legation at Vienna was used to carry Party instructions to the Austrian Nazis, whose headquarters had been transferred to Munich. It was announced that an S.A. legion was being formed in Germany for service against Austria.

To meet these new measures of aggression, Dr. Dollfuss sought and obtained the permission of the Great Powers to enlist a force of 8,000 men, in addition to the regular army of 22,000,[1] and to put them through six months' training (28th August). In conveying the approval of the British Government to this proposal, Sir John Simon wrote that no objection would be raised to the new force " so long as there continue to exist the ' special circumstances ', foremost among which the British Government count the Terrorist campaign conducted against the present Austrian Government and the defensive measures adopted, on the authority of the Chancellor, against the elements of disorder now in question ".

Placed geographically between two powerful neighbours, each having adopted a form of dictatorship, it was virtually impossible for Austria to remain the democratic State she had been since the Peace Conference. It was inevitable that Dr. Dollfuss should gravitate towards the influence of either Germany or Italy, and the former being clearly impossible he perforce chose the latter. He walked the tight-rope between Nazis and Fascists as long as it was possible, then, on 19th to 21st August, he spent a long week-end with the Duce at Riccione, in the course of which all the problems of Austrian politics, internal and international, were discussed and Signor Mussolini reaffirmed his previous pledge of support for Austrian independence.[2] On the Chancellor's return to Vienna it became known that he had made his choice, he had " gone Fascist " and Austria was to be constituted a Corporate State.[3]

[1] The regular army allowed to Austria under the Treaty of St. Germain was not to exceed 30,000 men, enlisted voluntarily.

[2] Signor Mussolini was said to have promised support of a most material kind for the Austrian Government in the event of a Nazi coup in Vienna.

[3] This was finally achieved when the new Austrian Constitution was promulgated on 1st May, 1934.

A reconstitution of the Government on "directorate lines" followed on 11th September, and though no Fascist principles were proclaimed, these were tacitly understood to be accepted. The opposition of the Social-Democrats to this new development was strong and the force of circumstances placed them in the ironical position of being allied with the Nazis " agin the Government ". For a while the position of the Chancellor seemed even more precarious than before, for the *Heimwehr* was also uncertain in their allegiance. Then occurred an event which had so often before saved a falling statesman from catastrophe. An unsuccessful attempt to assassinate Dr. Dollfuss on 5th October rallied the *Heimwehr* to his support and, on his recovery from his wounds, the Chancellor publicly allied himself with them and set about dealing with his Nazi and Socialist adversaries with redoubled vigour.[1]

3

To a Europe with nerves already strung to tension point, every act in the Austro-German drama was an added cause for alarm and misgiving. There began to gather again those dark storm clouds which had been temporarily dispersed by Herr Hitler's speech of 17th May. In every country the word " disarmament " vanished, if not from the official vocabulary, at any rate from the official mentality.

In Germany the word had for some time been replaced by " rearmament ". Germany had, in fact, made up her mind to rearm, largely because the others would not disarm. There was a time in Dr. Brüning's Chancellorship, or even at the moment when Herr von Papen made his offer in November, 1932, or even as late as the agreement of 11th December of the same year, when " military equality " at either level—all round disarmament or her own rearmament—was probably equally acceptable to her. But now the spirit of martial glory had descended upon her, and the way seemed opening for military expansion ; Germany could not, she would not, be baulked of it. Already the longing for military display, the swagger of a uniform, the glamour of a band, had been reawakened in the German people. New and smarter uniforms

---

[1] The friction with the Socialists came to a head in February, 1934, when a general strike was declared, and, after four days of bitter street fighting between the *Schutzbund* and the *Heimwehr*, supported by the Army with light artillery, the Socialist resistance was crushed and the party organization disbanded.

were making their appearance every day ; social distinctions between the S.S. and S.A., between staff and battalion, between Guard and Line, were manifesting themselves. Already many men, for whom life seemed to hold no other future than the unattractive, drab, humdrum existence of a clerk, were back in uniform as commanders of labour camps, as instructors in " war sport camps ", as experts in the secret areas where S.S. were being trained by N.C.O.'s from the *Reichswehr*. Thoughts of promotion were filling their minds, and they were looking eagerly forward to the day when the officer-corps of the *Reichswehr* should be doubled, in the hope that there would be a commission for them. Others were waiting to take their places in the labour-corps.

After fifteen years, the labour and effort which General von Seeckt had expended on the reorganization of the German Army were finding their reward. Not only was the *Reichswehr* the most efficient military force in the world, but it was no longer a disgraceful profession in Germany ; no longer was there the difficulty, as there had been in the early years, of getting the right type of young man as an officer. A commission was a greatly sought, highly prized privilege now. The Nazi revolution had restored to the Army its old prestige and honour, and, borrowing a leaf from the book of Mr. Flo. Ziegfeld,[1] was " glorifying the German soldier " ; the stigma of 1918 had been removed. " The German people know," had said the Chancellor, " that no new war will take place which will gain for our country more honour than was in the last war. Germany is not in need of rehabilitation on the battlefield, for there she should never have lost her prestige." [2]

But though Herr Hitler added that the Nazi revolution which had redeemed Germany was not " the expression of a desire to win new laurels on the battlefield ", the sentiment was not altogether shared by the rank and file of the S.A. and S.S. Many of the young men had been blooded for the first time during the Terror and their atavistic and combative instincts had been aroused. They had been hailed as the saviours of Germany from the degradation of Marxism and the Weimar System, and had been nurtured on the injustices which Germany had suffered under the Peace Treaty. They were young, they were ambitious,

---

[1] Mr. Florenz Ziegfeld, the great American theatrical producer, proclaimed to the United States, when he first produced the famous "Ziegfeld Follies ", that he was " glorifying the American girl ".
[2] See the Chancellor's speech at Nuremberg, 3rd September, 1933.

above all they were unemployed, and all the efforts of the Government had failed to absorb them into the economic life of the country ; what better glory then than to avenge Germany's external wrongs as they had purged her of internal pollution ? " When we've dealt with these Marxist swine," said one of them, " we'll have a slap at those —— Poles."

And the effect of all this was not lost upon France, where also the world disarmament was beginning to reassume that identical sense which it had acquired during the Peace Conference. It was impossible to ignore the fact that with the S.A., S.S., *Stahlhelm*, and Prussian Police, Germany had more than two million men in uniform, in addition to the very efficient *Reichswehr*, and, though it is by no means true that the uniform makes the man, it is truer in Germany than in any other country. It was impossible to ignore the fact that large numbers of the S.A. and S.S., armed with rifle, bayonet, and steel helmet, co-operated closely with the *Reichswehr*, and that they were organized in seven areas parallel to the seven military districts, and this despite the Chancellor's statement that " There is only one body in Germany which bears arms—and that is the Army ".

In Paris the facts were known and appreciated that German boys of between eleven and sixteen years were being given morning exercises in the technique of throwing hand-grenades, and that, in the curricula of German Universities and technical institutions courses in " Poison and Combat Gas ", " Military Utilization of Electrical Means of Transmission ", and " The Maintenance and Perfecting of the Military Aptitude of the Individual and of the People " were making their appearance.

More disturbing still was the large increase in German importations of nickel, leather, manganese, and other features more usually connected with the manufacture of munitions.[1] The military preparedness of German industry was a topic of continual

[1]   GERMAN IMPORTS OF NICKEL, TUNGSTEN, CHROMIUM, ETC., AND SCRAP IRON
JANUARY–SEPTEMBER

	1932		1933	
	Quantity Kilos.	Value Rm.	Quantity Kilos.	Value Rm.
1. GERMANY				
(a) Nickel : Crude, coins, waste, and scrap . . .	1,571,000	4,161,000	3,143,700	7,726,000
(b) Nickel : Bars, sheets, castings, forgings	56,800	254,000	109,600	450,000
(c) Chromium, cadmium, tungsten, and other base metals suitable for metal wares, crude and waste . . .	476,700	1,188,000	896,300	934,000
(d) Scrap and old iron, etc. . .	43,507,300	1,205,000	262,190,400	7,545,000

speculation and discussion in France. Germany, like other countries, had learned a hard lesson in the Great War and had not altogether forgotten it.   By reason of Treaty restrictions she had abandoned the maintenance of large peace-time effectives, and the equipment of her field army and of her national army no longer depended on warehoused stocks of material but upon industrial transformation for war production, and it was known that adequate plans for the organization of such a transformation existed.

To France it seemed as if her patience was being tried unduly highly, and to this M. Paul-Boncour made significant reference on 3rd September, at the unveiling of M. Briand's memorial at Trébenden.   " How easy it is to observe the contrast between a peaceful manifestation such as this and the agitations which surge to the very boundaries of our territories," he declared, and added that, if French patience with Germany were due to a feeling of weakness, that would be grave ; but France knew herself strong enough to resist violence, and the recent quiet visit of the Premier to the frontier defences was the best reply to proceedings of which the least he could say was that " they deeply trouble the atmosphere of peace so necessary to European restoration ".

In Great Britain the repercussions of the European situation were of a different nature, and produced amongst thinking people two divergent schools of thought, both of which were more long-sighted than the views expressed in Europe and treated the question of disarmament in relation to the whole vast problem of Treaty Revision.   The one school of thought held that, unless some specific guarantee were given, Europe would most certainly drift back to war which, as in 1914, would gradually engulf the whole world.   It was maintained that, even though minor rectification of the Peace Treaties were made, Germany would not be content, but would demand and would prepare to take more by force, unless it was made absolutely clear by Great Britain that she meant to oppose such forcible revision, if need be also by force. It was thought, therefore, that unless such additional guarantees of security were given, either France or Poland might precipitate war before Germany had had time to rearm, or that Germany, if given time, might re-establish a hegemony over Europe which would threaten the rest of the world as it did in 1914.

The second view was far more isolationist in character, and urged that Great Britain should resolutely refuse to form part of any special system of European security, and that the main object of her policy should be to co-operate with the Dominions and the United States in trying to form a non-European or Oceanic *bloc* actively interested in the prevention of war and prepared to carry out its obligations under the Covenant, " as these are generally understood to-day," but otherwise entirely unpledged to any special or automatic economic military action.

This school of thought—and in this particular aspect it was surprising to find the Round Table Group and the Beaverbrook Press in a startling degree of agreement—considered further that the provisions of the Locarno Treaty must in any case be reviewed, and that any special obligation which Great Britain might undertake on its own account in Europe as a modification of the Locarno system should be undertaken in the interests of her own security and should be limited to a renewal of the guarantee to Belgium and a declaration never to permit the return of Alsace-Lorraine to Germany. In no case, however, should Great Britain form part of a balance of power in Europe involving her inevitable liability to belligerency whenever a European war broke out.

There was no indication as to whether either of these views were held by the British Government, which still maintained a masterly silence on all subjects connected with foreign affairs, save that on 16th September at Cupar, in Fifeshire, Sir John Simon vouchsafed a gleam from the dark lantern, and disclosed the fact that he was shortly going to Geneva " to find out if there was even now some way in which we can secure an agreed Disarmament Convention ".

4

The three months' recess which the Disarmament Conference had given itself was drawing rapidly to a close and, despite the efforts of Mr. Henderson, there had been no real advance towards a compromise in the conflicting French and German views. No event had occurred during the interval which could in any way facilitate such a compromise, but rather the contrary, and it was apparent to all that the approaching session of the Conference would be far more critical than any that had preceded it. The note of tension was struck as early as 15th September by Baron von Neurath, who uncompromisingly asserted that the Conference must either produce equality for Germany or the collapse of the idea of disarmament, " with tragic circumstances."

The first definite step was taken on 18th September, when Mr. Anthony Eden began a series of Anglo-French discussions with MM. Daladier and Paul-Boncour, which lasted until

22nd September, and their scope eventually widened to include the American and Italian delegates. In these discussions it became evident that France was not prepared to take up the matter of disarmament where it had rested when the Conference had adjourned on 30th June, and was no longer willing to accept the provisions of the British Draft Convention as the basis of agreement. Three months' interval had convinced the French that, with a rapidly rearming Germany, it would be impossible to consider any immediate measure of disarmament at all. Instead, they advanced a new proposal—and one which was destined to wreck the Conference—that armaments should be stabilized at their present level, and that no disarmament should take place until after a four or five years' period, during which the supervisory machinery which the Convention would provide would have an opportunity of proving, or at least testing, its efficiency. In addition, the French urged that a clearly-defined system of sanctions must be included in the Convention for the purpose of dealing with potential violation of its provisions.

Though at the outset both the British and Italian representatives were not in harmony with the French proposals, Mr. Norman Davis, on behalf of the United States, warmly supported them, and at length, on 22nd September, a Four-Power Agreement was reached on the main heads of the policy which they were prepared to pursue at Geneva. It was agreed, therefore, that the proposed convention, which all were at one in feeling absolutely essential, should allow for two stages, the first to be a standstill period of from three to four years, during which it was hoped that Germany might substitute short-service troops for the present system of long-service enlistment. The second stage, also of from three to four years, would be one of actual disarmament, and it was held essential that the Convention should clearly specify what disarmament should be carried out during the second period.

The principle of supervision and control was undisputed, but, whereas the French desired it to be applied automatically and periodically, the British were more inclined to attach more importance to how much armament there would be to disarm than to a discussion as to what sort of supervision should be given to an undefined amount of disarmament. It was further agreed that no naval treaties should be changed before they expired.

All the participants in the Paris conversations then adjourned to the meeting of the League Assembly at Geneva, where they presented the fruits of their agreement to Baron von Neurath on

24th September. For four days the five Powers conferred together, whilst the German Foreign Minister made every effort to achieve a mitigation of the Allied proposals. The probationary period itself was unpalatable to Germany, for it virtually prolonged for a further three or four years the inequality of States created under the Peace Treaties. Moreover, the suggestion that during this period Germany should make the further gesture of transforming her army from a long-term into a short-term force without any corresponding gesture on the part of the Allies was greatly resented in Germany, especially as the French refused to agree to the possession by Germany of " samples " of the forbidden armament categories during this period.

In Germany itself opposition was rising and popular indignation was being fermented. Dr. Frick, the Reichsminister of the Interior, had told eighty thousand children that Germany would refuse to play the part of pariah any longer and that, if equality was refused her now, she would withdraw from all further international conferences. Dr. Rosenberg wrote in the *Völkischer Beobachter* that, if France refused to fulfil her disarmament obligations, Germany by international law would have the right to regard the Treaty of Versailles as revised and cancelled, and thus she would herself have no obligation any longer under the Treaty.

By the night of 28th September a complete deadlock had been reached at Geneva, and on the following morning Baron von Neurath and Dr. Goebbels left for Berlin, carrying with them the proposals at which the Four Powers had arrived in Paris and which they had since refused to modify. Throughout these conversations, Sir John Simon and Mr. Eden had urged the adoption of the British thesis that a decision be reached on the amount of disarmament to be attained rather than on the means of controlling its execution. The French Government, however, had been adamant on this point and also on that of sanctions, and on their refusal to allow " samples " of fighting-planes, light tanks, and anti-aircraft guns to Germany during the probationary period. Germany had also been denied the right to fortify the right bank of the Rhine, and, though certain Powers were prepared to concede this in return for some additional guarantee of security, France would have none of it.

There occurred now a week's interval during which, in Berlin, the Government of the Reich debated the situation, and on 6th October the result of the deliberations was communicated to the British and American Governments, though not to the French.

There is little doubt that the Italian Government had had private information.

The German *aide-mémoire*[1] took its stand upon the British Draft Convention which the Conference had adopted as a basis for agreement, and rejected the idea of a "probationary period". It accepted, however, the principle of a five-year period for the first step in disarmament, for this had been provided in the British Draft, and agreed that it might be by stages, of which the first should be two and the second three years. The German Government claimed that the principle of equality should be accepted from the start, and further agreed to transform the *Reichswehr* into an army of short-term recruits. With regard to material, Germany agreed not to demand any form of armament which other countries were prepared to abolish, provided that the actual abolition was to take place within the five-year period. But, where particular armaments were to be maintained, though limited, Germany asked that she should be entitled to possess such armaments, and that from the beginning of the five-year period. The quantity of such armaments was to be left over for further discussion. Finally, she claimed that, with respect to armaments which were not to be limited to other Powers, these also should not be limited to Germany. The *aide-mémoire* concluded " Merely to increase the quantity of arms allowed by the Treaty of Versailles by doubling the figures fixed in the Treaty would mean a discrimination which Germany cannot accept and would not satisfy her need for security. Germany wishes either to have full liberty or to be subjected to the same qualitative restrictions as other countries". The question of control was not mentioned, but, ever since the Chancellor's speech of 17th May, this had been accepted by Germany, provided that it was applied equally and impartially to all.

German diplomacy had shown an unusual and not customary adroitness. Their claim, always a strong one legally and morally, had the added advantage of being based upon the British Draft Convention which the Conference had accepted as a basis for agreement, and from which the Allied Powers, and not Germany, had departed. Moreover, on its own merits, the proposal was not unreasonable. It envisaged rather more concessions to Germany than the proposals of Dr. Brüning and Herr von Papen, but considerable time had passed since these had been made, and

[1] For text of documents concerning Germany's withdrawal from the Conference and the subsequent diplomatic negotiations, see *Documents on International Affairs, 1933*, pp. 279–324.

Germany, always in her own view the creditor in disarmament matters, regarded the Allied debt as accumulating at compound interest.   If the psychological change in Germany be left out of account, it would be difficult not to accept the justness of the German claim, but it was just that which the Four Powers found it impossible to do, and they made haste to restate their positions.

Mr. Baldwin at Birmingham on 6th October dealt a blow to the isolationist school in Great Britain, whose views he declared to be " both crude and childish ", and gave a categorical reaffirmation of Great Britain's pledges.   " What Great Britain has signed she will adhere to."   But he admitted that the Treaty of Locarno was " the most difficult " of the agreements entered into since the War.

This reference to Great Britain's obligation was described as " comforting " by M. Daladier, when he addressed the Radical Party Congress at Vichy two days later on 8th October.   France, he asserted, did not wish to threaten and humiliate anyone, and for that reason would accept no reduction of forces without an international agreement effectively guaranteed to organize progressive disarmament and establish permanent and automatic supervision.   Most countries had agreed on the principle of a period of four years, during which supervision would be organized and would begin its work, the various types of armies be re organized on a short-term basis, excluding the semi-military formations, and no more heavy materials would be constructed. Should supervision prove effective, all prohibited material would be destroyed.

What did Germany want ?   demanded M. Daladier, voicing the question all Europe was asking.   Publicly the German Government proclaimed its desire for peace, and by diplomatic channels its wish to draw closer to France.   Yet why was German youth trained for fighting ?   Why this refusal to take the first step towards disarmament ?   Why this demand of the right to construct material which would have to be destroyed soon afterwards if a Convention was signed [1] ?   That M. Daladier was speaking not only as a leader of the Radical Party but also as Prime

---

[1] The obvious German retort was that the Allied record of disarmament since the Peace Conference, and especially that of France, had not been conspicuously great, and that it was conceivable that, at the end of the four years' period, they might decide not to destroy their war material. This, as far as Germany was concerned, would perpetuate inequality of status, but if she already had her arms she would have achieved a marked step towards equality.

Minister of France was shown when on 10th October the Cabinet officially endorsed the attitude which he had taken up.

Events were now moving towards a climax with great rapidity.   Though all now knew that a crisis was inevitable, few, if any, had any conception of what its magnitude and gravity would be.

The Bureau of the Disarmament Conference met formally on 9th October and adjourned until the 14th ; a meeting of the General Commission was called for the 16th to begin the second reading of the British Draft Convention, which had been revised to include the amendments adopted during the first reading. For three days (9–11th October) the representatives of the five Powers conferred in an endeavour to secure a moderation of the German attitude as set out in the *aide-mémoire* of 6th October. But neither appeals, threats, nor cajoleries moved the saturnine Herr Nadolny ; moreover, the German Government had deeply resented the method followed by the Four Powers in consulting together, without the German delegate, and producing proposals which differed from those embodied in the British Plan.

On the evening of the 11th, Herr Nadolny received the final proposals of the Four Powers, which still contained the provision for a " probationary period " so abhorrent to Germany.   These he carried later to Berlin and placed before the Chancellor and the Foreign Minister.   Herr Hitler then took energetic action. He summoned a Cabinet meeting for the 13th, recalled the President from Neudeck [1] to Berlin, and ordered the legal expert of the Foreign Office, Dr. Gaus, to prepare a memorandum on the potential results in the event of Germany's withdrawal from the League of Nations.   He also authorized the issue of a semi-official statement pregnant with warning and foreboding.   The proposals for a disarmament agreement submitted by the Four Powers, it declared, constituted a withdrawal of the principle of equality as fixed by the Agreement of 11th December, 1932. " It is incompatible with the principle of international politics that certain Powers, as they are openly admitting, should want to bring into effect a disarmament convention yielding the obvious result that the most highly-armed Powers refuse to undertake even the slightest step towards disarmament."   German statesmen, it was added, observed with the gravest apprehension the methods " which have already caused the present grave situation and are most likely to jeopardize disarmament, which can be successful

[1] Neudeck about this time began to be known popularly as " the smallest concentration camp ".

only if the fundamental demands, a real and general disarmament and honest equality, are conceded ".

October 14th, 1933, may well go down as one of the outstanding dates in European history, for on that day the second or Locarno period of post-war history came to an end ; what may come forth from the period which then began is still thought of with fear and horror. It was a day of tremendous happenings and great decisions both in Geneva and Berlin, where, in full knowledge of what might be the outcome, both sides in the dispute went forward on the course which seemed to them best and most just. There is something most tragic, something of desperate futility, in the spirit of mutual distrust and suspicion which actuated the policies of both France and Germany, the one refusing to disarm because she believed the other to be rearming, the other rearming because of the refusal of the one to disarm.

At Geneva, despite the storm-signals in Berlin, the Four Powers could do nothing but hold on their course, and on the morning of the 14th, Sir John Simon rose in the Bureau, on behalf of his French, Italian and American colleagues, to put forward formally the proposals which they had evolved among themselves. It was necessary, he averred, that the British Draft Convention, put forward in March and adopted as a basis of agreement in June, must be in some respects recast. The time had gone past for glossing over difficulties by vague optimistic phrases. The unsettled state of Europe was a fact which must be faced, and the need, therefore, for modifying the Draft Convention was clearly established so as to accomplish by a process of evolution a programme which would gradually unfold in action.

It was, therefore, proposed to extend the period of evolution of disarmament from five years, as contemplated by the British Draft, to eight years, during which the time would be occupied by the fulfilment of a continuous programme designed to secure both disarmament, security, and equality.

" The proposed period of eight years would begin with the transformation of Continental armies on the lines set out in the British Draft, together with the setting up, through the medium of the Permanent Disarmament Commission, of an adequate system of supervision, so that the sense of security which the due observance of the Convention will afford should provide the groundwork for the practical attainment of the twin ideas of disarmament and equality. . . . .

" It is a matter for close consideration to determine how much of the eight years would be needed for the initial steps to which I have referred. . . . Transformation of armies involves technical questions which will govern the time-table. . . . I must repeat that the period of four years was mentioned by several Governments, though others have raised the question whether it could not be somewhat shortened."

Sir John Simon said that he had referred to the disarmament as substantial, and by that was meant either disarmament provided for in the British Draft or some comparable variation of it, and he continued, " I say quite definitely that the whole scheme would not be satisfactory to my Government . . . unless the degree of disarmament by the heavily-armed Powers is fully defined in the Convention and really adequate." Another feature of the second stage of the plan was that the result of the abolition of various kinds of armaments would be to constitute a common list of permitted arms which would become the same for all countries, and thus the differential position of the Powers whose arms were limited by the Treaties would finally cease.

This programme involved a feature which, he said, was essential. The scheme involved the principle that the Powers under restriction of the Treaties should not begin to increase their armaments forthwith, but should express their willingness to conform to a time-table such as he had indicated. He did not mean, however, to dispute the reasonableness, as the *Reichswehr* was transformed into a more numerous short-service army, of a proportional numerical increase in its armaments, and there should be from the beginning of the Convention an agreement that no Government would manufacture or acquire any further weapons of any of the types to be abolished.

Mr. Norman Davis immediately followed Sir John Simon, and briefly stated his complete approval and acquiescence in the sentiments which he had expressed. Delegate after delegate followed, French, Italian, Czech, and Polish ; there was a remarkable degree of unanimity ; only the German delegate, Baron von Rheinbaben, remarked darkly that the views of his Government were dominated by two essential claims—real and substantial disarmament on the part of heavily-armed Powers and the practical and immediate application of the principle of equality of status.

There was some little surprise at the restraint with which he spoke. Something more violent had been expected. But the Bureau had not long to wait for Germany's rejoinder, and it soon appeared that Baron von Rheinbaben's remarks were merely academic in character.

Almost as the meeting broke up, the President of the Conference received a telegram from the German Foreign Minister, in which he said : " In the light of the course which recent discussions of the Powers has taken in the matter of disarmament, it is now clear that the Disarmament Conference will not fulfil what is its sole object—namely, general disarmament. It is also clear that this failure of the Conference is due solely to the unwillingness on the part of the highly-armed States to carry out their contractual obligation to disarm. This renders impossible the satisfaction of Germany's recognized claim to equality of rights, and the conditions on which the German Government agreed at the beginning of this year to take part in the work of the Conference thus no longer exist. The German Government is accordingly compelled to leave the Disarmament Conference."

At the same time, in Berlin, the Government of the Reich gave notice of Germany's withdrawal from the League of Nations.[1]

A chapter of history had ended.

[1] On 16th October, the Bureau and the General Commission approved the terms of a reply, prepared by Mr. Henderson, to Baron von Neurath's telegram announcing Germany's withdrawal from the Conference. It pointed out that the German Government had taken this step at a moment when the Bureau had just decided to submit to the General Commission a definite programme. This programme, to be completed within a limited period, provided for the realization progressively, in accordance with resolutions of the Conference, in which Germany herself concurred, of reduction of armaments comparable to those contemplated in the Draft Convention submitted to the General Commission.

" This programme provided also, with corresponding measures of security, for the realization of equality of rights which the German Government have always placed in the forefront of their demands. I regret, therefore, that this grave decision should have been taken by your Government for reasons which I am unable to accept as valid."

Though the President's draft letter was approved by the General Commission, four delegates made reservations. The Hungarian delegate said that his country was in a special situation and must consider the disarmament problem from that special point of view. The Soviet delegate, while not objecting to the dispatch of the reply as a message from the President in his own name, said it should not be considered that his Government adhered to the text as it stood, because it was based on certain negotiations which had taken place on the margin of the Conference to which he had not been a party. The Polish delegate said a passage in the reply referred to a programme with which he was only partly acquainted, and the Turkish representative said his delegation had not been kept informed of the negotiations at all.

The General Commission agreed to adjourn till 26th October, but when that date arrived, and no progress had been made, it adjourned again until 9th November and 4th December respectively. The Bureau met in accordance with this plan and continued to function in a half-hearted manner, appointing new sub-committees which should carry on co-ordinating work during the interval. The December meeting of the General Commission was postponed until January, 1934, but no improvement in the situation had occurred by then and a meeting of the officers

5

Why did Germany withdraw from the Disarmament Conference and the League of Nations on 14th October ? For a full under-standing of the position to-day, with all its complexities, this question must be clearly and dispassionately answered.

Germany left Geneva for two different categories of reasons, external and internal ; both her foreign policy and her home policy were inextricably mingled in and deeply affected by the decision of the Bureau on 14th October. As far as foreign policy was concerned she withdrew because, as admitted by Sir John Simon, the basis of the British Plan—already accepted by all Powers, including Germany, as the " basis for the future Convention "—had been modified in a vital respect. The original draft, as accepted on 8th June, had proposed equality in armaments through disarmament by stages in five years within a framework of security. The modified Plan, as advanced on 14th October, proposed a preliminary period of probation of four years' duration, during which there should be limitation but no disarma-ment by the armed Powers, while the *Reichswehr* were to be organ-ized on a short-service basis, both limitation and reorganization being under the supervision of an international Disarmament Commission. The modified Plan was also decidedly vague as to the disarmament which was to be carried out by the armed Powers during the second period of four years, but was quite explicit that during the whole period of eight years there was to be no rearmament by Germany of any kind.

It must be said at once that there was never for one moment any possibility that Germany either would, or could, accept these new proposals. A Germany in the condition of 1918 might have done so, or they might have been imposed at the bayonet's point on States such as Egypt or the Philippines, but to expect it of a nation in such an exalted state of reawakened nationalism as was Germany in 1933 was little short of lunacy.

On the other hand, the Four Powers had been actuated in their stand at Geneva by the fact that, in its Note of 6th October, the German Government had made the claim for freedom to possess some quantities at least of all the arms allowed to the other Powers. This, it was asserted, went further than the previous demands of Germany, and it was this claim which had led to the

of the Conference on 20th January agreed that neither the Bureau nor the General Commission should meet again until after they, themselves, had conferred again in London on 13th February.

decision of other and smaller Powers to support the attitude represented by Sir John Simon on 14th October.

This point, and many others, were referred to by Baron von Neurath in a statement to the foreign Press on 16th October. The German Foreign Minister surveyed the whole position taken up by his Government at the Disarmament Conference, but especial importance attached to his reference to the Note of 6th October, since it gave the lie direct to the assertions of Sir John Simon with regard to previous German demands. The whole affair provides an outstanding example of the failure of German diplomacy to gauge or comprehend British psychology.

" I have never said," declared Baron von Neurath, " nor could have said anything else to Sir John Simon than what was contained in the instructions (to the German Chargé d'Affaires in London). For the standpoint laid down in these instructions arises self-evidently with compelling logic out of the principle of equality, and, moreover, only shows how moderate our attitude in regard to the concrete realization of this equality is."

Sir John Simon replied to this complaint in a broadcast statement made on 17th October. During the discussions, he said, the question which seemed likely to give most trouble was not the proposal of successive periods for the bringing into full operation of the Convention, but the question whether Germany should have from the very beginning what were called " samples " –i.e. types of weapons now prohibited to her.

" I had asked," he continued, " to be informed by the German Government exactly what they meant by samples. I had reminded her Foreign Minister that we had been promised this information. We were not, in fact, the only Government who were waiting for the information. What happened ? When at length the German claim was formally restated there cannot be the least doubt that, instead of defining what was meant by samples, the claim was for substantial rearmament from the very beginning. Now a Disarmament Convention cannot begin with rearmament.

" I very much regret to see that Baron von Neurath, in addressing the foreign Press yesterday in Berlin, has been accusing me of not only taking a false view as to this but of misstating the facts. Well, I am perfectly ready to publish the documents and records to show it, and indeed, in view of what he has said, the British Government are entitled to do so. There is not the slightest doubt in the mind of any of us who have been as closely in touch with these discussions on behalf of this country as I have, that the attitude taken up by the German Government at the last moment represented a further widening of the breach, and that all the hard work which has been put into recent conversations by all of us, with mutual good-will, was jeopardized, if not wrecked, by this new attitude."

The only reply to this account of the situation forthcoming from the German side was contained in a semi-official statement issued in Berlin on 18th October. In this, exception was taken to the statement of the Foreign Secretary that Germany had at first only demanded samples of the weapons which would in the Convention be allowed to other countries, but which remained forbidden to those disarmed under the Peace Treaties. It was objected that the idea and expression of " prototypes " had not been invented by Germany, and had only been used occasionally in negotiations. Sir John Simon had said that the German Note of 6th October had not gone into the definition of these sample weapons, but had demanded the rearming of Germany. To this it was replied that Germany had negotiated consistently on the basis of an immediate realization of her equality of rights. From this principle, once granted, it followed that weapons allowed to other nations should also be allowed to Germany. Her Government had beforehand insisted that it was ready to negotiate on the question of the number of the weapons to be allowed to Germany. That, and none other, it was claimed, was the case put forward on 6th October.

Now, when Baron von Neurath made his original statement on 16th October there is little doubt that he was in possession of reports from the agents of the German Government in London to the effect that Sir John Simon was the subject of considerable unpopularity in England ; that a section of the London Press had begun a " Simon must go " campaign ; that there was a division in the British Cabinet as to whether or not he should be promoted to the House of Lords if the position of Lord Chancellor became vacant ; and that in fact it needed only a push from outside to upset the Foreign Secretary once and for all.

Herein lay the proof of German ignorance of British psychology. All these circumstances might have been true, and Sir John Simon might have been in danger of being transferred to " another place," but it needed only the least suggestion of foreign interference to repair his position and to make it virtually impregnable for some time to come. British psychology had changed not one whit since Lord Landsdowne wrote, in 1905, of a similar —and in this case successful —German drive against M. Delcassé, that " if one of our Ministers had had a dead-set made at him by a foreign Power, the country and the Government would not only have stood by him but probably have supported him more vigorously than ever."

But there were other reasons of a domestic nature for the German withdrawal from Geneva. By October the Nazi Revolution had fetched up on a dead centre. The economic programme had not yet come into force ; the constitutional reforms were not ready and the political changes were over. The German people were being kept going on a policy of *panem et circences*, with the emphasis very much on the second element of the formula. There had been endless *Feste* throughout the summer, but now winter was in sight when bread would be more welcome than games. Moreover there had been ugly rumours of a " Second Revolution " emanating from the Radical Left Wing of the Party, and directed towards putting into force the Socialist, as opposed to the National, part of the programme of the Nazi Party. At the same time there were whisperings of a " Staats-Streich " organized by Herr von Papen with the support of the *Reichwehr*. In addition, the Reichstag Fire Trial at Leipzig had failed to produce that overwhelming degree of proof which should have convinced the German people of the danger of a Communist outbreak with which they were threatened in February, 1933, and from which they had only been saved by the Nazi Revolution.

The whole Nazi regime had entered into a very critical phase in October, and it was not to be wondered at that Herr Hitler leaped at the opportunity so gratuitously provided of appealing to the German people on an issue on which they could not possibly be divided. The withdrawal from Geneva provided just such an issue. No good German of whatever party could have accepted the proposals of 14th October ; the Nazi party could, therefore, go to the country as the paladins of German honour.

It was with these thoughts in mind that Herr Hitler, simultaneously with the withdrawal of Germany from the League and the Disarmament Conference, obtained from the *Reichspräsident* a decree not only providing for new Reichstag elections, but also for a referendum of the people in answer to the questions " do you approve the policy of the Government laid before you ? and are you ready to affirm and solemnly pledge yourself to this policy as the expression of your own view and your own will ? "

The election campaign which followed was carried out with " peace " as its keynote. The policy of the German Government was a peaceful one, peace at home and peace abroad,—but also equality, *equality*, EQUALITY! This word appeared on hoardings and kiosks, was written in the heavens, was printed in giant letters on the very streets and pavements. It cried aloud to heaven as witness to the demands of the German people.

All this was done in the name of world-peace. The Chancellor repeatedly declared the willingness of Germany to agree to disarmament, to *real* disarmament, and assured the world that there was no country which had the cause of peace more truly at heart than Germany. The President of the Republic, in an eve-of-the-poll address to the nation, summoned the people to support Herr Hitler and " subscribe to this policy of peace ". Unfortunately, on the same day, the Minister-President of Prussia, the recently promoted General Göring, told a tactlessly enthusiastic audience that " I only wish I could build another [German] army which would fill the world with fear ".

The campaign was successful beyond the expectation of the Government. On polling day, 12th November, 95·1 per cent of the valid votes cast were in favour of the Government's policy and 92·2 per cent were in favour of the candidates of the Nazi Party.[1] Herr Hitler could now demonstrate to Europe that he was indeed the leader of a united people and that, when he spoke, he spoke indeed for Germany.

But the victory had in some respects been too great. The excuse advanced on all occasions for the maintenance of the S.A., the S.S., the *Stahlhelm*, and the increased force of Prussian police was that they existed solely to defend Germany from the Communist peril, which, though temporarily repulsed, had but gone underground to recuperate against the day when it could catch its prey unawares. Now, however, it had been shown all too clearly that in an election in which 95·2 per cent of the electorate had voted, only a little over two million votes had been cast against the Government. Even supposing that all of these were ravening Communists, they were unarmed and dispersed over the country, and there seemed no adequate reason to maintain a semi-military force of over two million men to cope with them. The main drawback of propaganda is that it is impossible to calculate where its results will end.

6

The effect upon each of the Four Powers of Germany's withdrawal from the Disarmament Conference and the League of

---

[1] 2,101,004 votes were cast against the Government, and 750,282 voting papers, an unprecedented amount, were found to be invalid.

Nations gave in the majority of cases an indication of their future policies. To France the German action was corroboration of her worst fears and anticipations, and the French General Staff would willingly have indulged in a preventive war had they been sure of the willingness of the French Army to fight and of adequate support from Italy, the United States, and Great Britain.[1]

But no encouragement came from these quarters. Italy, though she had subscribed to the declaration of 14th October, was certainly not prepared to join in any joint action to penalize Germany for withdrawing from two organizations at Geneva of which Italy herself had long been sceptical and was later to become openly contemptuous. Italy's interests were concentrated in keeping the Nazis out of power in Austria, but apart from that Germany might count on her neutrality, though Signor Mussolini had been very seriously displeased that Germany had left the League without previously consulting him, and had rated his Ambassador for not keeping him better informed.

The effect upon the United States was as flame to flax in setting fire to the spirit of isolation in that country. Already deeply engaged with the programme of the Recovery Administration, public opinion was set even more firmly than ever against " entangling alliances ". All the energies of the nation were needed to pull it out of the grip of the economic depression, and the crisis of 14th October was the signal for an avalanche of letters and telegrams to descend upon the White House urging President Roosevelt to recall the American delegates to the Disarmament Conference and to cut loose from all connection with Geneva.

This sentiment was given official expression by Mr. Norman Davis, who, acting on instructions from the State Department at Washington, issued a statement at Geneva on 16th October to the effect that the United States delegation had crossed the Atlantic solely for the cause of disarmament. " We are not, however, interested in the political elements of the purely European aspects of the question. We emphasize once again

[1] There is every indication that Herr Hitler had fully anticipated such action on the part of France and her Allies, and had taken it into consideration before deciding on Germany's withdrawal. There was no more frightened man in Germany than the Chancellor for the few days succeeding 14th October, for he expected that every hour would bring him news of a French occupation of the Ruhr, of Czech troops in the brown coal country and of a Polish invasion of East Prussia. The realization that he was to " get away " with the German withdrawal without fear of sanctions materially affected Herr Hitler's future policy.

that we are in no wise politically allied to any European Power. Any unity of purpose that has existed is purely in the domain of world disarmament. As to the question of knowing whether there are favourable conditions for continuing the present efforts towards disarmament, that is a matter to be decided by Europe and not the United States."

Mr. Davis concluded by saying that the United States delegation did not wish to take an active part in the consultations which there would now be between the capitals of Europe, as they could only be of a political character, and having thus, in the manner of Pontius Pilate, publicly washed his hands, he departed with his delegation for Washington.

In England the immediate reaction to the events of 14th October was one of anxiety as to whether they would entail war, and, if so, whether England could keep out of it. Popularly there was a sense of keen resentment against Germany for having precipitated the crisis, and a widespread feeling that, had the Germans been genuinely anxious to bring about general disarmament and not general rearmament, they would not have bolted the Conference ; a feeling that was in no way diminished by Baron von Neurath's allegations against Sir John Simon. Certain extremist factions publicly advocated the use of sanctions against Germany, ranging from economic boycott to thoroughpaced intervention and preventive war. To meet this blast of anger, Mr. Vernon Bartlett made his now historic broadcast of 21st October, in which he put with admirable clearness the force of the German claim for equality.

From then on, rival schools of influence battled in England for the soul and attention of the thinking public. Mr Rennie Smith, a pacifist turned warrior, organized the " Friends of Europe ", and warned England and the Continent of the ever-increasing danger of German rearmament, calling for action to prevent it. Mr. Vernon Bartlett, a warrior turned pacifist, both in his book *Nazi Germany Explained*, and in the columns of a daily paper, drew attention to the virtues of the Nazi regime, to the unjust treatment of Germany in the Peace Treaty, and urged patience and a new deal. Mr. Wickham Steed, ever a warrior before the Lord, demonstrated, in a series of lectures at King's College, London,[1] the challenge which Nazi ideology constituted to the ideas and institutions which form the basis of Western liberal civilization.

[1] Subsequently published in book form as *Hitler, Where and Whither ?* (Nisbet, 1934).

In contrast to these conflicting theses, the British Government maintained its attitude of masterly inactivity, and, despite a certain amount of parliamentary discussion and some political addresses in the country, gave no public indication of where it stood in regard to the situation. It would seem that Great Britain, exhausted in childbirth, had only had strength sufficient to nurse its Draft Convention through its first reading and to help to wrap it in its winding-sheet. Now, if ever, was surely the moment for a definite statement of policy by the British Government in defence of the collective European system of consultation against which Germany had transgressed. Such a statement, including a clear assertion that no violation of Austrian independence would be tolerated, would have done more to ease and clarify the situation than any number of diplomatic exchanges in ambiguous formulas.

For all Europe at that moment—in October, November, and early December—was looking to England for a lead. Dr. Dollfuss in Vienna, General Gömbös in Budapest, and Dr. Beneš in Prague all wondered, each for a different reason, whether Great Britain was for him or against him, and in Paris, Rome, and Berlin it was the same. Any British political observer in Central Europe at that time had the galling experience of hearing his country's lack of policy abused in every Chancellery in no uncertain terms, without having any defence ; and American observers coming to London declared that they could discover no British policy, but that every Englishman they met told them what he thought ought to be done. But the opportunity for action was allowed to pass unheeded.

Such then were the results of Germany's diplomatic *coup* of 14th October. By reason of French unwillingness to act single-handed, of Italian reserve, of American lack of interest, and of British inactivity, Germany had been able to take the first trick of the rubber and to call the Allied bluff thus far. Fortified by his electoral victory of 12th November, Herr Hitler proceeded to play his cards in the new game with a certain unexpected dexterity.

7

The keynote of the German elections of November had been *Frieden und Gleichberechtigen*, and it was in this same order that the Chancellor pursued his new policy ; first must Germany's desire for peace be established and then the demand made for Germany's equality of status. In accordance with this

programme the German Government prepared and launched a
" Peace Offensive " reminiscent of similar activities in the latter
years of the Great War.

The first step was taken on 15th November, three days after
the elections, when the Chancellor summoned the Polish
Ambassador to a conference, at the end of which it was announced
that full agreement had been established and that both countries
would take up direct negotiations on all German-Polish problems
" in order to consolidate peace in Europe. They renounce the
use of force in adjusting their mutual relations ". Nothing could
be more gratifying and, flushed with success, Herr Hitler next
approached Czechoslovakia with a similar proposal for a joint
declaration denouncing the use of force. But whether the
Czech diplomacy was more wary than the Polish, or whether it
was that Czechoslovakia had less to gain than Poland by a
reaffirmation of Germany's Eastern Locarno obligations, the
German proposals, though renewed on three separate occasions,
met with no success in Prague, where the indefatigable Dr. Beneš
continued to keep watch and ward over the heritage of the
Little Entente.

Somewhat abashed, Herr Hitler turned his attentions to
France. Franco-German relations were anything but friendly,
and the fact that in the course of one Sunday afternoon's drive
the French Ambassador's car had been stopped and searched by
Nazi patrols five times had done little to improve them. An
attempt, however, must be made to demonstrate the peaceful
intentions of Germany towards her, and to this end the Chancellor
received the Comte de Brinon, of the *Matin*, on 16th November,
and gave him an interview, in which he surveyed the points at
issue between France and Germany, asserting that he was only
pursuing the policy of Stresemann and Brüning, and that
Germany had abandoned all claims to Alsace-Lorraine. His
predecesssors had not had the whole German people behind them
as he had, for now the whole nation had approved his policy and
knew what he wanted. " I am deeply convinced that once the
question of the Saar is settled there will be nothing, absolutely
nothing, to divide France and Germany."

There was no dispute in Europe sufficiently important to
justify a war. A bad treaty was responsible for the
difference between Poland and Germany, but this dispute
was not worth a war. He was not quite mad—"a war would not
settle anything ; it would only make matters worse—it would
mark the end of our races, which are the *élite* of humanity, and

in time Asia and Bolshevism would rule Europe. . . . I have
a great deal of work to do at home. I have restored the German's
sense of honour; I want to restore his joy of life . . . I shall need
years to restore Germany's prosperity. Do you really think I
want to upset my work with a new war ? "

Herr Hitler summed up his attitude in the words " Not a
single German for a new war ; every German for the defence of
the Fatherland ". If France wished to make of Germany's
helplessness the keystone of her security, no agreement could be
reached between them, " but if France is prepared to look for
security in a free agreement with Germany, I am willing to
listen, to understand, and to act. The equality demanded by
Germany is absolute moral equality. As for practical equality,
it can be achieved by stages, and we are prepared to discuss the
details."

In conclusion, he said that in leaving Geneva he had done the
right thing, for in doing so he had helped to clear up the situation.
" We shall not return to Geneva," he said. " The League of
Nations is an international Parliament in which the conflicting
groups of Powers can only quarrel. The differences, instead of
being settled, only grow worse. But I shall be only too glad to
enter into negotiations with anyone who wants to talk to me."

In England the method was more indirect, and the Ministry of
Propaganda made great use of those Englishmen who had been
carried away with the more emotional and sentimental aspects of
the Nazi regime and were prepared to undertake " conversation
work " in their own country. In addition, the frequent visits to
London of Herr Hanfstängel, Herr Hitler's romantic *alter ego*,
won many converts in Mayfair. Many Englishmen who had at
first been convinced that the " new presbyter was but old priest
writ large ", and that the Nazi regime in Germany was but a
recrudescence of pre-War Prussianism, began now, under the
force of the German " peace offensive ", to waver in their opinion
and to wonder whether, after all, there was not something fine
and genuine and hardy about the Nazi movement, which only
wished to be let alone to purge Germany from the decadence of
the post-War years. It is said that the chairman of a well-known
peace organization was only with difficulty dissuaded from
sending a congratulatory telegram to the Chancellor on the spirit
of his peace policy.

It will at once be seen that it was profoundly difficult to
counter the German " peace offensive ". If Germany's neighbours
rejected her advances they laid themselves open to the charge

of deliberately *sabotaging* the peace of Europe by refusing to enter into *bona fide* negotiations for a settlement. If, on the other hand, they accepted the German proposals, they placed themselves in a position of disadvantage in the event of Germany's bad faith, which they more than suspected. Never was it truer that Europe feared—in this case—the Germans even when they brought gifts, but on the whole it was felt better at least to discuss the gifts even though it meant looking them in the mouth rather more than was generally considered courteous.

By the close of November, Herr Hitler considered the ground sufficiently well prepared to proceed with the second item of his programme, that of equality, and he, therefore, in the course of conversations with the British and American Ambassadors, put forward the views of his Government regarding the conditions on which disarmament negotiations might be resumed. The French Ambassador also had two long interviews with the Chancellor and, in course of time, the German proposals were crystallized into the form of an *aide-mémoire* which reached Paris on 18th December.

These new German proposals were more far-reaching than anything which had been put forward in the previous negotiations for equality in armaments, and definitely envisaged a very marked degree of rearmament. Germany offered a ten-year non aggression pact with France, Poland, and her other neighbours. In return, however, the provisions of the Treaty of Versailles prohibiting Germany from maintaining troops in or fortifying the demilitarized Rhineland zone must be abrogated, and Germany must be entitled to fortify her Eastern and Western frontiers. The *Reichswehr* of 100,000 men, enlisted for twelve years, would be reorganized into a conscript army of 300,000 men engaged for one year, and permitted all categories of weapons (field artillery up to 6-inch guns, light tanks, scouting planes), forbidden under the Treaty but defined as " defensive " by the Disarmament Conference. It was hinted that German rearmament might be restricted to a certain proportion of the total " defensive " weapons now possessed by France, Poland, and Czechoslovakia. The destruction by an early date, to be determined, of all the " offensive " weapons of the Powers, and the abolition of air-bombing and chemical and bacteriological warfare was demanded, but civil aviation must be free from supervision and restriction. Automatic and full control of armaments was agreed to, but on condition that it was applied to Germany only after she had attained equality with other Powers, and it was further stipulated that the S.A., S.S., and *Stahlhelm* were to be regarded as non-military organizations and outside the scope of a Disarmament Convention.   Finally, it was requested that the Saar Basin Territory should be returned to Germany immediately, without waiting for the plebiscite in 1935, and that the ownership of the coal mines should be the subject of further negotiations.[1]

The French Ambassador who, during his two conversations with the Chancellor, had amassed a wealth of explanatory and complementary information, brought the *aide-mémoire* to Paris in person in order that he might take part in the discussions regarding it which took place at the Quai d'Orsay.

It was clear at the outset that the German demands constituted a great degree of rearmament and that any real hope of disarmament for the rest of Europe was out of the question.   A German conscript army of 300,000 men a year, taken in conjunction with the fact that the present 100,000 men of the *Reichswehr* were experts who could immediately become highly efficient commissioned and non-commissioned officers, produced for France a prospect of a very terrifying nature.   One thing was absolutely necessary if an even approximately conciliatory reply was to be returned by France, and that was the answer to the questions—What does Great Britain mean by Article 16 of the Covenant ?   Will she carry out her obligations under the Locarno Agreement and the Pact of Paris ?   And, above all, What is her attitude towards the Treaty of Versailles ?

The British Government, torn between the Prime Minister's emotional sympathy for Germany and the Foreign Secretary's departmental orientation towards France, succeeded in evading the return of a direct answer to any of these questions, but was nevertheless unsuccessful in its attempts to induce the French to temper the asperity of their reply, which was handed to the Chancellor on New Year's Day (1934).

In the French view a new and limited pact of non-aggression was regarded as less binding than Germany's obligations under the Locarno Agreement and the Pact of Paris, and the Note was

[1] The Saar Basin territory was placed by the Treaty of Versailles under control of the League of Nations, which administered it by means of a Governing Commission.   This form of Government was to continue for fifteen years after the coming into force of the Treaty (i.e. 10th January, 1935), at which time a plebiscite would determine whether the territory would go to France or to Germany or remain under the League.   The mines were handed over to France, in full and absolute possession, in compensation for the damage done to the French pits of Lens and Valenciennes by the German Army.

equally definite in its refusal to countenance any revision of the
Peace Treaty except as provided for under the British Draft
Convention. The *Reichswehr* must be transformed into a short-
term militia of 200,000 men, as proposed in the British Draft. A
hint was given, however, that France might agree to a gradual
increase to 300,000 men, on condition that the para-military
organizations were disbanded. If this were not done, however,
they were to be considered as trained reserves and subject to
international supervision and control. The transformed *Reichswehr* might have only the weapons strictly necessary to its training
as a defence force ; that is to say, it might have rifles, machine
guns, and light artillery, but not military airplanes or tanks.
The Powers now armed would reduce their effectives by stages
to the number prescribed in the British Draft Convention, but
the " probationary " period of the proposals of 14th October was
tenaciously retained unmodified. France agreed to abolish
chemical and bacteriological warfare, and offered to " lay-up "
50 per cent of her heavy bombers. She insisted, however, that
there must be international supervision of civil aviation and
immediate international control of the armies and armaments of
all Powers, and that para-military organizations, such as the
S.A., S.S., and *Stahlhelm*, should be included in such a scrutiny.
The future of the Saar, it was submitted, was a matter not for
France or Germany but for the League of Nations, and, finally,
France refused to discuss further with Germany alone any
question involving her rearmament or the abrogation of the
Treaty of Versailles, for such discussions affected all parties to
the Disarmament Conference and the League of Nations.

A period of three weeks elapsed before the German counter-
reply was received in Paris, a period during which Sir John
Simon visited Rome, and on his return claimed to have convinced
the Duce that the question of disarmament must be settled before
the world embarked upon his pet scheme of reforming the League
in such a way that Japan and Germany could return, and the
United States and the Soviet Union could come within its
compass and remain undefiled.

When, however, the counter-reply was received at the Quai
d'Orsay on 21st January, it was found that Germany had abated
none of her claims and that the position remained substantially
unchanged. The main differences between the two countries
was the size of the transformed *Reichswehr* ; the German right
to possess immediately all defensive arms sufficient for the
augmented army, which was completely inacceptable to France ;

and the " probationary " period, which was summarily rejected by Germany.   On these points both parties remained adamant.

There were, however, certain new elements introduced by Germany, which gave the Note an appearance either of delaying, or wrecking, tactics.   For the first time the question of naval rearmament was raised, though not in detail.   The German Government then restated their belief that the ideal solution of the armaments problem would be the reduction of all national forces to the level imposed upon Germany by Part V of the Treaty of Versailles, and, in defence of their claim for rearmament, repeated that this claim was only based on the patent disinclination of the other European Powers to disarm, which had destroyed all prospect of a general and drastic reduction of armaments.

In addition, the German Government, in their defence of the claim to maintain the S.A. and S.S. as well as the 300,000 men of the reorganized *Reichswehr*, referred to the question of French Colonial troops ; for the rapid transport of which from Africa to Europe in case of war, a complete and detailed organization was, it was alleged, already in existence.

It was agreed in Paris that these new aspects of the problem had merely been interjected at this moment by Germany in an effort to gain time and save the negotiations from complete collapse, for it was clear that after a month of diplomatic exchanges the French and German points of view were as widely separated as ever.

By the end of January, 1934, a complete deadlock had been reached in the disarmament negotiations, and the air seemed heavy with the portents of crisis.   As on a similar occasion in the previous May, the German Chancellor announced his intention of making from the tribune of the Reichstag a statement of policy to Germany and the world.   The date chosen for this pronouncement was 30th January, the day on which Germany celebrated the first anniversary of the Nazi Revolution and the inauguration of the *Dritte Reich*.   But, before this speech was made, there had occurred a number of events which materially affected the general situation.

First amongst these, both in chronological order and in order of importance, was the declaration signed on 26th January between Poland and Germany, constituting a new era in their political relations, and affording the first example of the new diplomatic bi-lateral procedure which Germany intended to substitute for the multi-lateral and more complicated methods of Geneva.

The German-Polish declaration of 26th January was the actual corollary to its predecessor of November.[1] It did, however, mark a far greater departure than the first from the system of political alignment then obtaining. Ignoring all reference to the Covenant of the League or the Locarno Treaties, the Declaration was based upon the Pact of Paris, its general object being to " define more precisely the application of these principles in so far as the relations between Poland and Germany are concerned."

Both Governments declared that it was their intention to reach direct understanding on problems concerning their mutual relations, but that, in the event of disputes arising between them on questions which could not be settled by direct negotiations, they would in no case have recourse to force, but would seek to find a peaceful solution either by the means provided by already existing Treaty obligations or, failing this, by any other means which might present themselves. The Declaration was to remain valid for ten years.

Europe was startled by this new manifestation, and at once sought to find an explanation for this seemingly inexplicable *rapprochement*. The reason, however, was not far to seek. Herr Hitler had taken thought as to how best he could meet the powerful diplomatic and military Franco-Polish combination opposed to him, and on due consideration had decided that Poland was the weaker vessel of the two. Fortune had favoured him. Poland had never really been reassured on the matter of the Four-Power Pact, and deeply resented even this very circumscribed excursion of France into the field of Treaty Revision. Moreover, Franco-Polish friendship had been cooling for some considerable time. France had begun to regard her Eastern European *protégé* as rather more a liability than an asset, and Poland, for her part, had gradually become convinced that a *rapprochement* with Germany was better policy than a precarious hostility, maintained with the uncertain support of French bayonets. The failure of the French Government in the matter of the Gdynia Loan had added further fuel to the already smouldering fires. And thus, when presented with an opportunity of securing a temporary respite on his western front similar to that which had already been achieved by the *rapprochement* with the Soviet Union.[2] Marshal Pilsudski made haste to take advantage of it.

For Herr Hitler, however, the *volte-face* was even more complete. One of the salient points of his programme had been

---

[1] See above, p. 192.
[2] Ibid. p. 155.

the restoration to Germany of the Corridor, and one of the fears which had been entertained by many people during the early days of the Nazi Revolution had been that over-zealous bands of German patriots might be impelled to make something in the nature of a Jamieson raid into the Corridor, which might precipitate a European crisis of the first magnitude.

Now, however, Herr Hitler had deliberately delayed any hope of Treaty Revision in this quarter for a period of ten years, and by so doing had driven a most formidable wedge between the two partners in the former Franco-Polish alliance.   For, although the Declaration averred that it did not infringe nor contradict any of the international obligations which the contracting parties might have entered into with third parties, the effect upon Franco-Polish relations was fully apparent nevertheless.

There has been no more striking example of the power which Herr Hitler exercises in Germany than this new Pact with Poland. No previous Chancellor, neither Stresemann nor Brüning, could have negotiated this Agreement and survived an hour, and though it must have been a bitter pill for many of his followers to swallow, they swallowed it and smiled, albeit perhaps a trifle wryly.

In addition to this success in the field of foreign affairs, Herr Hitler during the same week-end achieved two signal triumphs in internal politics.   On the same day (27th January) he destroyed the two remaining remnants of opposition within the Reich, for on this date not only were the Monarchist societies dissolved and prohibited, but the opposition of the Protestant clergy to the *Gleichschaltung* of the Lutheran Church was ruthlessly attacked, and its leader, Pastor Niemöller, a former U-Boat Commander who had refused to surrender his craft after the Armistice of 1918, was placed under temporary arrest.

It was, therefore, with no mean record of achievement that Herr Hitler faced the Reichstag on 30th January, and the renewed applause which greeted every item of his speech, save one, bore witness to the enthusiastic loyalty of his hearers.[1]   Having announced the long-awaited reorganization of the Reich on tribal lines, and made reference to the achievement of the Nazi Government in its economic efforts and of its unification of the Protestant Church, the Chancellor turned to the field of foreign politics and indulged in an attack upon familiar lines on the Treaty of Versailles.   He repudiated all German guilt for the war, and

[1] The exception was the reference to the Agreement with Poland, which was received in silence.

invoked the Polish Pact as a pledge of his Government's desire
for peace, passing then to an impassioned and eloquent plea for
an understanding with France. " France fears for her security,"
he declared, " no one in Germany wants to threaten it, and we
are ready to do everything to prove that. Germany demands
her equality of rights. No one in the world has the right to
refuse that to a great nation, and no one will be strong enough
to obstruct her indefinitely."

He then explained the considerations which had led him to
propose that France and Germany should settle between them the
question of the Saar at once, for it was the only territorial problem
still outstanding between them, and, once it was settled, Germany
was ready to accept not only the letter but also the spirit of the
Locarno Treaty. If a solution equally satisfactory to both sides
could be obtained, if the hatchet could only be buried between
them, then France would see that Germany's demand for equality
of rights was the obvious right of an independent people. The
Chancellor then referred to the new British Disarmament
proposals, which had been presented to him on the previous day,
and thanked Great Britain for the effort she was making to pave
the way to an understanding.

In conclusion, he declared :—

> " I can only once again repeat to the world at this moment that
> no threat and no force will ever move the German nation to give
> up those rights which cannot be denied to a sovereign nation.
> I can, however, also give the assurance that this sovereign nation
> has no other wish than to apply joyfully the strength and weight
> of her political, moral, and economic resources, not only for the
> healing of wounds which the past has inflicted on the human kind,
> but also towards the co-operation of all cultured and civilized
> nations."

8

The British Disarmament proposals which were handed to the
German Government on 29th January, and were made public
two days later, had their origin in a conversation between the
British Ambassador in Berlin and the Foreign Minister at the end
of November, in the course of which the German proposals were
intimated.[1] As a result of the report of the Ambassador, the
British Government addressed a Note to Berlin on 20th December,
to which a reply was received on 22nd January, and it was in
response to this that the British proposals were made.

They had, therefore, been some considerable time maturing,
and were undoubtedly the subject of discussions between Sir

[1] See above, p. 194.

John Simon and Signor Mussolini at their Conference in Rome during the first days of the New Year.[1] In the course of these conversations, the Duce put forward the Italian proposals for disarmament which were subsequently addressed in the form of a Memorandum to the Powers attending the Disarmament Conference and their text made public simultaneously with that of the British proposals.

Signor Mussolini's views were based upon the fundamental belief that any appreciable degree of disarmament was for the moment impossible of attainment and, further, that a protracted search for an illusive formula at the present moment might be more dangerous to the cause of disarmament than not. At the same time he was anxious to go as far as possible to meet the German claim for equality, and believed that the " final counterpart to the acceptance of the German demands " should be an undertaking by Germany to return to Geneva not only to sign the Disarmament Convention but also to resume her place in the League of Nations.

With this general end in view, therefore, the Italian Memorandum contained the following seven proposals :—

(1) Any Convention now realizable should remain in force until the end of 1940.

(2) Chemical warfare should be abolished, and there should be proper methods of control.

(3) The bombardment of civilian populations should be prohibited.

(4) The military expenditure of the Powers not bound by the Peace Treaties should be limited at the present level, subject to expenditure on replacements and the completion of defensive works.

(5) The land armaments of these Powers should be similarly limited at the present level.

(6) The German claim to a remodelled force of 300,000 men should be accepted. The German readiness to reconsider this figure if the other Powers were prepared to reduce their armaments was recalled.

(7) Discussion of naval armaments should be adjourned until the next Naval Conference (in 1935).

It was argued that, though the proposals outlined above would demand of France certain concessions, she would, nevertheless, be compensated for the granting of these by the fact of retaining the whole of her present state of armament, and this should suffice to guarantee her security for the duration of the proposed Convention. Italy's loyalty to the provisions of the Pact of Locarno were emphatically reaffirmed, and attention was drawn

[1] See above, p. 196.

to the further elements of security which were contained in the
Pact of Rome, a meeting of the signatories of which, it was
suggested, would be justified, and to which the representatives of
the other principal Powers concerned might be invited.

With this Memorandum in his pocket, and with the satisfaction
of knowing that Signor Mussolini and he were in agreement that
the question of the reform of the League should be postponed
until after the settlement of the disarmament problem, Sir John
Simon returned to London, where already the Foreign Office
experts were at work preparing the preliminary draft of the
statement of the attitude of the British Government, for it was
at last felt that the time had come when Great Britain should
make a final effort to effect a compromise, upon the basis of
which a Disarmament Convention of some sort might be
negotiated.

On January 28th, therefore, a Memorandum was addressed by
the British Government to all other States taking part in the
Disarmament Conference, and was handed to the German
Chancellor in time for its consideration before his speech to the
Reichstag on 30th January. The proposals contained therein
were of such a nature as to justify Herr Hitler in thanking Great
Britain for the effort she was making to pave the way to an
understanding.

The British Memorandum was at the same time more drastic
and more precise than the Italian proposals, though it was
evident that it had derived certain principles from them. His
Majesty's Government prefaced their views with the general
statement that arms of a kind permitted in one State could not
be indefinitely denied to another, and that, further, the alternative to a Disarmament Agreement was an armaments race, " the
end of which no man can see." The choice that lay before
Europe, therefore, was two-fold :—

> (1) " To reach agreement in a Convention which will involve
> the abandonment of certain classes of weapons by the most
> heavily-armed Powers, or
> (2) " To reach agreement on the basis that the most heavily-
> armed Powers, while unable or unwilling to disarm, will at any
> rate undertake not to increase their present armaments."

It was this latter course that had been indicated in the Italian
proposals as the most to be hoped for, but the British Government earnestly pressed on other Governments that the first
course, " which they most strongly prefer and regard as more in

accord with the main object to be attained, should not be abandoned but should be actively pursued." It was further emphasized that the British Government had never departed from the principles and purposes of the British Draft Convention of March, 1933, nor had sought to substitute a second and contradictory draft for it. " If there were any misapprehension in any quarter on this score the Declaration they are now making will finally remove it."

The proposals put forward fell under the three heads of Security, Equality of Rights, and Disarmament, and under the first of these it was proposed to add to the first four Articles of the British Draft Convention [1] a further three, the first of which would declare that the loyal execution of the Convention was a matter of common interest to all signatories ; the second would provide for immediate consultation if the Permanent Disarmament Commission reported a failure by one of the parties loyally to execute the Convention ; and the third would define the object of such consultation, which was to exchange views as to the steps to be taken to restore the situation and to maintain the Convention in operation.

The insertion of these new Articles would, it was submitted, emphasize the inescapable duty of all signatories to the Convention to keep in the closest touch with one another, and to do whatever was right and possible to prevent or remedy any violation of so important an international treaty, and, taken in conjunction with the existing treaty obligations incurred by the signatories of the Covenant of the League, the Pact of Paris, and the Treaty of Locarno, together with the willingness expressed by the German Government to conclude pacts of non-aggression with all Germany's neighbours, would present a sum total of security worthy of general acceptance.

The principle of the Five-Power Declaration of 11th December, 1932, was reiterated and re-emphasized, and the practical application of the principle of equality of rights was declared to be no less essential in a disarmament agreement than that of the principle of security. It was urged that the disarmament proposals which followed were conceived in that spirit and constituted a practical fulfilment of that principle.

On the assumption that the Disarmament Convention when concluded should remain in force for ten years—and not for five, as originally proposed in the British Draft of 1933—the British Government suggested that, though the figure of effectives

[1] See above, p. 108.

proposed in the Draft Convention was 200,000 on the basis of eight months' service, and that suggested by Germany was 300,000 on a basis of twelve months' service, the difference, " though difficult and serious," did not present an insuperable obstacle to an agreed compromise. It was not so much the figure as the principle of parity, fairly calculated and applied, which was the essential and unalterable element in fixing the effectives between France, Germany, Italy, and Poland, and, if the figure of 200,000 was found to be too low, accommodation could surely be found between this and that of 300,000, though the British Government frankly preferred the first. It was also prepared to acquiesce in the longer period of service if such was the general desire, but the process of standardization at the agreed figure should be completed in four years.

With regard to the " para-military training ", that is to say, the military training outside the army of men of military age, the British Government welcomed the promise of the German Chancellor to supply proof, through the medium of control, that the S.A., the S.S., and the Labour Corps were not of a military character, but suggested that any training outside the Army should be prohibited, and that this prohibition should be checked by a system of permanent automatic supervision " in which the supervising organization should be guided less by a strict definition of the term ' military training ' than by the military knowledge and experience of its experts ".

In the matter of land war material, attention was drawn to the fact that under the British Draft Convention restrictions on Germany in the matter of anti-aircraft guns would disappear, and it was now suggested that the maximum calibre of guns in permanent frontier and fortress defensive systems should be fixed by international agreement   All tanks over 30 tons should be destroyed by the end of the first year after the coming into force of the Convention, those over 20 tons by the end of the third year, and those over 16 tons by the end of the fifth year. A further international examination should be completed by the end of the third year by the Permanent Disarmament Commission, and it was agreed that the new German short-term service Army should be equipped with tanks up to 6 tons, as proposed by Germany.

Though the British Government would have preferred to adhere to the maximum limit of 115 mm. as provided for in the British Draft Convention, they were prepared to concur in the German proposal that the newly constituted *Reichswehr* should be equipped with 155 mm. guns, in which case all those over 350 mm. belonging to the armed Powers should be destroyed by the end of the first year, those over 220 mm. by the end of the fourth year, and those over 155 mm. by the end of the seventh year.

It was in the proposals for aerial armaments that there remained the last vestige of the probationary period theory which had been so great and fatal a factor in the proposals of 16th October. Now it was proposed that, if the Permanent Disarmament Commission could not decide on abolition at the end of two years, all countries should be entitled to possess military aircraft. Countries would reduce or increase by stages, as the case might be, in the following eight years, so as to attain eventually figures to be agreed upon. Germany would, therefore, acquire parity with the principal air Powers by these stages, but in any case the present restrictions imposed by the Treaty of Versailles would remain in force for two years.

The British Government were not prepared to make any further alterations to the naval chapter of the Draft Convention, but would make proposals for a simpler arrangement if it were thought that by this means the situation prior to the assembling of the Naval Conference of 1935 could be more appropriately dealt with. And, finally, they were prepared, if agreement were reached on all other issues, to agree to the application of a system of permanent automatic supervision to come into force with the obligations of the Convention.

In conclusion, the British Government stated that its proposals must be considered as a whole, and that they were framed in the endeavour to meet in a fair manner the essential claims of all sides. They were not the terms of agreement which could be most desired without regard to the claims or needs of others, but were propounded as a basis of compromise on which a general agreement could and should be reached. The return of Germany to Geneva and to the League of Nations ought to be an essential condition of such an agreement.

It will be seen at once that the British proposals went very much further towards meeting the German case than the French. With the exception of the aviation clauses and the provisions regarding the " para-military " organizations, the German claims of 19th December had been virtually granted, whereas the only concession to France was the proposal for a General Pact of Consultation in the event of a breach of the Disarmament Convention. Though this went further than the accepted British policy of undertaking no other commitments than those concluded in the Covenant and the Treaty of Locarno, these new proposals fell very far short of French desires.

It was natural that, from their very nature of compromise, the British proposals should come under a hot fire of criticism both in Great Britain and abroad, and perhaps the most common ground for censure was the fact that they represented so complete an abandonment of the position which His Majesty's Government had held but three months before.   In October, Great Britain, in company with Italy and the United States, had appeared as a whole-hearted supporter of the new French disarmament thesis, and Sir John Simon had been the spokesman of the Powers at Geneva ; now the British Government had to all appearances embraced with equal warmth the German thesis, and had destroyed the united front which French diplomacy had been at such pains to build up against the menace of a rearming Germany.

There were not wanting those who imputed more Machiavellian designs to His Majesty's Government, in that, having offended the Capulets in October, they had now estranged the Montacutes in February in order to be able to say " a plague on both your houses ".   As a result of this policy these critics feared that in the day of battle Great Britain would be numbered amongst those " cross-bench or Mugwump angels " who were neither on the side of Jehovah nor yet on that of Satan.[1]

A more technical criticism was that, whereas the Italian Memorandum had included budgetary limitation, the British proposal made no mention of it, but to this Mr. Eden, speaking in the House of Commons on 6th February, replied that it had not been included because there had been no general agreement on it.   There had, however, been agreement on publicity, and this might be the first step ; the *principle* of budgetary limitation had never been rejected, but at present the technical difficulties in its way were too great.

In Europe the reception of the British proposals was not enthusiastic.   In Paris, though the general public were too much concerned with the sudden disclosures of the Stavisky scandal, which had swept M. Chautemps from office and was to cause so soon the tragedy of 6th February, the Press proclaimed the impossibility of their acceptance by France.   It was argued that,

---

[1] An interesting by-product of the British proposals was the great interest displayed in them throughout Great Britain, where they became the topic of heated criticisms and defence alike on public platforms and around dinner tables.   At one of the latter, when it was advanced in support of the proposals that Great Britain now had clean hands, at once the rejoinder came that " so had Pontius Pilate."

apart from any other consideration, there was no assurance given
that the British Government would abandon its opposition to the
necessary condition of effective control, such as the licensing of
armaments factories, and that no sanctions for a violation of the
Disarmament Convention were proposed.   In the *Echo de Paris*,
" Pertinax " declared " Sir John Simon has presented the French
with a magnificent stuffed crocodile purchased cheap in the
Caledonian Market ".

In Germany the British Plan received, as was natural, a slightly
more warm reception than in France, but it was greeted only as a
basis of discussion, and not as a proposal which must be accepted
or rejected as a whole.   For this reason all discussion of Germany's
return to the League was omitted, and it was felt by many that
any slight hope that might have been entertained of Germany's
possible return was doomed when it became known that the very
Powers who asked her to do so, at the same time gave their
consent to the Austrian appeal to the Council against alleged
German aggression.   In any case, it was considered impossible
for Germany to accept either the probationary period as regards
aviation or the provisions concerning the S.S., S.A., and *Stahlhelm*.

All doubt as to the first of these vanished when on 19th
February the Reichsminister for Air, General Göring, gave to
the Correspondent of the *Daily Mail* an outline in unequivocal
terms of his views of the numbers of war-planes required by
Germany for her adequate defence.

" Germany," said he, " must have a defensive air fleet, unless
the other Great Powers are prepared to give up their bombing
machines, which I do not believe they will.   We have common
frontiers with France, Belgium, Czechoslovakia, and Poland, and
I must have between 30 and 40 per cent of the total aeroplane
strength of those four countries.   That is the most modest
defensive air force that will ensure the national safety of
Germany." [1]

In defence of the British proposals it must be said that they
represented for the first time a realization of fact which was most
salutary, if unpalatable.   Germany's rearmament had been in
process for the past 18 months, or at least a year, and as a result
Europe was faced with two alternative policies, either to prevent
such rearmament by means of force, that is to say, to take up

[1] The latest published figures give the air force strengths of France
as 2,375 machines, Poland 700, Czechoslovakia 546, and Belgium 195 ;
a total of 3,816 machines.   According to General Göring's statement,
the minimum German air force would consist of between 1,150 and
1,525 planes.

arms in defence of the military clauses of the Treaty of Versailles ; or, alternatively, to recognize German rearmament as an inevitable fact and to legalize and, if possible, control it.

The Disarmament Conference had wavered between these two decisions, and had finally compromised in bluff on 14th October, which same bluff Germany had called by abandoning the Conference. By its Memorandum of 28th January the British Government had faced the problem squarely, had recognized that no one, least of all itself, was prepared to go to war or even to impose economic sanctions in support of the Peace Treaty, and had, therefore, made a determined and honest effort to accept as much as possible' of the German rearmament programme, to legalize it, to secure certain concessions from Germany, and, finally, to offer an additional, though very slightly additional, guarantee to France.

In this aspect the British proposals were welcomed as an awakening from the fool's paradise into which the Disarmament Conference had almost succeeded in lulling Europe. On the other hand, however, it must be admitted that the British concessions to Germany constituted, together with the Japanese and German withdrawals from the League, a tremendous blow to that structure and to the whole theory of a collective system of security. Within a year the world had been provided with two examples of the fact that, when a State was sufficiently determined to flout the combined public opinion of the world, it could do so with impunity. That great weapon of public opinion in which the pacifists had put their trust had proved but a stage sword, incapable of combating the sharper weapon of determined Nationalism as exemplified by Japan and Germany.

It will be remembered that on 21st January the German Government had addressed a further *aide-mémoire* to France in continuation of the correspondence which had been initiated on 16th December.[1] In it they had reiterated their previous demands for a transformed *Reichswehr* of 300,000 men, and their claim to possess immediately all defensive weapons for such an augmented army ; at the same time they finally and summarily rejected the French proposals of a " probationary " period, inquiring caustically whether " the other Powers can find any justification for a plan which it is so hard to reconcile with the honour and security of the German people ? " An annexed Memorandum, however, submitted to the French Government

[1] See above, p. 196.

thirteen questions intended to elicit information which would elucidate the whole disarmament situation.[1]

The French Government did not reply until 13th February, partly because the points raised in the German *aide-mémoire* necessitated considerable study and consideration, and partly because, in the swift and tragic passage of events in Paris during the first days of February, the reorganization of the French Government under M. Doumergue rendered the further postponement of the reply necessary. With the replacing at the Quai d'Orsay of M. Paul-Boncour by M. Louis Barthou, a veteran Premier and Minister for Foreign Affairs, a new and sterner tone crept into the correspondence. M. Barthou was a man of an older school, and few are likely to forget the masterly way in which he carried out his mission of wrecking at the Genoa Conference of 1922.

In their Reply of 13th February[2] the French Government stated that, in accordance with the resolutions of the Disarmament Conference, they had put forward a programme providing by stages, and with corresponding guarantees of control and security,

[1] These questions were :—

(1) What will be the total strength of the French home and overseas effectives ?

(2) To what extent are the overseas effectives and the trained effectives to be included in the calculation proposed by France ?

(3) In the event of Germany transforming her army into a short-term service militia, is France prepared to guarantee neither to station nor use overseas troops in France ?

(4) What will become of transportable artillery guns exceeding 6 inches calibre ? Will they be destroyed or will they be further available for training purposes ?

(5) What is the highest tonnage proposed for tanks, and what will be done with tanks exceeding that tonnage ?

(6) Does the French Government suggest for all countries a limitation of specific types of arms, including the reserve material, and what types are meant ?

(7) With what material will those French troops be equipped which are not included in the standardization of the Army ?

(8) In what period would the reduction of military planes in service by 50 per cent be carried out ? Will the surplus be destroyed or what will be done with them ?

(9) What is the nature of the control proposed for civil aviation and the manufacture of planes ?

(10) Will the general abolition of military aircraft be concluded within a definite period, and, if so, what will be the length of that period ?

(11) Will the prohibition of bombing be of a general and absolute character, or will there be certain agreed limitations ?

(12) Is it to be understood that France is only willing to submit to a control of the manufacture and import of arms, or will the control be extended to stocks in use and in store ?

(13) What is the French attitude regarding naval armaments ?

[2] This Reply was published on 15th February.

for substantial reduction of armaments as well in the matter of
effectives as in that of land and air material. The German Government, however, had thought fit to reiterate that " the principal
interested Powers which are in possession of powerful armaments
are not inclined for any really effective measure of disarmament ".
The French Government, therefore, left to Germany " the full
responsibility for a conclusion to which they for their part cannot
subscribe, if only because it is directly contradicted by their own
proposals ".

The Reply continued that the French Government could not
accept the German point of view in any important respect, and
insisted on absolute guarantees of security, declining to consider
any further disarmament by France, if such disarmament were to
be accompanied by any rearmament of Germany.   They further
declined to answer the extensive *Questionnaire* annexed to the
German Memorandum, as they did not understand what chance
of progress it could offer.

> They continued, " The French Government cannot but feel
> the difficulty of a discussion limited to two Governments when
> various and complex questions which affect all the Powers
> assembled in conference are at issue.   These problems can be
> brought to a useful conclusion only with the participation of all
> the interested States, and the Franco-German examination of
> these questions, undertaken as a preliminary process, would
> have no useful purpose unless agreement already existed between
> the two countries on precise principles which would no longer
> be called in question. Unfortunately this is far from being so as
> may be seen from facts which are only too clear."

In conclusion, it was stated that the French Government
ardently desired to collaborate, with sane comprehension of
European feeling, in the necessary improvement of the political
atmosphere.   They believed that a complete and sincere understanding with Germany would be the condition and the guarantee
of such improvement ; on the other hand, nothing could be more
dangerous than misunderstanding.   " It is for the German
Government to dissipate or prevent it by explanations which
they may be sure will be examined justly and without prejudice.
It is the duty of the French Government to maintain the point
of view for which the reasons have been given."

The French Reply terminated the Franco-German exchange of
views on the subject of Germany's rearmament, and the way was
now clear for the second step to be taken by the British in their
last desperate effort to secure some degree of limitation of
armaments.   Mr. Anthony Eden, the Lord Privy Seal, was

entrusted with a mission to the French, German, and Italian capitals to explain and elucidate the British Memorandum and to elicit the views of the three Governments concerned on the proposals contained therein. As Mr. Arthur Henderson, the President of the Disarmament Conference, had embarked upon a similar Diogenic journey in the previous July,[1] so Mr. Eden started forth on 16th February, and proceeded first to Paris.

If there was a member of the British Government who could single-handed achieve this mission it was Mr. Anthony Eden, whose continually adroit handling of a most difficult position at the Disarmament Conference had won him great personal popularity, confidence, and trust throughout Europe. But even Mr. Eden's charm failed to win any great degree of support for the British proposals. In Paris, M. Barthou demanded sanctions as well as consultation, and drew Mr. Eden's attention to the declaration sent on 15th February to M. Doumergue by the Military Committee of the Senate, emphasizing the impossibility of further reductions in the defensive forces of France having regard to the present state of Europe and the world.[2]

From Paris, Mr. Eden passed to Berlin, where he found the Chancellor accommodating in attitude, particularly in the matter of the control of the para-military organizations, but firm on two major points. These were the German demand for immediate right to rearm in the air to the extent of at least 1,000 planes, and the flat refusal of Germany to consider a return to Geneva until after a Disarmament Convention satisfactory to her had been signed elsewhere.

In Rome, Signor Mussolini was, on the whole, helpful, for, while preferring his own plan, which he believed to have more practical chances of success, he was perfectly prepared to abandon it in favour of the British proposals if there was the least chance of a general agreement being reached on such a basis. France alone remained mute.

By the time that Mr. Eden returned, therefore, the sequence of diplomatic exchanges lacked two documents, namely, the French comment on the British proposals of 29th January and the final German *riposte* to the French Note of 13th February. This latter was delivered in Paris on 13th March and was made public five days later. It was conciliatory in tone, and recapitulated at some length the differences which existed between the

---

[1] See above, p. 164.
[2] Similar declarations were sent to the Prime Minister by the Naval and Air Committees of the Senate on 22nd and 24th February respectively.

French and the German points of view, and the reasons of the German Government for adhering to their own.   Tribute was paid to the efforts of the British and Italian Governments to secure a basis of compromise, and in the final paragraph it was pointed out to France that there now lay before the nations two alternative paths along which a solution might be found.   The first led to a short-term convention, for about five years, confined to the limitation of the highly-armed countries to their existing level, and the second to the embodiment of certain measures of disarmament by the highly-armed Powers in a convention which would consequently be of longer duration.   In either case the level laid down for Germany would have to be much the same, as, even under the second alternative, disarmament measures of such an extent as to contribute materially towards the realization of German equality could not be counted on.

Inspired comments in the German Press pointed out that Germany had not insisted on the reduction of French armaments, but had suggested the maintenance of the *status quo*, and had, herself, renounced all the heavy offensive weapons which France and others would keep.   In the view of the *Börsen Zeitung*, on 18th March, the German reply was regarded as "a last attempt at understanding", and if there followed no clear reply, or a definite negative, there was nothing left for Germany but to do, without French consent, that which her honour demanded, that which was dictated by the most primitive needs of the nation's security, and that which, moreover, had already been acknowledged as fair by the British and Italian Governments.

The German reply was in the hands of the French Cabinet before the text of their own Note to Great Britain had been finally agreed upon, but, before the receipt of the German Note, there had been provided an unexpected factor which had given M. Louis Barthou very furiously to think.

Speaking in the Belgian Senate on 6th March the Prime Minister, the Comte de Broqueville, made a statement of the greatest importance with regard to the general attitude of his country in the matter of German rearmament.   There were only two ways, he declared, by which Germany could be compelled to respect the military clauses of the Treaty of Versailles, namely, an investigation ordered by a majority vote of the Council of the League of Nations under Article 213 of the Treaty, or, alternatively, a preventive war.   The first would not be agreed to by at least two Powers—Great Britain and Italy—and the second was a remedy worse than the evil it sought to cure.   After maintaining that the existing situation was due to the delusions of the authors of the Treaty, who believed that it was possible to keep a great nation indefinitely disarmed, M. de Broqueville said that the Powers had recognized Germany's right to equality and, as all recourse to force was excluded, there remained only the friendly negotiation of a convention to limit armaments. There could be no true peace in Europe so long as Belgian security was threatened, and the Government would use its utmost efforts to bring about the successful conclusion of a Disarmament Convention with the minimum of sacrifices and the maximum of guarantees.

The effect in Paris of this statement by the Belgian Premier may well be imagined, where already there was sufficient dejection at the defection of Poland from the French orbit.   Now it seemed that Belgium, too, would join the ranks of France's doubtful allies.   Some little consolation was, however, gleaned by reason of the fact that there were grounds for believing that the Comte de Broqueville had made his statement without previously consulting his Ministerial colleagues, and this belief gained ground when two days later, on 8th March, the Foreign Minister, M. Paul Hymans, when taxed in the Chamber with the Premier's declaration, described as an *absurdité* any interpretation of it as favourable to German rearmament, thus covering his French flank.[1]

The French Note of comment on the British Memorandum was received in London on 19th March and made public on the 23rd, and in it the French Government virtually rejected the British proposals, which, it was argued, while legalizing German rearmament, would result in limiting French armament without guaranteeing French security. The French Government, therefore, " could accept no proposal which would render more serious the disarmament of France, while granting, on the other hand, to Germany an immediate legalization which could only be limited with difficulty, of a rearmament already realized in violation of the Treaties."[2]

France was not hostile in principle to a further degree of

[1] A subsequent resolution passed by the Belgian Senate indicated that the Prime Minister's statement had not meant quite what it appeared to mean.

[2] The anxiety of the French Government was to stress an aspect which in their view was increasingly in danger of being ignored, namely, that in the general discussion on German rearmament the unilateral abrogation of the Peace Treaty by Germany was being condoned.

disarmament if her security were not imperilled, and in this connection the British proposal for consultation was designated as " a step forward ", but the view was taken that something more was needed than an agreement to consult in the event of a violation of the Convention. Signatories should recognize their imperative duty to " rectify without delay that infraction by all methods of pressure which would be recognized as necessary ". The League of Nations, it was urged, remained the only organization capable of a collective guarantee of peace, and there could be no better guarantee of world stability than Germany's return to Geneva, where a reversion to the principles of the Disarmament Conference " will enable the common effort of all countries to produce the solution which will reconcile equality with the right, no less inalienable, of security ".

The contents of the French Note scarcely came as a surprise either to its immediate recipient or to the world at large, since it frankly and publicly put forward a view which had long been expressed in private discussion. In London it was accepted with almost fatalistic resignation, and with very considerable depression in Washington, where it was regarded as having completed the transfer of world disarmament out of the realm of practical possibility, at least for the immediate future. In Rome it confirmed the Italian point of view that progress could only be made along the lines of the Italian Memorandum, while the French demands for further guarantees for the execution of the Disarmament Convention were regarded as inacceptable, the Government considering that the Locarno Agreements were the limit to which it was possible to go in the way of guaranteeing other people's security.

In Germany, the reaction was one of bitter antagonism. The *Völkische Beobachter* characterized it as " the most dishonest production of Parisian post-war politics ", and declared roundly that " it is difficult to consider in detail the sum of frivolity and malevolence which the French Note represents ". The *Angriff* added that France " must take the responsibility for a new armaments race ", and the *Morgenpost* expressed the opinion that the French Note marked " a relapse into a time everybody believes to have gone long ago ". Even in the more moderate *Berliner Tageblatt*, Herr Paul Scheffer descried in the French Note proof of the correctness of the German view that the question of disarmament had already been sufficiently thrashed out, and that now a definite agreement to disagree was all that was lacking. In his opinion the renewed demand for sanctions was nothing more than an attempt to keep Europe in the position where the Treaty of Versailles had placed her.

In the terms of the French Note of 19th March the British Government were brought squarely up against the problem of whether or not they were prepared to increase the political and military obligations of Great Britain beyond those already incurred in the Covenant of the League of Nations and the Locarno Agreement.   In the French view any serious violation of the Disarmament Convention by a signatory must be met by concerted action by the other signatories in the following order : (a) systematic representation ; (b) financial and economic sanctions, and (c) war ; and it was firmly believed in Paris that a potential transgressor would be effectively restrained by the knowledge that these sanctions would be the inevitable consequence of his transgression.   The British Government, on the other hand, had to reckon with the strong body of opinion in Great Britain, which found utterances in the Beaverbrook Press, for the abandonment of even those guarantees contained in the Locarno Agreement, and had at the same time to take into account those who were urging, not only an addition to British commitments in regard to the Disarmament Convention, but also a definite offer of an alliance to France.

The Government, therefore, moved with considerable circumspection, and, after consideration by the Disarmament Committee of the Cabinet, three questions were submitted to the French Ambassador, to which replies were returned on 27th March.

Question.	*Answer.*
(1) Does the French Government distinguish between guarantees for the execution of the eventual Disarmament Convention and general guarantees in case of aggression ?	(1) France admits a theoretical distinction, but believes that there is no difference in practice, because, in case the Convention was violated, sanctions would have to be taken, presumably with armed force.
(2) If a distinction is made, what kind of guarantee does the French Government esteem necessary in such an instance ?	(2) To this the French replied with a counter-question as to what guarantees Great Britain was going to offer.
(3) Is the French Government willing to subscribe to a regional instead of a general guarantee system ?	(3) France agreed to accept a regional agreement but inquired how far Great Britain was prepared to extend the regional system.

The trend of the French replies indicated a definite change of front, which in a large measure may be attributed to the visit

which M. Barthou had paid to Brussels a few days previously
(27th March). There he discussed the whole question of
M. de Broqueville's bombshell of 6th March, and is believed to
have found singularly little support for any measures to prevent
German rearmament. The emphasis of French policy was,
therefore, changed, and it became apparent that whereas the chief
previous objection had been to the controlled increase of German
armaments, it was now the reduction of their own armaments
below the present level which the French were most anxious
to avoid.

This view was still further confirmed by the receipt on 7th April
of a further Note from Paris, in which it was understood that
the French Government expressed its willingness to recognize
some measure of German rearmament, provided that it was
limited, and that its limitations were subjected to full international control and supervision, the same control and
supervision to be applied to all other signatories of the
Convention. Full guarantees were, however, to be provided
within the framework of the Convention for its execution.

This most recent of French memoranda was of an interim
nature, and foreshadowed the dispatch of a further and longer
Note in the same vein in the near future.

Thus the position stood on the eve of the meeting of the
Bureau of the Disarmament Conference on 10th April. The
British Government was confronted with two vital questions.
Already committed by the British Memorandum to consultation,
they had now to decide, first, whether they were prepared to agree
in advance to the principle of sanctions being written into the
Convention ; and, secondly, if so, what test was to be accepted
by which an aggressor might be established.

In regard to the first of these problems, it was impossible to
avoid the issue that the demand for security on the part of France,
whether within the framework of the Disarmament Convention
or outside it, was hardly distinguishable from a demand for an
undiscriminating maintenance of the *status quo* for all time ; and
again the question arose, as it had arisen during the negotiations
of 1922 and 1925[1]; was the British guarantee to extend to
Eastern as well as to Western Europe ? Was it to be an automatic
sanction coming into force on the vote of the signatories of the

[1] Both in the negotiations at Cannes in 1922 and in the early preliminaries
of the Locarno Agreement of 1925 the French were anxious to obtain the
guarantee of Great Britain for the German frontier of Poland and Czechoslovakia.

Disarmament Convention or the Council of the League, or was each signatory to retain the right to satisfy itself that an act of violation had taken place ? and, finally, was the form of sanction to be that of economic boycott or military action ?

There seemed to be no doubt that any further obligation which Great Britain assumed must be limited in scope and regional in application. The unpopularity with which any extension beyond this point would be greeted in the country as a whole was unquestionable. The scope, therefore, of any further British guarantee appeared to be limited essentially to the same area as the Western Locarno Pact of 1925.

In the matter of the application of sanctions also, the post-war policy of Great Britain had been to reject any proposal which involved the granting of a " blank cheque " for the use of armed force, whether in the application of a general guarantee or of a special agreement. For example, Article 16 of the Covenant of the League of Nations provided that :—

> " It shall be the duty of the Council in such case to *recommend* to the several Governments concerned what effective military, naval, or air force the Members of the League shall severally contribute to the armed force to be used to protect the Covenants of the League,"

and, again, Paragraph 3 of Article IV of the Locarno Treaty of Mutual Guarantee provided that :—

> " In case of a flagrant violation of Article 2 of the present Treaty or of a flagrant breach of Articles 42 or 43 of the Treaty of Versailles by one of the High Contracting Parties, each of the other Contracting Parties hereby undertakes immediately to come to the help of the Party against whom such a violation or breach has been directed *as soon as the said Power has been able to satisfy itself that this violation constitutes an unprovoked act of aggression . . .*"

In each case the signatory Powers reserved the right of judging each case upon its own merits. This view was also held by the German Government, and it was improbable that any system of automatic sanctions would be agreed to by Germany. It appeared therefore that, in the event of the principle of sanctions being written into the Disarmament Convention, it could only follow a period of consultation between the High Contracting Parties.

There arose also the vexed question as to whether signatories of the Convention should undertake the possible obligation of employing military as well as economic sanctions, but it had become increasingly clear to many students of the problem that economic sanctions could not be embarked upon without at least involving the possibility of military sanctions following. As Mr. Rudyard Kipling has written, " If you take the first step you must take the last," and in this respect the policy of Great Britain was deeply affected by the attitude of the United States.

When in May of 1933 Mr. Norman Davis announced to the Disarmament Conference that, in the event of a State being declared by the other signatories of the Disarmament Convention to be guilty of a breach of its obligations, the United States would, if they concurred in the judgment, refrain from any action tending to defeat the collective effort which the other States might make to restore peace, it almost seemed as if the traditional American policy of isolation had been abandoned.[1] But the value of Mr. Davis' announcement was greatly diminished when, a few days later, the isolationists on the Senate Committee on Foreign Relations so amended a Resolution intended to prohibit the export of arms to a transgressor State that it finally prevented any assistance being rendered to any belligerent party in the event of war or the application of sanctions.[2] This action was taken with the expressed intent of securing the preservation of American neutrality and isolation, and, though it met with the disapproval of President Roosevelt, it was finally passed by the Senate (though not yet by the House of Representatives in its amended form) in February of 1934.

If America could be persuaded to forego her neutral rights in the event of the enforcement of a financial and commercial boycott of an aggressor State, one of the principal objections on the part of Great Britain to participating in a system of sanctions would have been eliminated, but the action of the Senate gave little hope that this would be achieved, and as lately as 24th March a statement was issued by the White House, following the publication of the French reply to the British Memorandum, to the effect that " President Roosevelt has indicated that the United States maintains the attitude which it adopted at the beginning of the negotiations on disarmament, namely, that the United States would join other nations in a Consultative Pact to discuss international problems, but it would not sign any accord obliging it to use its armed force for the settlement of any dispute whatever ". Without the participation of the United States, any system of sanctions, even if it were agreed to by other Contracting Parties to the Convention, would inevitably prove useless in any event of application.

[1] See above, p. 121.   [2] See above, pp. 124–5.

There remained for consideration the vital and all important question of the definition of aggression upon which so many proposals for mutual security and guarantee have broken down. In its Memorandum of 19th February, in reply to the British Disarmament proposals, the United States Government urged that a universal Pact of Non-aggression should be included in the Disarmament Convention " in which an undertaking would be given that the armed forces of no State should invade the territory of another country in violation of treaty rights ". A similar definition of aggression had also figured in the Soviet proposals of February, 1933, and had been adopted in the Report of the Politis Committee on Security set up by the Disarmament Conference in May of the same year. As such it has found its place in the series of Conventions signed by the Soviet Union in July, 1933, with Poland, the Baltic States, the Little Entente, Turkey, Persia, and Afghanistan,[1] and remains, therefore, the one definition of aggression, in addition to that of Locarno, which is in active operation.[2]

9

Meanwhile, in Europe there were evident and unmistakable signs of unrest and anxiety. In Great Britain the demand by a section of the popular Press for increased armaments was but slightly appeased by the increase in the naval, military and air estimates put forward in March. In France the Service Commissions of the Senate and Chamber reaffirmed that it was impossible to reduce the armed forces of the Republic. New Parliamentary Bills were announced providing for the extension of a new line of fortifications to link up with and strengthen the Belgian defences as far as the sea, and for the laying down of a cruiser of the *Dunkerque* type, one destroyer, and two submarines. The naval estimates showed an increase of 30 million francs on those of 1933,[3] and a special article of the Budget authorized the Air Ministry to spend 400 million francs on new equipment and 90 millions on technical development. Moreover, on the same day that the text of the Memorandum to Great Britain was published,

[1] See above, p. 154.
[2] The text of the " secret " protocol annexed to the Balkan Pact of 9th February, 1934, was published in *La Macedoine* of 1st April, and showed that in this document also the Politis definition of aggression had been accepted.
[3] The total Naval Estimates of 2,742 million francs included 50,000,000 francs for the upkeep of personnel in the Naval Air Service, which had formerly been included in the Air Estimates ; it did not, however, include 20,000,000 francs to be spent in 1934 in beginning the construction programme outlined above.

the Ministry of War announced its intention to call up for the
current year of training more reserves than in recent years, by
enforcing the second period of training, which was to take the
form of a mobilization rehearsal.[1] Not lacking in significance,
moreover, was the speech of the Minister of War, Marshal Pétain,
to the National Union of Reserve Officers on 24th March, in which,
citing the example of Germany where the pre-military and
para-military education of youth was counted among the most
important of national duties, he appealed to the teachers and
professors amongst the reserve officers to use their influence in
the direction of giving to youth a sound physique and a *moral*
capable of standing any test ; and of developing among the
youth of France a taste for and knowledge of military matters in
order to prepare them for that most sacred of duties, the eventual
defence of the country.

Meanwhile Germany, whilst London, Paris and Rome discussed
whether or no she should be allowed to increase her armaments,
pushed ahead, as she had so often warned them that she would
do if the rights which she claimed and which had been admitted in
principle were not granted in practice.   The heavy increase in
the armaments expenditure published at the end of March spoke
for itself, and it was difficult to imagine that academic discussion on
German rearmament could be much longer protracted after the
publication of the military budget, which showed an increase in
air estimates alone from 44 million Reichsmarks in 1932–3,
and 78 millions in 1933–4 to 210 millions (£10,500,000 gold).
The *Reichswehr* estimates amounted to 574,545,000 Reichsmarks,
as compared with 344,900,000 in the previous year, and showed
clearly that military expansion was confidently foreseen.   The
increase in the German service estimates was the subject of
Parliamentary questions when the House of Commons reassembled
on 9th April.   In reply the Foreign Secretary announced that
the Government were giving " very serious consideration " to
Germany's increased expenditure on armaments, and that the
British Ambassador in Berlin had been instructed to make
inquiries of the German Government on the subject.

Within a few hours of Sir John Simon's reply, an official
communiqué was issued in Berlin pointing out that the Treaty of
Versailles placed no restriction on military *expenditure*, and
explaining the increase in the Army Estimates as being due to the
reorganization of the *Reichswehr* on a short-term basis.   The

[1] It had been the custom for most reservists to be excused from the
second period of service.

Navy, it was explained, was dangerously antiquated and must be reconditioned ; and the increased expenditure in the air was accounted for by the replacement of single-engined transport machines by multi-engined planes.[1] Despite these explanations, the impression still obtained in many quarters that the next few months would see the German Army openly doubled in size, and that the increased estimates were to equip the second 100,000 men.

Confirmation of this indication was found in an interview which the *Reichskanzler* gave to the Associated Press on the same day as the publication of the estimates (29th March), in which he declared, " I have no intention of accepting an Army of 250,000 men and in no circumstances will I submit to the orders of anybody. . . . All that I shall do will be done openly.   For example, I do not intend to accept with goodwill 150,000 men as the basis of our Army, and then proceed to arm 150,000 more secretly . . . I do not want to expose Germany to the possibility of any foreign attack or an air raid over our industrial centres, or to a so-called preventive war with no other aim but to divert attention from internal troubles.   For this reason, and this alone, do we want an Army adequate for our defence."

The publication of the German military estimates was probably the most important event of this particular phase of the whole disarmament problem.   By this means the German Government served notice on the armed Powers that, so far as she was concerned, the period of discussion and consultation was at an end and that she intended to go forward with the programme of rearmament which she had frequently and repeatedly declared.

For France, too, it was a turning point.   French diplomacy had been placed at a definite disadvantage by the admittedly moderate proposals which Herr Hitler had made to Mr. Eden regarding the Storm Troops and the S.S., which were repeated in the German Note to Great Britain of 16th April.[2]   France was in danger of being cornered, for Great Britain had gone so far as to ask what kind of guarantees of security France required, and

---

[1] This explanation was repeated officially by the German Foreign Minister to the British Ambassador on 11th April, and was communicated to the House of Commons by the Foreign Secretary on 16th April.

[2] This moderation was somewhat tempered by the tone of an address by Captain and Reichsminister Röhm before the Diplomatic Corps and foreign journalists on 18th April, in which he declared that " the existence of the S.A. will make any future illegal attack on Germany such a risk that any aggressor will have seriously to consider whether the possible gains are worth the risk ".

the latter was ever unwilling to put her actual demands on paper. For France, therefore, the publication of the German Estimates came at a most opportune moment, for it allowed her to shift from the discussion of guarantees to her old, and much better known, ground of the inviolable legality of the Treaty of Versailles, which Germany had deliberately announced her intention of infringing. To France this action meant that she had regained her liberty of action and she regarded this course justified in law by the violation of existing treaties.

There was, however, a further factor upon which French diplomacy based much of its expectations. From their latest information from Germany they had gained the impression that the Nazi Government would in fact be hard put to it financially to carry out their programme of rearmament much beyond the point which it had already reached. If this were true, Herr Hitler was bluffing. To legalize German rearmament would be to present him with a diplomatic victory. To call his bluff might be to turn the tide of Nazi ascendancy.

It was, therefore, with these thoughts in mind that the French Government composed its final Note to Great Britain which was delivered in London on 17th April. It began by recounting the recent inquiries made by Sir John Simon, and pointed out that on the very day they were made the German Budget figures were officially announced. The British Government had been no less concerned than the French at the size of the increase in expenditure (352 million marks) and had made representations in Berlin. The explanations which they received in return were " less a justification than a confirmation ".

" In reality," said the Note, " the German Government, without waiting for the results of the negotiations which were in progress, has wished to impose its determination to continue every form of rearmament, within limits of which it claims to be sole judge, in contempt of the provisions of the Treaty, which, in the absence of any other convention, continue to govern the level of its armaments. The German Government intends to increase immediately on a formidable scale, not only the strength of its army, but also that of its navy and of its aviation. So far as this last is concerned, it is all the less permissible for the neighbours of Germany to disregard the menace that hangs over them, in that numerous aerodromes have recently been organized in the demilitarized zone, also in violation of the Treaty. . . ."

Facts of such exceptional gravity could lead to only one conclusion ; they proved that the German Government, whether of set purpose or not, " has made impossible the negotiations the basis of which it has by its own act destroyed."

The duty and the reply of the Government were dictated by the recognition of this fact, and, before seeking to discover whether agreement could be reached upon a system of guarantees of execution, " France must place in the forefront of her preoccupations the conditions of her own security, which, moreover, she does not separate from that of other interested Powers."

The return of Germany to the community of States was an essential condition to the signature of a Disarmament Convention, and her presence in the Geneva Assembly would be no less indispensable for the realization of a satisfactory system of guarantees of execution. On this point of capital importance, however, Mr. Eden had not been able to bring from Berlin any favourable solution.

The Government could not abandon this essential and necessary condition, and " even less can it assume the responsibility of so dangerous a renunciation at the very moment when German rearmament is being claimed, prepared, and developed without any account being taken of the negotiations entered upon in accordance with the wishes of Germany herself ".

France's will to peace must not be confounded with the abandonment of her defence, and she regretted that " the action of a third party should abruptly have rendered vain the negotiations undertaken by the two countries with equal good will and good faith ".

In conclusion, the Note stated that it would be the duty of the Disarmament Conference to resume its work. That work should not be abandoned, but taken up at the point at which the Conference left it when it invited Governments to proceed to an exchange of views, which had not produced a result.

The Note conveyed a decision from which, so long as the circumstances remained unchanged, no retreat could be expected, and the stand of the French Government was further affirmed when M. Barthou appeared on 9th May before the Foreign Affairs Committee of the Chamber and declared that France could under no circumstances give legal sanction to the rearmament of Germany ; the Government would await the course of events and the decision of the British Government.

This, however, did not entirely represent the course of French policy. Convinced that when the General Commission of the Disarmament Conference met on 29th May it would be merely to record its own demise, the French Government set about preparing for the period which would follow the collapse of the Conference. The French naval and air estimates had already been increased,[1] and it was now stated that the period of military service would be lengthened to two years, and that plans were already being made to complete the great line of fortifications on the eastern frontier at an additional cost of some £13 millions.

But the Government was not content with these material precautions, and M. Barthou set about shoring up the somewhat ramshackle edifice of French alliances in Central and Eastern Europe. This very closely resembled the entry of the trainer into a lion's cage, the occupants of which had shown too great a lack of docility. Poland, by her Non-Aggression Agreement with Germany, had registered her disapproval of French participation in the Four-Power Pact and in other aspects of French policy ; while Czechoslovakia had caused a flutter in the dovecotes of the Quai d'Orsay when, on 21st March, Dr. Beneš had informed the Foreign Affairs Committees of Parliament of the amazing fact that he was not irrevocably opposed to an Austro-German *Anschluss*, of which he and President Masaryk had been in favour at the Peace Conference, but had withdrawn their support therefrom out of deference to the attitude of the Great Powers.[2] Well might M. Barthou direct towards Prague a glance of " *et tu Brute* ". Moreover, the Belgian *démarche* of 6th March [3] had given the Quai d'Orsay a considerable shock, though matters had been comparatively satisfactorily adjusted during M. Barthou's visit to Brussels on 27th March.

No doubt with some trepidation, therefore, M. Barthou set out for Warsaw on 21st April, but it is believed that he achieved a greater degree of success than might at first have been expected. Humble-pie had undoubtedly to be eaten by the French Foreign Minister, who had to announce that France regarded Poland " as a great and independent Power ", and to give assurances that in future France would do her utmost to carry out the economic and financial agreements between the two countries. In return, Marshal Pilsudski promised his support at Geneva for

[1] See above, p. 219.

[2] This statement by the Foreign Minister of Czechoslovakia was doubtless prompted by the frequently appearing rumours of a Habsburg restoration in Vienna, and Dr. Beneš was well known to prefer, as a choice of evils, a Nazi Austria to a Habsburg. The wisdom of this choice may be questioned since, in the event of Austria becoming a Nazi state, Czechoslovakia would be in imminent peril of sharing a like fate.

[3] See above, p. 212.

the new French disarmament policy.   It was finally agreed that
" there had been faults on both sides " and that the Franco-
Polish Alliance remained intact and indissoluble.[1]

From Warsaw M. Barthou passed on to Prague, arriving on
26th April, and there discussed with Dr. Beneš all the international
questions in which the two countries had common interests.
Dr. Beneš went so far as to recede from his previous viewpoint
and to acquiesce in the French thesis that the peace of Central
Europe depended upon the maintenance of Austrian independence.
As to disarmament, the two statesmen found themselves in
agreement that it was impossible to sanction a policy which,
under the shibboleth of equality, would permit rearmament
instead of disarmament.

On his departure, M. Barthou was accompanied as far as the
frontier by Dr. Beneš, in marked contradistinction to the
circumstances of his arrival in Warsaw, where he was not welcomed
by representatives of the Polish Foreign Office.

M. Barthou returned to Paris, therefore, after a week of
Central European travel, with the prestige of French diplomacy
considerably enhanced and having gone far to re-establish the
former French *bloc* at Geneva, though now with France not so
much in the position of mentor as of *primus inter pares*.

10

Meanwhile in London the effect of the French Note of 17th
April had been to clear the air.   There was an increasingly active
school of thought which considered that the farce had now been
played out and the sooner the curtain were rung down the better.
The publication of the German estimates had conveniently
presented the opportunity of fixing the blame for the failure of
the Disarmament Conference on Germany, and it was urged that
the whole thing should be wound up at the forthcoming meeting
of the General Commission on 29th May.

[1] M. Barthou's visit, however, did not extend to the military aspect
of the alliance, and, to strengthen this, General Debeney, a former Chief
of the French General Staff, went to Warsaw in June.   Despite these
visits, however, real confidence had not been established between the two
countries, as was shown by the Polish attitude to the proposals for an
Eastern European pact of security, and the strained relations which
resulted from the arrest in August by the Polish of the French directors
of the French-owned Zyrardow textile mills.

More vocal was that section of opinion which called for the building up of the air forces of Great Britain from the lamentably low point to which optimistic anticipation of disarmament had reduced them, and very great satisfaction was felt when on 11th May Mr. Baldwin renewed publicly the pledge which he had already given to the House of Commons, that, " In the event of no agreement being come to, and particularly no agreement in the air, this country will be satisfied with no less position in the air than a position of equality with the greatest Power within striking distance of our shores."

Some substantiation was given to the French case by the mysterious flying visit to London of Herr von Ribbentrop, the recently appointed Reichscommissar for Disarmament, on 9th May. Herr von Ribbentrop's mission was to ascertain what would be the position of Great Britain in the event of Germany finding herself at grips with France. He left on 11th May with his curiosity unsatisfied, nor had he been able to give a satisfactory answer to the counter-question put to him in London as to Germany's intentions towards the Disarmament Conference and the League of Nations. The impression left behind him was that the Chancellor was seriously concerned at the position in which the new departure on the part of France had placed Germany.

And indeed within the Reich itself all was not well. The bitter struggle within the National-Socialist Party between the Radical and Conservative elements had virtually paralysed the progress of the revolution. The white heat of enthusiasm, which had followed the withdrawal from Geneva and the elections of November, had cooled off by now, and the reaction which followed was proportionate to the fever of hysteria which had preceded it. The German people were looking for the implementing of some of the many promises which had been made to them during the preceding fourteen months, and in this respect the speeches of the Chancellor on 21st May, at the opening of the new motor road, and on May Day, gave very real disappointment, since they held out no hope of further benefit. Instead, the German people were urged to make use of *Ersatz* (substitute) commodities, a word which conjured up before the eyes of the older generation memories of the hardships and privations of the war years. A foreign observer in Germany in the Spring of 1934 could not but be impressed with the sense of depression and the degree of disappointment and open criticism with which he met. Ardent supporters of the Party in December now shrugged their shoulders in questioning uncertainty. Despair was not yet apparent, only

the beginnings of a doubtful wondering as to whether the dream
were really going to come true.

But throughout this period it was of interest to note that the
personal popularity and prestige of Adolf Hitler himself scarcely
suffered at all.   He was still the *Führer*, and even those who had
been his political opponents agreed that " without Hitler we can
do nothing ".   It was against the Party machine as a whole, with
its petty tyrannies and impositions, that the criticism was
directed ; the differentiation between the Leader and the Party
was clearly defined.

11

The respective positions of the Great Powers, therefore, on the
eve of the reassembly of the General Commission of the Conference
on 29th May was as follows :—

Germany, in the Note to Great Britain of 16th April, had
assumed a not unreasonable attitude.   She had agreed to the
postponement of the reduction of armaments of other Powers for
five years after the signature of a Convention ; had accepted the
proposals for supervision and control of armaments contained in
the British Memorandum of 29th January,[1] and was agreeable,
on the basis of reciprocity, to the regulations suggested by the
British Government for ensuring the non-military character of
the S.A. and S.S.[2]   On the other hand, she had insisted upon her

[1] See above, p. 202.
[2] These regulations provided that the S.A. and S.S. would possess no
arms ;   receive no instruction in arms ;   not be concentrated or trained
in military camps ;   not be, directly or indirectly, commanded or instructed
by officers of the regular Army ;   not engaged in or take part in field exercise.
The fulfilment of these regulations was to be verified by a system of
supervision.
There was ample evidence that Herr Hitler would welcome an opportunity of lessening the power of the S.A., who under Röhm were coming
into constant friction with the *Reichswehr* authorities, who refused to take
S.A. troops *en bloc* into the enlarged army and insisted that every new
soldier must undergo the regular course of training regardless of the
number of years he had served in the S.A.
The struggle between Hitler and Röhm for the control of the S.A., and
for the final decision as to whether they should remain a purely political
force or receive military training, had been in process since the first organization of the S.A. in 1921.   The dispute had been the cause of the Berlin
Revolt in 1930 and of many subsequent disagreements.   In each case
Hitler triumphed.   The final round in the fight came with the Röhm
intrigue of June, 1934, in the suppression of which not only Röhm
himself, but also Heines, Police President of Breslau, Ernst, S.A. leader
of Berlin-Brandenburg, General von Schleicher (and his wife), and more
than fifty other leaders were summarily shot.

300,000 men for the *Reichswehr* and upon " a defensive air force
of short-range machines, not including bombing planes, from the
beginning of the Convention, the numerical strength of which
would not exceed 30 per cent of the combined air forces of
Germany's neighbours or 50 per cent of the military aircraft
possessed by France (in France itself and in the French North
African territories) whichever figure was the less ". This would
suffice Germany for the first five years of a ten years' Convention,
" but after those five years she claims that the necessary reduction
and increases should be made so that she should attain full
equality of numbers with the principal Air Powers at the. end of
the ten years of the Convention." She refused to discuss the
question of her return to the League until after the question of
disarmament and of equality of rights had been settled, and by the
publication of her military estimates on 29th March had given
notice to the world that in her claims and intention to rearm she
remained adamant, and had thereby further demonstrated the
knack of those who rule Germany of providing material for those
who distrust her.

Great Britain, though her action had been belated, had made
an honest effort to bridge the gulf between Germany and France.
She had gone a long way in her concessions to the German point
of view regarding rearmament and, in the matter of French
security, had made a considerable departure from her traditional
policy, first in offering to participate in a Pact of Consultation
and, later, in asking France what form of " guarantees " she
really did consider necessary to her security.

France alone had remained consistent and had steadfastly
refused to consider any agreement which recognized the immediate
rearmament of Germany. She had considered the British offer
to consult in the event of a breach of the Disarmament Convention as insufficient and, by a familar perversity, her interest in
" guarantees " had waned as British interest in that subject had
increased. Finally, she had seized upon the publication of the
German military estimates to terminate the diplomatic exchanges
and to call for a return to Geneva and the policy of October,
1933.[1]

The attitude of *Italy* had perhaps been the most helpful of all,

---

[1] These tactics recall the similar occurrence of March, 1931, when the
French Government of the day utilized the publication of the Austro-
German *Zollunion* Agreement as a reason for breaking off the naval
disarmament conversations with Italy. See *Disarmament and Security*,
pp. 225 and 334.

for she had not only put forward a very practical plan of her own,[1] but had also declared her willingness to agree to any formula acceptable to the other nations.

In effect, therefore, the position had undergone little change since the withdrawal of Germany from the Conference, save that she had made further progress towards her own rearmament. No success had attended the efforts to bridge the gap between Paris and Berlin, and in endeavouring to do so a definite rift had occurred between Great Britain and France.   Failing to secure the required degree of support from her former ally, France had turned more and more towards the Soviet Union, and was not unhopeful of securing not only the entry of the U.S.S.R. into the League of Nations, but also a pact of mutual guarantee with that country which should also embrace Poland and the Little Entente.[2]   She was, however, somewhat deterred by the manifest desire of the Soviet Union to extend the scope of such a pact to include her eastern as well as her western frontier, and for this there was little enthusiasm in France, who was interested solely in maintaining what remained of the European *status quo* created by the Peace Treaties.

The proposals of the *Soviet Union*, which were discussed by MM. Litvinoff and Barthou in a conversation of great importance on the evening of 18th May, were for a definite European Pact of Non-Aggression and Mutual Assistance.   In their preparation, M. Litvinoff had gone back to the idea of the French Plan submitted to the Conference in November, 1932,[3] which provided for a series of interlocking " circles ", the first of which consisted of a Pact between France, the U.S.S.R., Poland, the Little Entente, the Baltic States and Germany,[4] and was to remain open for adherence by other Continental States.   The second " circle " consisted of an agreement to cover the Mediterranean area and would presumably require undertakings of naval action by Great Britain and Italy, which the French Government was in hopes of obtaining.   Finally, there was a somewhat vaguely

---

[1] See above, p. 201.
[2] As a step towards paving the way for this agreement the French Government persuaded two out of the three Governments of the Little Entente, Rumania, and Czechoslovakia, to recognize the Soviet Union on 9th June.   The third party, Yugoslavia, however, refused to follow suit.
[3] See above, p. 77.
[4] The invitation to Germany placed that country, perhaps designedly, in a peculiarly difficult position.   If she accepted, it would mean for her the recognition of the *status quo* based upon existing Treaties ; while her refusal might be interpreted as an admission of aggressive designs and an added reason for refusing all rearmament to her.

defined third " circle " termed a " Naval Locarno in the Pacific ",
in which Great Britain and the United States, and even possibly
Japan, would be asked to join, as soon as agreement had been
reached on the European problem.

Both M. Litvinoff and M. Barthou, when taxed, vehemently
denied that these proposals could in any sense be described as a
" policy of encirclement ", but it is impossible to ignore the
similarity between this new diplomatic departure and the
Franco-Russian policy of the pre-War era.

12

The General Commission of the Disarmament Conference
reassembled on 29th May,[1] after an interval of seven months,
in an atmosphere of gloom and fatalistic pessimism.   On all
sides it was felt that the meeting partook of the character of a
" wake ", and interest was concentrated mainly upon the
nature of the funeral orations.   Disarmament had been dead
for some considerable time ; the chances of limitation of
armaments were by this time of the slimmest, and rearmament
seemed to be the word of the moment.

The sense of unreality which overhung the whole proceedings
was reflected in the speeches of the first session ; in Mr. Henderson's
review of the position since October, 1933 ; in Mr. Davis'
reiteration of the willingness of the United States to co-operate
in the preservation of peace but of her firm intention not on any
account to send any of her forces anywhere for the settlement
of disputes ; and of M. Litvinoff's happy suggestion that the
Conference should perpetuate itself in a permanent body " for
the preservation of security and the safeguarding of universal
peace ".[2] The world at large and the delegates in particular
were waiting for the statements of policy from Great Britain
and France, to know whether the body should be given decent
burial or cast out into Aceldama.

Sir John Simon, who spoke first on the following day (31st May),
gave a sober and moderate restatement of the British case as it
stood since the end of the direct negotiations and the French
Note of 17th April, and showed clearly that the British Govern-

---

[1] The meeting of the Bureau of the Conference on 10th April had convened the General Commission for 23rd May, but the date was later
advanced a week in deference to the wishes of the French Government.

[2] Apart from this somewhat fantastic proposal, M. Litvinoff's bitter
criticism of the failure of the Disarmament Conference is among the
most accurate appraisals of the work of that body.

ment had no further proposals to make. The only thing that mattered, he said, was to try to find a possible bridge between the conflicting French and German points of view, and His Majesty's Government still regarded the Draft Convention submitted to the Conference in March, 1933, together with the modifications proposed thereto in the British Memorandum of January, 1934, as being the best possible basis of agreement. Indeed, if it were not possible to agree on that basis, he himself did not believe that a Convention could be realized.

He indicated that the British Government was in general agreement with the Memorandum put forward by the Danish, Spanish, Norwegian, Swedish, and Swiss Delegations on 14th April,[1] and warned the Conference that his Government could not and would not lend themselves to vague and indefinite discussions inspired by no more than a pious hope of success.   Finally, he made an appeal that by combining such agreements as had already been reached with new concessions, there was material to hand for reaching an agreement, and proposed that in any case protocols should be made ready for signature providing for the prohibition of chemical warfare and budgetary control of arms and the appointment of a Permanent Disarmament Commission.

M. Barthou's first appearance before the Disarmament Conference will long be remembered.   Even in the fifteen years' experience of oratory at Geneva it had no equal, for the seventy-four years old French Foreign Minister called into play every artifice of Parliamentary rhetoric, making full use of dramatic appeal, bitter irony, and caustic humour.   Speaking with dynamic energy and without notes, M. Barthou proceeded to give coldly and clearly a far more definite exposition of the French case than could have been gathered even from the note of 17th April, and to a castigation of Sir John Simon and Sir John Simon's policy.

The French Government, he declared, would not consent to any system involving an immediate measure of German rearmament, and by implication, therefore, they would not accept the British

[1] The Memorandum of the Scandinavian, Spanish, and Swiss Delegations was put forward in an effort to secure a basis of agreement for a short-term Convention which should be limited to certain branches of armaments.   The problem of naval armaments, for example, should be left to the Naval Conference of 1935, but the Convention must contain a measure of disarmament, if not coming into force immediately, at least provided for within its ambit.   The Conference, it was urged, must take into account in conventional form the situation resulting from a *de facto* rearmament, and the Convention must contain some proposals under the head of security.

Memorandum as a basis of agreement, even if it were accompanied by agreed guarantees of security.   This gave the reply, which had hitherto been lacking, to the British offer of March.[1] France, he said, had her own concrete plan for the limitation of all arms —the plan of 1st January, 1934,[2] which provided for a parallel, progressive reduction of armaments, accompanied by the necessary guarantees of security.

Referring to the Locarno Treaty and the position of the British Government—Sir John Simon had said : " What His Majesty's Government have promised they will perform "— M. Barthou remarked scornfully that it would not be very difficult to go further than the British Government in the matter of security,[3] but he made no suggestion of his own as to how security should be organized, contenting himself with the remark that French policy was " to refuse no suggestion, to devote full attention to any proposal that might be made ".

This brilliant oratorical *tour de force* was received by the Conference at first with artistic appreciation and then with grave concern, for M. Barthou had showed with brutal frankness how deep was the cleavage between the British and French theses and how apparently impossible it was to find a basis of compromise between them.   To many it appeared that the speech had destroyed the last vestige of hope of a fruitful prolongation of the efforts of the Conference, and on all sides it was admitted that the crisis was more acute and the deadlock more complete than at any time in the past two and a half years.[4]

So great was the consternation that the President suspended the session until the afternoon, and later until the following day (Friday, 1st June), to allow of an interval for reflection, and in the hope that in private conversations a means might be found to mend the Anglo-French rift.   When this interval proved too short, Mr. Henderson grimly adjourned the Conference over a long week-end.

But meantime the Bureau continued to meet, and at its session the situation began to clarify and the crisis to crystallize. It became clear that within the Conference there were two clearly

[1] See above, p. 215.
[2] See above, pp. 195-6.
[3] This remark, which had its clear effect upon the British delegation, was deleted from the shorthand report of M. Barthou's speech.
[4] Broadcasting from Geneva on the night of 31st May, Mr. Anthony Eden, the Lord Privy Seal, made no attempt to minimize the gravity of the situation, and frankly told his hearers that " at no time has the outlook been as black as it is now ".

defined schools of thought, those who regarded a disarmament agreement, however limited, to be an immediate essential, and were prepared to make certain concessions to secure the participation of Germany therein ; and those who considered that some further agreement on security must be arrived at before any adequate degree of disarmament could be achieved.   This body of opinion was opposed to an early return of Germany to Geneva because they believed that, given sufficient time, Germany would come back to the Conference as a penitent and unconditionally.

Leading the first group was Great Britain, supported by the United States, the Scandinavian Powers, Switzerland and Spain. They submitted to the Bureau on 4th June a programme of work based upon the discussion of the disarmament proposals put forward by the British, French, Italian, and German Governments between December, 1933, and April, 1934, from which they believed the basis of compromise could be evolved, not only for a Convention but for the return of Germany to the Conference.

Opposed to them was the Security group, led by France and comprising the Soviet Union, Turkey, the Little Entente and the Balkan *bloc*, who were convinced that further discussion of the Notes which had passed between the Powers concerned during the past five months was fruitless and that the Conference should adjourn pending an agreement on Security.

M. Barthou, fortified by the fact that on 31st May the French Cabinet had unanimously endorsed the expression of policy which he made, maintained an adamant attitude with regard to the further concession to Berlin which Mr. Henderson was anxious to make.   " I will," he declared " accompany the President anywhere else but not there ; we should only return with empty suitcases "

Despite the efforts of Mr. Henderson, the 4th of June passed without any indication of a break in the deadlock.   It was succeeded by a day of crisis and acrimony which threatened to bring the Conference to a peremptory termination.   In a final effort at compromise the President himself put forward a draft resolution for the consideration of the Bureau on the following lines :—

That the Soviet proposal for a permanent Conference be referred to the Governments concerned, together with the proposal for pacts of mutual assistance ;

That all the Powers concerned should affirm their intention to discuss the proposals ;

That the question of guarantees of execution be referred to the existing Committee on Miscellaneous Provisions ;

That further negotiations should take place on the basis of the British, French, Itsalian and German notes ;

That the question of disarmament be referred *en bloc* to the General Commission of the Conference and that of security to the Political Commission.

That further political preparation, for which the President should be responsible, was necessary before useful discussions could again take place.

The resolution, which was tantamount to a proposal for adjournment and was an attempt by Mr. Henderson to secure the return of Germany, had been accepted in advance by the British, American, and Italian delegates and by the six small Powers. It was summarily and categorically rejected by M. Barthou in terms which brought to a head the ill-feeling which had existed between himself and the President since the opening of the session, and which provoked Mr. Henderson to threaten to resign the chair.

M. Barthou gave as his grounds for rejecting the proposals of the President the fact that, though Mr. Henderson had laid such stress upon security in his opening speech, this question, " which dominates the discussion ", was mentioned only at the end of his draft resolution. Unlike the French, therefore, the President had been inconsistent and not impartial.

This brought Mr. Henderson to his feet with an impassioned defence of his own conduct. M. Barthou, he declared, had, during the last few days, steadily impugned his impartiality, an impartiality which had never been questioned before ; " if this is called in question I will willingly resign this task." Rather ungraciously M. Barthou withdrew his personal imputation against the President, but refused to be moved from his negative attitude towards the resolution ; whereupon, quite unmollified, Mr. Henderson called the attention of the Bureau to the fact that M. Barthou had successively refused to be a member of a drafting committee, to accept the President's programme of work, and to draw up a programme of his own. Under the circumstances he declared the meeting adjourned.

The deadlock remained unbroken, the gloom deepened.

But, just when it seemed that all that remained to be done by the delegates was the packing of their bags, there came the al- most inevitable compromise. Mr. Norman Davis, the peacemaker of the Conference, had been quietly at work behind the scenes and had discovered that, all appearances to the contrary, a basis of compromise did exist. Despite the fact that the Cabinet had given their support, there were those in Paris who were seriously alarmed at the effect of M. Barthou's speech on the British delegation. Word came to Geneva that if it were possible to win the French case for security by compromise, it were better to do so. Moreover, the agreement secured with Germany on 1st June in the matter of the Saar gave reason for hope that the National-Socialist regime was beginning to realize the difficulty of its position both at home and abroad and to act accordingly.

Mr. Davis' task was, therefore, less difficult than at first appeared, and M. Barthou was persuaded to present a counter-proposal to the resolution submitted by Mr. Henderson on the previous day. So successful were his efforts that, at the opening of the meeting of the Bureau next morning (6th June), the President appeared smiling once more and announced " The storm has passed."

The French proposal was a piece of very skilful drafting. It made the greatest possible concessions to Mr. Henderson's views and accepted his three essential points. But it kept security in the foreground, urging that the Political Commission should also complete the measures of supervision of armaments and study guarantees of execution. At the same time the French proposals avoided any mention of the return of Germany to the Conference, but in his *exposé*, M. Barthou made it clear that he was not opposed to such a return, but did not think it should be bought or begged for.

Mr. Eden frankly expressed his preference for Mr. Henderson's resolution, and insisted that provision should be made for the discussion of the British, French, German, and Italian Notes. With the intention of harmonizing the two sets of proposals, Mr. Henderson adjourned the Bureau for forty-eight hours, during which private discussions took place in the hotels of the delegations. In the meantime, the German Government issued an authoritative denial of the rumours of any immediate intention of Germany's return to Geneva or participation in pacts of security. Through unofficial channels and inspired articles in the Press, the German conditions for return, namely the realization of equality, were restated.

The compromise resolution agreed upon by the British, French, and United States was adopted both by the Bureau and the General Commission on Friday, 8th June. It represented a very fair combination of the Henderson-Barthou resolutions, and by it the General Commission decided to " continue without delay the investigations already undertaken " and :—

(1) Invites the Bureau to seek, by whatever means it deems appropiate and with a view to the general acceptance of a disarmament convention, a solution of the outstanding problems, without prejudice to the private conversations on which Governments will desire to enter in order to facilitate the attainment of final success by the return of Germany to the Conference.

(2) Having regard to the peculiar importance presented by the study and solution of certain problems to which attention was drawn at the beginning of the general discussion, takes the following decisions :—

(i) SECURITY.—(a) Since the results of the earlier work of the Conference have enabled certain regional security agreements to be concluded in Europe during the past year, the General Commission decides to appoint a special committee to conduct such preliminary studies as it may consider appropriate in order to facilitate the conclusion of further agreements of the same nature which may be negotiated outside the Conference. It would be for the General Commission to determine the relationship, if any, of these agreements to the general Convention. (b) The General Commission decides to appoint a special committee to study the question of guarantees of execution, and to resume the work relating to supervision.

(ii) AIR FORCES.—The General Commission instructs the Air Commission to resume forthwith the study of the questions mentioned in its resolution of 23rd July, 1932, under the heading " Air Forces ".

(iii) MANUFACTURE OF AND TRADE IN ARMS.—The General Commission requests the Special Committee on questions relating to the Manufacture of and Trade in Arms to resume its work forthwith and, in the light of statements made by the United States delegate at the meeting of 30th May, 1934, to report to it as early as possible on the solutions it recommends. These committees will carry on their work on parallel lines ; and it will be coordinated by the Bureau.

(3) The General Commission leaves it to the Bureau to take the necessary steps at the proper time to ensure that when the President convenes the General Commission it will have before it as far as possible a complete draft Convention.

(4) Recognizing that the proposal of the U.S.S.R. Delegation that the Conference be declared a permanent institution under the title of the Peace Conference calls for careful study, the General Commission requests the President to submit that proposal to the Governments.

Reservations were made to the resolution by the Italian and Polish delegates ; the one on the ground that essential political problems were still unsolved, and the other on the ground that the Notes of the Four Powers could not be accepted as expressing the views of every section of the Conference.

The General Commission met again on 11th June to appoint

the Chairman of the four committees set up by virtue of the resolution of 8th June [1] and then adjourned *sine die.*

13

The record of achievement was not a great one. The Conference itself had been saved from collapse, and had been thrown once more into a state of suspended animation while innumerable Committees deliberated and discussed. Franco-British good feeling, after undergoing a period of severe tension, had taken on an improved tone. France, at the expense of accepting the extra-security considerations which M. Barthou had at first rejected, had retained British friendship without sacrificing that of the Soviet Union, and had registered a further success in placing the clear burden of responsibility upon Germany. For Germany's open professions and Geneva's open emendations left no present reason, except that of bad will, why Germany should not return to Geneva, and the next move lay with Germany.

As against this meagre record of achievement, there remained the dominant fact that no step had been taken to dispel the atmosphere of suspicion and fear which had gradually enveloped Europe since January, 1933. All that had been done was to give one more injection of vitality into a moribund body without attempting to eradicate the cause of the disease. No progress had been made in this last session of the Conference and the position remained practically the same as before 29th May. For, though the Anglo-Franco-American formula had left the back door open for the return of Germany, Mr. Henderson's closing remarks were not conspicuous for their confidence of success in the future. He expressed the fervent hope that the Governments would " do something ", and thought that the Conference must wait until it was seen what the Governments could do.

Mr. Anthony Eden put the position candidly, in all its gravity, before his constituents on the night of 9th June, less than twenty-four hours after the compromise had been effected at Geneva.

---

[1] The chairmen appointed were as follows : Security Committee, M. Politis (Greece) ; Guarantees of Execution, M. Bouquin (Belgium) ; Air, Señor de Madariaga (Spain) ; and Manufacture and Sale of Arms, M. Scavinius (Denmark). The Italian and Hungarian delegates refused to be represented on the Security Committee except as observers, and the United States not at all. On the other hand, the Soviet Union, who had refused to take part in the work of the Security and Arbitration Sub-Committee set up by the Preparatory Disarmament Commission in 1927, was now prepared to participate.

"We have," he told them, "in no sense solved the main difficulties of the European situation, which consist in the present relations of the chief Powers of Continental Europe. Unless they can be improved, there will be no disarmament agreement, no political entente, and in consequence no extension of international trade recovery in Europe. . . . This is the problem which European statesmanship has so far singularly failed to solve."

After two and a half years of discussion the disarmament problem was as barren of solution as it had been at the opening of the Disarmament Conference in February, 1932. By the summer of 1934 the deadlock was complete. All hope of disarmament had vanished, that of limitation of armaments had grown tarnished and faded, and the fear of general rearmament and its possible ghastly results had become a threat and a nightmare before the mind of the world.

Chapter X

YESTERDAY AND TO-MORROW

1

At the moment when this book is concluded (August, 1934), the two dominating factors in European politics are the proposed Eastern Locarno Pact of Mutual Guarantee and the effect produced both in Germany and abroad by the events of 30th June, and the two are not unrelated.

The proposals for a Pact of Mutual Guarantee in Eastern Europe had their origin in the conversations which took place between M. Litvinoff and M. Barthou in Geneva during the League Council Meeting and the Session of the Disarmament Conference at the end of May and the beginning of June,[1] and the first draft had been rejected by Germany on 13th June on the grounds that it amounted to the revival of the pre-War Russo-French policy for her encirclement. This refusal had found the support of Italy, and at the meeting in Venice[2] Herr Hitler and Signor Mussolini had agreed in their mutual dislike of regional pacts of Security.

In the latter part of June and the early days of July the proposal had undergone a process of redrafting at the hands of the Quai d'Orsay in collaboration with the Soviet Embassy in Paris, and M. Barthou made a triumphal progress through Rumania and Yugoslavia to win their approval for the new project. In this he was fully successful, and reinforced by this support he came to London on 8th July to acquaint the British Government with the results of his recent conversations and to explain to them in detail the revised version of the Franco-Soviet proposals.

The plan which M. Barthou outlined and to which Sir John Simon ultimately agreed, and commended to the House of Commons on 13th July, was as follows :—The existing Eastern Locarno Pact of 1925, whereby Germany and Poland and

---

[1] See above, p. 229.

[2] On the suggestion of the German Government the long deferred meeting between the two dictators took place at Venice on 14th–16th June. The two leaders discussed a number of subjects of mutual interest, and reached a " Gentlemen's Agreement " regarding Austria to the effect that a halt should be called to the Nazi campaign of terror in that country.

Czechoslovakia agreed not to alter the territorial *status quo* other than by peaceful means, and France undertook reciprocally to guarantee her two allies against unprovoked German aggression, would be supplemented by a new agreement involving Germany, Poland, Czechoslovakia, the Soviet Union, and the Baltic States. France herself would not be a signatory of the pact.[1] The new agreement, however, was presumably to be modelled on the Western Locarno Pact of 1925, that is to say, the contracting parties would definitely accept the present territorial *status quo*, though this was not mentioned in the original draft, and would agree to come to the assistance of any co-signatory who might become the victim of aggression by any other signatory or non-signatory State.

In addition to this there was to be another pact between France and the U.S.S.R. in which France would give a guarantee in respect of the frontiers of the Soviet Union and also the frontiers of Germany in the east ; at the same time the Soviet Union would become a co-guarantor, with Great Britain and Italy, in the Western Locarno Pact. In other words, if France were the aggressor, the Soviet Union would go to Germany's assistance or to the assistance of France if Germany were the aggressor. A further condition of the negotiation of the Pact was that the Soviet Union should join the League of Nations.

In commending these new proposals to the House of Commons on 13th July, Sir John Simon stated clearly that the approval of the British Government had only been given on certain conditions, namely that Great Britain should incur no further obligations and that the agreement itself should be based primarily upon the principle of reciprocity and that there should be nothing in the nature of a selective alliance directed against any Power or group of States. Great Britain, he indicated, would have no part in the formation of a programme for the encirclement of Germany, and assured the German Government—and in this he stated that he spoke also for France—that any agreement reached must be in conformity with the formula embodied in the Five Power Agreement of December, 1932, the realization of equality of rights within a system of security for all nations.[2] He hoped most sincerely that this new development if consummated would result in giving a fresh opportunity of " promoting the objects

---

[1] It would, however, be inevitable that, in the event of the pact being put into operation, France would be involved by reason of her commitments to Poland and Czechoslovakia incurred under the Eastern Locarno Treaties of 1925.

[2] See above, p. 84.

for which the Disarmament Conference was called ''.   Finally, he stressed the importance of bringing the U.S.S.R. within the circle of the Nations.[1]

Just how hopeful the British Government were for the success of the Conference may be more accurately gauged from the closing sentences of Sir John Simon's speech, in which he declared that all consideration of national defence could not be postponed until the end of the Disarmament Conference, which so far, in spite of valiant efforts, had reached no results, and he promised that a statement on air policy should be made to the House before the recess.   When the statement was made by Mr. Baldwin a week later (19th July), it showed that over the current and the four following years it was proposed to build 41 new air squadrons comprising some 460 planes, and in many quarters this programme was regarded as insufficient.

A further factor of the greatest importance with regard to the proposed Eastern European Pact was the changed attitude of Italy.   From the negative policy agreed upon with Herr Hitler at Venice, in June, Signor Mussolini had become so sympathetic towards the revised French proposals that he communicated with Sir John Simon immediately before the latter's speech on 13th July and authorized him to express to the House of Commons the warm approval of Italy as a guarantor of the Western Locarno Pact for the furtherance of the new project.

This change of front was explained by the Italian Foreign Office as being occasioned by the fact that the alterations made had robbed the proposals of their objectionable features and showed them to be no longer concerned with the intention of being employed against Germany, but it may also be believed that other considerations played their part, as, for instance, the events in Germany of 30th June and the failure, or inability, of Herr Hitler to fulfil the '' Gentlemen's Agreement '' of Venice and call off the terrorist activities of the Nazis in Austria.[2]

[1] The Foreign Secretary also took the opportunity to give a virtual reaffirmation of the pledge given to Belgium under the Western Locarno Pact, saying that '' the territorial integrity of Belgium is no less vital to the interests and safety of this country to-day than it has been in the past . . . changed conditions, especially in connection with the air, have not altered that historic fact at all ''.

[2] As time progressed these continued activities still further estranged Germany from her one possible friend in Europe.   On 20th July, in an inspired article in the *Giornale d'Italia*, Signor Mussolini issued a strongly worded warning to Germany that neither the Austrian people nor international public opinion would tolerate further the '' bestial '' terrorist outrages of Nazi agitators and bluntly asked the German Government whether it had a share in the campaign.

In Germany the new proposals were greeted with the same suspicion and hostility which had been accorded to the original suggestion put forward by M. Litvinoff, and there was anger mixed with dismay in the Wilhelmstrasse when it became known that England, and even Italy, were sympathetic to the idea of the new pact. Particularly unexpected and unwelcome was the fact that the draft instruments of the new agreement were brought to the German Foreign Office on 13th July not by the French, but by the British Ambassador, thereby showing that Britain was not merely disposed to play the rôle of benevolent onlooker, but intended to carry out to the full the part of sympathetic supporter.

To the German Government the new proposals, like the originals, seemed to be merely a veiled design for the encirclement of Germany and the prevention of her political expansion to the north-east and south-east of Europe. But their position was essentially a difficult one. To accept meant the abandonment of all hope of regaining the Corridor, not for ten years, as was provided in the bi-lateral agreement with Poland,[1] but indefinitely, since the new agreement, if modelled upon the Western Locarno Pact, would have no time limit. In addition, though Sir John Simon had given assurance that the new agreement would be actuated by the spirit of the formula of December, 1932, and had declared that he spoke also in the name of France, M. Barthou's statements in Paris after his return from London did not seem wholly in accordance with this attitude, and showed quite plainly that France was prepared to discuss her own disarmament and Germany's equality only after the Eastern European Pact had become a *fait accompli*.[2] Moreover, it was made clear to Germany that her acceptance of the pact must be unconditional and that she must give this proof of her pacific intentions before her armaments position could be discussed.

On the other hand, refusal on the part of Germany to accept the proposals would at once lay her open to the charge of harbouring aggressive intentions and would at the same time remove any obstacle in the path of a definite Franco-Soviet *entente*, which

[1] The attitude of Poland towards the new proposals was also unfriendly, for she feared that in any struggle in which the pact was likely to become operative her territory would be the cockpit. Like Germany, she was anxious to make reservations in the spirit of Annex F of the original Locarno Treaty, which took into consideration the geographical position of the Contracting Parties.

[2] It is not impossible that this declaration of M. Barthou may have sounded the death knell of the pact.

might form part of a larger Little Entente-Baltic-Balkan *bloc*, with the sole object of isolating Germany.

Rather than be faced with this second alternative, the German Government might well agree to swallow the pill, despite the very meagre amount of jam surrounding it, and to signify their acceptance with reservations, if Poland and certain Baltic States had not expressed their opposition to the proposed pact. The opposition from three potential contracting parties, taken in conjunction with the apparent disagreement regarding the application of the formula of December, 1932, shown by M. Barthou's statement on 15th July may, however, well foreshadow the abandonment of the project in its present form. One important development may still result, the entry of the U.S.S.R. into the League of Nations and her reassociation with Western Europe.

2

It is not the intention of the author to retail here the horrors which attended the events in Germany of 30th June, but merely to present them in their relation to the problem of disarmament. In passing, however, it is permissible to say that the deliberate substitution by Herr Hitler of gangster methods for the processes of law have lost for him the last vestige of support and sympathy abroad, and have so damaged the prestige of the Revolution at home that, had it not been for the providential opportunity for concentrated propaganda presented by the Referendum of 19th August, following the death of the President and Herr Hitler's assumption of supreme power as *Reichsführer*, it might well have proved impossible to recast the spell over the German people.[1]

[1] The death of the President and the consequent opportunity for propaganda presented a further example of the phenomenal good fortune which has played so important a part in the history of the National-Socialist Party. Time and again, when the fortunes of the Party seemed at their lowest ebb, some fortuitous circumstance has occurred to redress the balance. After the fiasco of the Munich *putsch* it was the premature release of Herr Hitler which enabled him to reorganize the Party in 1926 ; and, when it seemed in 1929 and 1930 that the Party would be destroyed by so many internal dissentions, the national opposition to the Young Plan and the Hague Agreements provided the opportunity for the Nazis to come to the fore as the champions of German honour. Again, when, after the General Election of November, 1932, the Party seemed bankrupt in every sense of the word, the unexpected collaboration of Herr von Papen not only revived their fortunes but actually placed them in power. When in October, 1933, the Revolution had reached a very critical period and support for it was on the wane, events in Geneva and Germany's withdrawal from the Disarmament Conference provided the chance for

Very early in 1934 it became apparent that the long-standing dispute between the *Führer* and the Chief of Staff of the Storm Troops as to the functions and position of the S.A. within the *Dritte Reich* was approaching a climax.   Ever since the formation of the S.A. in 1921 there had been disagreement between Hitler and Röhm, first as to their control and then as to their duties. To the Leader they were merely the militant wing of the Party, concerned only with political activities ; to their organizer and *Stabchef* they represented the nucleus of that reorganized and rearmed *Reichswehr* which it was his ambition to see created.

With the advent of the Nazi Party to power this clash of opinions became intensified, and when, after the second withdrawal of Germany from the Disarmament Conference, the question of German rearmament became a practical one, it was soon evident that an explosion was inevitable.   With the conclusion of the " revolutionary period " of the National-Socialist regime the Storm Troops became an incubus, and it was clear from the Chancellor's conversations with Mr. Eden in February, 1934, that he would welcome any opportunity to reduce their number and to render them a non-military organization.   This desire was still more apparent in the Note to Great Britain of 16th April, the contents of which in a re-emphasized form were repeated, it is believed, by Herr von Ribbentrop to the French Government during his visit to Paris on 16th June.

In taking up this attitude Herr Hitler had the substantial support of the *Reichswehr* High Command, who harboured the greatest contempt for Captain Röhm and his " amateur soldiers " and flatly refused to consider their incorporation in the army except as individual recruits who must undergo the regular training in which their length of service in the S.A. availed them nothing.   Furthermore, by the summer of 1934 the financial maintenance of two and a half million S.A. men became so great a drain upon the finances of the Party and the State that their disbandment, or at least their very material reduction, became an imperative economic necessity.

There was, however, a further complication.   The S.A. formed the bulk of the supporters of that Radical wing in the Party which looked to the coming of the Second Revolution which

Herr Hitler to restore again the united national front by the Referendum of November.   So now, when the prestige of the Revolution had been seriously shaken by the events of 30th June, the death of the President and the assumption by Herr Hitler of supreme national power as *Reichsführer* provided just that fillip which was so urgently required, although the opposition vote was considerably greater than in the previous November.

should implement the " Socialist ", as opposed to the " National ", aspect of the party programme.   These men looked with angry dismay at the gradual swing of the Revolution towards the Right, at the apparent domination of the Chancellor by the great industrialists, and particularly at the exalted position of General Göring and of their deadly rivals the S.S., now led by Herr Himmler.

To the S.A., who had been brought up on the propaganda doctrine of the pre-Revolutionary era, there had come a period of•bitter disillusionment.   They had been promised the return of the Polish Corridor and they had seen a ten years' Pact of Non-Aggression concluded with Poland ; they had been promised " socialism in our time " and they had seen the great industrialists and landowners become still more strongly entrenched ; worst of all, they had been promised glory and honour as soldiers of the Revolution and now they were faced with disbandment. In short, the appalling number of inconsistent promises which Herr Hitler had made in order to gain popular support were now arising like spectres about him, and he was not in a position to meet his obligations.

There arose amongst the High Command of the S.A. and the leaders of the Left Wing a strong desire, in which General von Schleicher agreed, to set the Revolution upon a more radical course and ensure the position of the Storm Troops. Thanks to the unsurpassed clumsiness of German intrigues— only equalled by the indomitable stupidity of German diplomacy—the affair became commonly known in Berlin before it had reached any grave stage of development, and it did not present great difficulty to the fertile imagination of General Göring and Herr Himmler to magnify it into a plot of gigantic ramifications, with the most diabolical and murderous intentions.   Having created this bogey for them- selves, it was comparatively easy for them to justify meeting the menace with similar methods, and with the approval of the Chancellor they indulged during 30th June and the two ensuing days in an orgy of murder which nauseated the civilized world.

Amongst the immediate victims who were shot without trial were Röhm, Heines,[1] Police-President of Breslau, Ernst, S.A.

---

[1] It is impossible to regret the elimination of either Röhm or Heines, whose homo-sexual activities amongst the Storm Troops had been an open scandal for years past, and the latter of whom was a convicted murderer.   So common had been the knowledge of their excesses that it is

Leader of Berlin-Brandenburg, and General von Schleicher and his wife. In addition, the list of victims [1] included adherents of the Right and of the Nationalists who had pleaded for moderation and the toleration of constructive criticism, and also the victims of a number of old scores, some of which had waited as long as ten years to be paid off. [2]

The opportunity was at once seized to disband two-thirds of the Storm Troops and to reorganize thoroughly the remainder on a non-military basis. Herr Hitler, in a speech before the Reichstag on 13th July, informed a bewildered Germany, and a shocked and incredulous world, of how he had saved his country from the perils of a national rising very similar, strangely enough, to that which had been threatened at the time of the Reichstag Fire.

But the illusion which had been created by the elections of November, 1933, of a Germany standing firm and united behind her Leader had been destroyed both at home and abroad. Within the Reich itself, Herr Hitler had, by his actions following 30th June, dangerously imperilled his connections with the proletariat and with the lower middle class from which the popular support for his Party had been originally so largely drawn. To the disgruntled elements of the Socialists, Communists, Jews, Catholics, and Protestants he had now added many disappointed Storm Troopers and disillusioned Nationalists, and was dependent upon the support of the S.S., the *Gestapo* (Secret Police), and the *Reichswehr*. Germany had temporarily been handed over to the tender mercies of General Göring and Herr Himmler, and it seemed even possible that there was a danger that the S.S. might become as great a threat to the Leader's position as the S.A. had been.

Moreover, the rapidly increasing gravity of the economic position made it necessary for further and greater sacrifices to be called for from the German people, and there was nothing to offer them in return. For the time being the negotiating power of Germany abroad was of the weakest, and it seemed more and more probable that Herr Hitler would be forced to throw himself into

impossible that it should have escaped the notice of the Chancellor, who had been associated with Röhm for more than fourteen years. In any case their conduct had not been such as to preclude even the formality of a trial.

[1] The exact number of these will never be known, but it certainly exceeded the 77 admitted by the Chancellor in his speech to the Reichstag on 13th July.

[2] Mention should be made here of the death of Herr von Kahr, who, as Reichskommissar in Bavaria, was accused by the Nazis of having betrayed the *Putsch* of 1923.

the arms of the *Reichswehr*, as being the one stable force in Germany.[1]

These factors in the political situation were evident in the results of the Referendum of 19th August, for, despite the whirl-wind campaign of concentrated propaganda which was let loose upon the German people, the returns were significantly less satisfactory than in the previous November. For though the number of those who went to the polls was larger, the number who voted " Yes " decreased by over two million, the opposition had more than doubled itself, and the number of invalid votes had appreciably increased.[2] It is calculated that as many as seven million signified their disapproval. It should, moreover, be noted that whereas the November Referendum was a vote of confidence in the policy of the Government as a whole, that of August involved the personal prestige of Herr Hitler himself and a substantial increase in hostile votes weighed all the heavier for that reason.

Thus Germany's attitude towards the proposals for a new Eastern Locarno was materially affected by the position of her Government both at home and abroad, a position which

---

[1] There is ample evidence to show that the High Command of the *Reichswehr* is playing a far greater political rôle to-day than at any time since 1918. The outward and visible signs of this were the fact that General von Blomberg was selected to convey the congratulations of the Cabinet to the Chancellor after 30th June, and his subsequent declaration of the loyalty of the Army to Herr Hitler. The meticulous manner in which the Chancellor returned these compliments in his speech of 13th July was also significant, and the indications have become multiplied since Herr Hitler became Commander-in-Chief. German history has a strangely disturbing parallel. In 1813 the General Staff of the newly reorganized Prussian Army " captured " the somewhat nebulous movement of German regeneration inaugurated by the *Tugend-bund*. The results were the re-establishment of the military caste in control of Prussia, and of Prussia's foreign policy. Is it possible that Generals Blomberg, Reichenau, and Fritsch will play the parts of Scharn-horst, Gneisenau, and Blücher, with Adolf Hitler as the shadowy well-intentioned figure of Frederick William ?

[2] The following is a comparison of the voting in the Referenda of November, 1933, and August, 1934 :—

November, 1933.		*August*, 1934.	
Total of the Electorate	45,004,793	Total of the Electorate	45,473,635
Votes cast (96·3 per cent of the elector-ate) . . .	43,460,529	Votes cast (95·71 per cent of the elector-ate) . . .	43,529,710
" Yes " (95·1 per cent of valid votes) .	40,609,243	" Yes " (84·3 per cent of valid votes) .	38,363,760
" No " (4·9 per cent of valid votes) . .	2,101,004	" No " (9·4 per cent of valid votes) .	4,294,654
Invalid . . .	750,282	Invalid . . .	872,296

had become very much worse as a result of the brutal murder
of the Austrian Chancellor, Dr. Dollfuss, by Nazi desperadoes on
25th July. Despite all Herr Hitler's desperate efforts to clear
Germany from any direct complicity in the plot for a general
Nazi rising in Austria and for the assassination of the Chancellor,
he could not exonerate his own Party from a very grave degree
of moral responsibility for the death of Dr. Dollfuss. For a
year or more no effort had been spared by the Nazi Party in
Germany to incite the Austrian people to rise against the Federal
Chancellor, who was frequently and openly stigmatized as a
traitor. The result of the events in Vienna was greatly to
exacerbate the general European situation and to render the
chances of success for the negotiation of the new Eastern Locarno
Agreement even slighter than they had been before.

3

In the present state of development of this possible new
departure in European diplomacy it is unwise to make any
definite comment save that of speculation on the potential
results. Has France really got her own way at last, and would
the conclusion of this new agreement really open the door, as
Germany avers, to the French hegemony over Europe ?
Admittedly, it would seem that, so far as Germany is concerned,
French diplomacy has won a signal victory ; for whether Germany
accepted or rejected the plan she was placed at a disadvantage.
But may it not be that the advantages to France of her new
friendship with the Soviet Union are not altogether certain ?
It must be remembered that the initative in the original proposal
came from the U.S.S.R., who is afraid not of Germany but of
Japan, and if Germany were ever to become dangerous to the
U.S.S.R. it would be when she was engaged with Japan. An
entente with the Soviet Union, taking the definite form of a
guarantee of her western frontier, might in such case prove more
of a liability to France than an asset. It might prove a very
serious business indeed, committing her even to an attack on
Germany's western frontier, which, in any case murderous,
might, if unsuccessful, provoke a counter-attack. In such an
event, would the Western Locarno Pact of 1925 become operative ?
And would Great Britain and Italy become involved ? And in
any case who would be the aggressor ?

These are questions which merit the greatest consideration, and
their answers do not tend towards a breaking of the disarmament deadlock. If the new agreement now under discussion

is really calculated to provide France with that elusive degree of security necessary before she can discuss disarmament, then not only is there no objection to it but it must be furthered in every way possible. If, however, by reason of its complications it merely increases the unrest and suspicion in Europe, it may well prove a danger. For it is not inconceivable that, faced with the dread of encirclement and in the grip of a serious economic crisis, the same leaders of Germany who shot down the " conspirators " of 30th June without trial might, in a last desperate attempt to rally the country to them, indulge in some international excess, and thus, Samson-like, precipitate disaster. For, taken in conjunction with the events of 30th June, the wanton killing of Dr. Dollfuss on 25th July has shown to the world all too clearly the ruthless methods which National-Socialism, whether German or Austrian, will not hesitate to employ to attain its set objectives. All hope of disarmament, or even of security, is vain until the gangster element has been eliminated from international politics. For if war was possible before, it has become one hundred per cent more so since the introduction of this new development.

In the words which Signor Mussolini has used so recently (24th August), " Nobody in Europe wants war, but war is in the air and might break out at any moment."

APPENDIX I

THE YEAR 1931

1

Almost from the beginning of the year there began a series of events all tending towards the aggravation rather than the amelioration of the European situation, until in the autumn a concatenation of circumstances had placed France in a position in which, both from a military and a financial view-point, she could virtually dictate to the rest of Europe. Indeed, even by the summer, the idea of disarmament had been forced into the background of public interests by the more pressing matter of the general economic and financial crisis, which in the course of a few short weeks brought Germany, Austria, and Hungary to the brink of bankruptcy, forced Great Britain to abandon the Gold Standard, and involved the £ sterling in a fight for existence such as it had never previously experienced.

Early in 1931 it became evident that the result of German extravagance in state and municipal works and social insurance, to which the Agent-General for Reparations had called attention in his Reports,[1] taken in conjunction with the effect of the world-wide economic depression, would render Germany unable to meet her reparation obligations, and would necessitate a revision of the Young Plan Agreements reached at The Hague in the previous year. A moratorium from her debts and the obtaining of credits or a long-term loan were essential for the preservation of the economic life of Germany, and it was therefore a singularly unpropitious moment to throw a bomb-shell into the camp of those who alone could grant her these necessities.

On 19th March, 1931, there was signed and published in Vienna an Austro-German Protocol for the establishment of a Customs Union. It embodied proposals for an Agreement between the two countries under which a single customs law and a single customs tariff would be put into force in their territory, and in accordance with which no customs duty on imports or exports would be levied on exchanges of goods between them.

The effect on Europe of the announcement of this action was symptomatic of the very real feeling of insecurity lying dormant therein, and it is difficult to over-emphasize the lack of wisdom displayed by the German Foreign Office in taking such a step.

The idea of such a Customs Union revived, not only the old bogy of the *Anschluss* to terrify the Little Entente, but also rekindled in French minds the fear of German economic superiority. At the same time it alienated from Germany a measure of Italian sympathy.

The reaction on the disarmament situation was disastrous. The French Government took the opportunity to break off the naval conversations with Italy on 28th March,[2] and on 9th April the President of the Republic delivered a speech at Nice, the more important because of the rarity of M. Doumergue's political utterances. After reproaching Germany for her latest step, which, the French Government claimed, had taken them completely by surprise, the President struck a note of warning in the matter of disarmament which was maintained in all subsequent French announcements on this subject. " So long as the League of Nations—to which she (France) is so loyally attached—has not at its disposal a military force sufficient to enforce the execution of its decisions on all not willing to accept them voluntarily, she must keep vigilant watch and ward and rely to a large extent upon herself. . . . A country like ours, which has been taught by bitter experience the cruel surprises to which it may be exposed, must not, so long as no powerful international force has been set on foot, allow itself to reduce its own forces below the level demanded by the needs of the security and integrity of the Mother-country and the Colonies." [3]

The situation was acerbated rather than palliated by the statement of the German Government that they were prepared to conclude similar Customs agreements with any other country who might wish to do so. In this suggestion the French at once saw a challenge to the plans put forward in M. Briand's European Federation Movement.

So strained did the European situation become, that the advisability of postponing the Disarmament Conference was debated in the English Press and was even discussed in official circles.

At the request of the British Government, the question of the Customs Union was placed on the Agenda of the May Session of the Council, on the ground that it might be found to be contrary to the stipulations of certain international instruments, namely, Article 88 of the Treaty of St. Germain and Protocol No. 1 signed at Geneva on 4th October, 1922.[4] On the motion of the British representative the question of the legality of the proposed Austro-German Customs Union was referred to the Permanent Court of International Justice for an advisory opinion, it being understood that there would be no further negotiations until the Court had given its opinion (19th May, 1931).[5]

A further series of events occurring almost at the same time
did little to improve the situation. Towards the end of April
it became known that the first of the German 10,000-ton
" pocket-battleships ", constructed within the scope allowed by
the Treaty of Versailles, was nearing the moment of launching,
and it was understood that the German naval architects had
succeeded in creating a war vessel which was superior in
every way to anything in its own class. It could sink anything
that could catch it and could escape from anything that could
sink it.[6]

Nowhere were the possibilities of this new craft more appreciated than in Paris, where it was realized that, if Germany
built up to the full naval strength allowed her by the Treaty,
she would, in the event of the General Disarmament Conference
abolishing capital ships, become once more a first-class naval
Power on a scale very much superior to that of France. The
French reply to this new potential threat was contained in
the Naval Budget presented to the Chamber on 7th May, wherein
provision was made for a battleship of 23,000 tons. The report
on the building programme, issued on 11th June, showed that,
whereas the previous apportionment had been 70 per cent
of light vessels and 30 per cent of submarines, the new programme was divided into 60 per cent of battleships, 40 per cent
of light vessels, and no submarines. The necessity for this
change was attributed to the construction of the *Deutschland*.[7]

The debate which followed the presentation of this report
disclosed in the Chamber an unexpectedly friendly attitude
towards the policy of disarmament. The full consequences of
the projected construction of a 23,000-ton battleship and its
probable effect on the construction programme of other naval
Powers were fully debated, and from more than one quarter
came the opinion that such an action on the eve of the Disarmament Conference would be absurd and out of keeping with the
spirit of that gathering. On 18th June, therefore, the Chamber
passed the budget with a cut of more than 50 per cent. (£4
million instead of £8,799,680) and agreed to refer back the
appropriation for the new battleship for further study.

This conciliatory gesture on the part of the Lower House was,
however, offset by the action of the Senate, which, on 2nd July
(in the midst of the Franco-American negotiations for the
adoption of the Hoover proposal), rejected the modified Naval
Budget, accepted a motion calling on the Government for the
immediate laying down " of a cruiser designed to reply to the
construction of the *Deutschland*," and two days later passed
an additional appropriation of some £20 million to complete
the chain of fortifications on the Eastern frontier, a project on
which nearly £11½ million had already been spent.

2

To return now to Germany, where the financial and economic situation had rapidly worsened. No longer was it a question of *will* Germany declare a moratorium, but rather of *when* will a moratorium be declared. The Chancellor and the Foreign Minister were due in England for a conference early in June, and it was felt that, if possible, no irrevocable step should be taken until after this meeting.[8]

Drs. Brüning and Curtius visited England from 5th to 9th June and conferred frankly and freely with Mr. MacDonald and Mr. Arthur Henderson at Chequers. The main advantage of this Conference was that for the first time the German statesmen were enabled to explain personally to their British " opposite numbers " the full gravity of their position.[9]

At the same moment the German Government in Berlin issued a new Emergency Decree—the third since July, 1930— imposing heavy increased taxation and stringent cuts in salaries and social insurance. This was accompanied by a Manifesto to the Nation signed by President von Hindenburg, designed alike for internal and external consumption, and containing a warning to the world at large that Germany had reached her ultimate capacity to pay :—

> " We have made every effort to fulfil obligations resulting from a lost war. We have, too, made use of foreign help for this purpose to a large extent. That is no longer possible. The mobilization of the last forces and reserves of all sections of the population gives the German Government the right, and renders it its duty to its own people, to declare to the world : The limit of the privations which we can impose on our nation has been reached ! The assumptions upon which the New [Young] Plan was based have been proved erroneous by the course taken by world developments. The alleviation which it was the intention of all concerned that the New Plan should bring to the German nation, and which at first it gave promise of doing, has not been brought by it. It is clear to the Government that the economic and financial situation of the Reich, which is menaced in the extreme, inevitably compels the relief of Germany from the intolerable reparation obligations. The economic recovery of the world is also involved." [10]

It was confidently hoped and believed in Germany that, as a result of the Chequers Conversations, a moratorium would be declared, and it therefore caused the greatest disappointment that, on his return to Berlin, the Chancellor made no statement to this effect. As a result there occurred a political crisis which in its turn so affected foreign confidence in German credit as to occasion very considerable withdrawals of gold. It was

estimated that the political uncertainties of 10th to 19th June
cost the Reichsbank a milliard marks and it seemed certain
that a financial crash in Germany was inevitable.

Then on the morning of Sunday, 21st June, appeared those
Extrablätter containing the welcome news of President Hoover's
proposal for a " War-debt Holiday " and the clouds lifted almost
visibly from the German horizon.[11]

In effect Mr. Hoover proposed " the postponement during
one year of all payments on inter-Governmental debts, reparations and relief debts, both principal and interest . . ." and
gave a lead in that, " subject to confirmation by Congress, the
American Government will postpone all payments upon debts
of foreign Governments to the American Government, payable
during the fiscal year beginning July next, conditional on a
like postponement for one year of all payments on inter-
Governmental debts owing to the important creditor-Powers."

Great Britain and the Dominions,[12] Italy, and Japan gave
immediate approval and adhesion to this proposal, but France
demurred, being anxious to secure the guarantee of the continuance of the unconditional annuities under the Young Plan
and of the return into operation of the full Plan at the conclusion of the Hoover Year. The essential value of the Hoover
Proposal clearly lay in its psychological effect, and speedy
action was necessary if the full benefit was to be derived from
the offer.

For this reason it was the more regrettable that the Franco-
American negotiations in Paris relative to the French adherence
to the Hoover Plan should have dragged on until 5th July, by
which time developments in Germany had so seriously affected
that country's financial condition that, within the space of
a few days, the problem Mr. Hoover's proposal was intended to
solve reappeared in a form even more acute than before.[13]

The delay in putting the Hoover Plan into operation resulted
in Germany in an increased loss of confidence in the mark and
an accentuated flight of capital abroad. The emergency measures
taken by the Government failed to have an immediate effect,
and an aerial dash by Dr. Luther, President of the Reichsbank,
to London and Paris on 8th–9th July, in an attempt to gain
further credits abroad, though a complete and signal failure,
served to re-emphasize the necessity of further and immediate
action.[14]

It was at this moment that a rather more sinister note crept
into the course of events. It became known officially that
France was prepared to give financial assistance to Germany—
but on her own terms, terms which included the giving of
certain " political guarantees " by Germany. The German-
Austrian *Zollunion* was to be abandoned ; all work on the

construction of the second " pocket-battleship ", the *Ersatz Lothringen*, due to be launched in 1934, must cease ; a " political moratorium " must be declared, meaning that all Treaty Revision agitation must stop, and Germany must dissolve (forcibly if need be), such militant organizations as the *Stahlhelm*.[15] Last, but not least, Germany was to guarantee the integrity of her Eastern frontier by the signing of a Pact similar to the Western Locarno Pact of 1925.

The German Government contended that the acceptance of any of these conditions would endanger the Brüning Cabinet and so open the door to the possibility of serious international complications. Moreover, the case of the Customs Union was *sub judice* and the construction of the battleship was already employing a considerable number of men who would be thrown out of employment were it scrapped, while no Government could agree to an Eastern Guarantee. Pact and survive in office twenty-four hours. Apart from this, the view in official circles in Berlin was that Germany was already disarmed to the bone, and that the French demands placed a highly disagreeable extra burden on her internal policy because they emphasized and increased the German feeling of helplessness and inequality with other nations.

Thus matters stood on the eve of the Conferences of Ministers held in Paris and London (18th–22nd July).[16] Germany was definitely not prepared to accept the French conditions of assistance and some other method had to be found. As a result no long-term loan was secured, but the London Conference closed with a recommendation for a " Stand-still " Agreement, whereby no further short-term credits still with Germany should be withdrawn and the £20 million credit to the Reichsbank, falling due on 16th August, should be extended for a further ninety days. It was also agreed that the Bank for International Settlements should appoint an expert committee to go into the wider question of the future financial position of Germany, and to examine the question of the possibility of converting the existing short-term credits into long-term loans. This Committee sat at Basle from 8th–17th August and produced the Layton-Wiggin Report, recommending to the statesmen of Europe an early settlement of the whole question of inter-governmental payments.[17]

3

It has been necessary to trace the course of events during the summer of 1931, partly because it is impossible to ignore the most momentous happenings of the post-war period, and partly because of the very strong though indirect influence which these happenings have had on the disarmament problem. For one of the most salient factors which have emerged from the welter of financial chaos in which the world is still floundering is the financial and political predominance of France in Europe, which has had its inevitable effect on the future of disarmament.

France at the close of the London Conference occupied a position in Europe unequalled since the Great War. A large portion of the gold of the world lay in the vaults of the Banque de France,[18] French unemployment was negligible, French currency stable, and the French Army and Air Force the largest (with the exception of the Red forces) on the Continent. At a moment when many European States needed financial assistance and needed it desperately and speedily, France, alone of the Great Powers, was in a position to supply it—but on her own terms. In every case political conditions accompanied the granting of aid. In return for French loans Hungary departed from her Italian and German orientation, dispensed with the services of Count Bethlen, and modified her Treaty Revision agitation ; Austria renounced, in the most humiliating circumstances, the Customs Union with Germany, and Yugoslavia returned from the dictatorial to the constitutional form of Government.

Even before the draining of her reserves forced Great Britain to abandon the gold standard, on 19th September, France had established her dominance in Europe, and if ever she had attained her long dreamed of state of security it was in the summer of 1931.[19]

What then was the effect on the disarmament problem of this attainment by France to the pinnacle of power ? Was she urged by the other Great Powers to utilize her unique position by making a gesture ? Or did France herself, in the surety of her national security, take the opportunity which presented itself by taking the lead in disarmament ? Far from endeavouring to persuade the French to modify their attitude towards the problem at issue, the only publicly expressed views on the subject went in the opposite direction. In the course of the disarmament debate in the House of Commons on 29th June, both the Prime Minister and the then Leader of the Opposition, Mr. Stanley Baldwin, went out of their way to send a remarkable message of sympathy to France in her nervousness regarding disarmament.

No doubt the Quai d'Orsay was greatly pleased with this unsolicited testimonial of appreciation from across the Channel, and any illusions as to whether French policy had undergone any modification as a result of the London Conference must have been shattered on 21st July by the publication of a Memorandum on the reduction and limitation of armaments prepared in response to the request of the Council of the League at its January session.[20]

The Memorandum contained a full statement of the land, sea, and air forces of France, but included sections dealing with the political aspect of the problem, and here the French views were an elaboration of those set forth by President Doumergue on 9th April,[21] or in a word—Back to the Protocol.

" Within a system of international co-operation (*solidarité*) such as the League of Nations, a reduction of armaments might become more important for each State as mutual assistance against aggression became better organized, more certain and more rapid. . . . Insecurity for one State means insecurity for all. . . . By reason of the dangers threatening the weaker or more exposed States, the general reduction of armaments lays upon the stronger or less threatened Powers responsibilities which they cannot elude."

The French Government was convinced of the

" necessity of a security guaranteed to every State by assistance which should be mutual, effective and prompt. . . . By such assistance alone can the League of Nations be given sufficient strength, material and moral, to prevent the launching of an aggression."

Such a revival of the ideas of 1924 was completely at variance with the foreign policy of Great Britain, which had, since Locarno, been based on the Chamberlain formula of " special agreements to meet special needs ", and was essentially opposed to the undertaking by this country of fresh security obligations of a general nature.

It was, however, to Germany that the most important passages of the Memorandum referred :—

" Reduction of armaments implies confidence. Can that confidence be expected to prevail, so long as the feeling is abroad that, in the eyes of many, the problem is not so much one of organizing peace for the benefit of all, as of modifying the existing order for the benefit of a few, and so long as it is possible for some States to feel that the very existence conferred upon them by the Treaties is threatened ? The decision of the Conference must be based upon respect for the Treaties.

" Should an attempt be made, for instance, in the name of a theoretical principle of equality, to modify the relative situation created by the provisions of Part V of the Peace Treaties, it would prove impossible to maintain the reductions already accomplished and still less practicable would become the general limitation of armaments."

Elsewhere the Memorandum dealt even more definitely with the German theory of equality.

" It by no means follows, however, that the Member States of the League, whose standards of forces have not been expressly defined by the Treaties, are under the obligation of adopting either the methods or the figures laid down in Part V of the Treaties as regards the general limitation of armaments. When the Treaties were framed, at no time and at no place was the agreement advanced, either in speech or in writing, that other States should in their turn place their armaments on the level prescribed for certain States. . . . Were it to be admitted that the standards prescribed in Part V of the Treaties for certain States should apply in an equal and uniform manner to other States, Article VIII of the League Covenant would clearly be bereft of all value and all significance."

A week later, addressing a reunion of officers of the National Reserve at Arcachon on 27th July, M. Maginot, French War Minister, further emphasized this latter aspect. At the Disarmament Conference, he said, France would demand that in the military stipulations laid down for certain nations the strength of their respective forces must be excluded from the discussions. France had only been able to reduce her forces owing to the limitation of armaments imposed on Germany by the Treaty, and if Germany were to be free to re-arm, France would be obliged to increase her armaments. In any case, no contribution could be made by France to a general limitation of armaments unless guarantees for the maintenance of international order were to take the place of the guarantees of security represented by military forces.[22]

Taken in conjunction the French Memorandum and M. Maginot's speech represent the most depressing contribution yet made on the subject of disarmament. Here is found the seal of official approval set upon M. Massigli's statement of 27th November, 1930, at the last session of the Preparatory Commission, when he assured his hearers that, only on the condition that Germany formally re-affirmed her disarmament obligations under the Treaty of Versailles, could France come to the Disarmament Conference :—

> "When the Conference meets, a certain number of Powers, including France, will submit proposals in figures for the limitation of their armaments. These proposals will be calculated in relation to a given condition ; they will correspond to a given degree of security. In determining this degree of security, the regime which results from the strict application of the military clauses of the Peace Treaties forms an essential factor."

Of the two conditions demanded as the price of French disarmament, the first, a general guarantee of security, was inacceptable to Great Britain, and the second, the perpetuation of the *status quo* in regard to the disarmament of the ex-enemy States, was impossible for any German Government to agree to, since the granting of the principles of equality was the one concrete achievement which Germany expected to gain from the Conference.

In view of this intransigent attitude officially adopted by France, the advisability of holding the Conference at all began to be questioned in various quarters, and indeed rumour began to circulate that the postponement of the Conference was really the aim of the French Government, who had launched their Memorandum in the nature of a torpedo. To many of the more earnest proponents of disarmament, on the other hand, it seemed that it would be better to postpone the Conference rather than to hold it in face of its almost certain failure, a failure which would almost certainly entail the withdrawal of Germany from the League of Nations.

Thus the summer of 1931 closed, and the September Assembly of the League of Nations opened, with a deep depression blanketing the world and the prospects of the Disarmament Conference as dark as they well could be.[23] It seemed that the one consideration which might induce the peoples of the world to reduce their armaments would be the sheer inability to find sufficient funds to continue their construction.

4

The Twelfth Assembly of the League of Nations held at Geneva in the month of September 1931 made three important contributions to the programme towards disarmament. These were, first the definite statement by M. Briand that France did not propose that the Disarmament Conference should be postponed [24] ; secondly, the participation of a United States representative in the discussions of the Third Committee, thereby ending the existing anomaly that that body should discuss the reduction of armaments without the presence of delegates from certain countries which were already associated with the work of the Preparatory Commission and had every intention of taking part in the Disarmament Conference ; and, thirdly, the Italian proposal for an Arms Truce until after the close of the Conference.

Though the first and second of these events had their own importance in that, respectively, they ensured the meeting of the Conference and re-emphasized the keen interest of the United States in its work and success, it was around the Italian proposal that the main interest concentrated.

In a speech to the Assembly on 8th September, Signor Grandi, Italian Minister for Foreign Affairs, conveyed the Italian proposal to the League that, from that date, until at least the end of the Disarmament Conference, there should be a " real and effective truce in armaments ".[25] This suggestion, arising in part out of the Conference held earlier in the year (9th-14th July), between Signor Mussolini and Mr. Stimson, American Secretary of State, was warmly supported in subsequent speeches by Lord Cecil and Dr. Curtius. The latter took the opportunity of recalling to the League its particular responsibility for disarmament and of warning it of its loss of authority if it failed in this task. In fact failure might be disastrous for it—a point which the speaker emphasized and repeated.

The Italian proposal received the general approval in nearly all the speeches made in the earlier Plenary Sessions except that of M. Briand, in which mention of it was conspicuous by its absence.

The first step towards implementing the proposal was taken by the Neutral *bloc* (Denmark, Norway, the Netherlands, Sweden, and Switzerland) by putting forward a draft resolution calling on the Assembly to request the Council

> " To urge all Governments convened to the said Conference to show their firm determination to support the efforts to ensure peace and re-establish mutual confidence by abstaining, pending the result of the Conference, from any measure leading to an increase in the present level of their armaments."

This resolution was referred to the Third Committee for discussion, as a result of which it was agreed to invite the representatives of non-member States to take part in the deliberations of the Committee.[26] After two days' debate, the Italian representative, General de Marinis, in support of his contention that the Resolution of the Neutral *bloc* was inadequate, presented one of his own, which represented the Italian form of the proposal for an Arms Truce.

The Italian draft Resolution contained four main points :—

> (1) Each Government undertakes not to increase the expenditure on land armaments already authorized for the current financial year and likewise not to exceed the total of such expenditure during the next financial year until the expiration of the Truce.
>
> (2) Each Government undertakes not to place any warships on the stocks, until the expiration of the Truce, provided always that vessels under construction may be continued and completed. [27]
>
> (3) Each Government undertakes to suspend the construction of additional military aircraft during the Truce, except to replace machines which are placed out of commission during the Truce.
>
> (4) The duration of the Truce shall be one year, dating from 1st November, 1931.

In the ensuing discussion on the two draft Resolutions, it became clear that while the five original sponsors of the first Resolution preferred their own draft, the remainder of the

Committee were principally concerned with the Marinis proposal.
The United States and a number of smaller Powers were supported
by Italy, while France, with Yugoslavia and Rumania, were
opposed.   Lord Cecil declared that the British Government
favoured the Italian draft, provided that all other countries
agreed to it as well.   The Japanese, with a certain *naïveté*,
advocated the postponement of the whole question until
February 1932.

In consideration of the divergency of views it was at length
agreed to refer the two Resolutions to a drafting committee with
the hope that a compromise text acceptable to all might thus be
evoked.   This method proved successful, for on 29th September
the Third Committee adopted unanimously the new draft Resolution, which two days later received similar approval from the
Assembly.[28]

The Resolution, after its preamble, reads as follows

" In view of the fact that an undertaking on the part of all
States not to increase their armaments would help to create an
atmosphere of confidence, to prevent competition in armaments,
and to prepare the ground for the forthcoming Conference, the
Assembly requests the Governments invited to the Disarmament
Conference to prepare for this event by means of an armaments
truce, and accordingly requests the Council to urge the Governments convened to the said Conference to give proof of their
earnest desire for the successful issue of the efforts to ensure an
organized peace and, without prejudicing the decisions of the
Conference or the programmes or proposals submitted by each
Government, to refrain from any measures involving an increase
in their armaments.

" The Assembly likewise requests the Council to ask the Governments to state, before 1st November, 1931, whether they are
prepared for a period of one year as from this date to accept
this truce in armaments."

In its accompanying Report the Third Committee showed
clearly that " this Resolution aims at preventing any increase
of the efforts at present made in respect of the whole of each
country's armaments ".

Apart from its value as a mark of progress on the road towards
disarmament, the Arms Truce may be regarded as a high point
scored by Italy in her continuous diplomatic conflict with
France.   The fact that Italy was enabled to take the lead for
the first time, and to establish her position before the world
as a peace-seeking nation, was a considerable achievement for the
diplomacy of Signor Mussolini.

As to the effectiveness of the Truce, this may best be judged
from the fact that on 30th November fifty nations had
accepted the proposal.

5

As the year drew on towards its close, circumstances became no more favourable for the Disarmament Conference.   The practical relationship between the reduction of all international War Debts (as a possible solution of the world's economic difficulty) with the reduction of armaments had been equally emphasized by President Hoover in his Address on 4th May to the Congress of the International Chamber of Commerce at Washington.   Co-operation between the European countries, or between Europe and the United States, undertaken with a view to ameliorating the economic depression, was, he argued, futile, and would be futile, until such a time as action had been successfully taken to reduce armaments.[29]

The acceptance by Europe of the Hoover Moratorium of 1st July was the first material advance on this line of policy, and M. Laval was anxious to be quite clear in his own mind as to whether Mr. Hoover intended to pursue this policy further or not.   He went to Washington in October, therefore, with the hope of converting official opinion in the United States to the French disarmament thesis and of ensuring the resumption of operation of the Young Plan at the end of the Hoover Year. M. Laval regained for France the initiative in the matter of reparations, but at the same time found himself " left with the baby ", for, at a later date, when France hoped for action on the part of America, Mr. Hoover reminded M. Laval that the initiative must now come from Europe.[30]   In addition he received very little encouragement for his disarmament policy in Washington, since, on his return to Europe, he made a declaration to the Press on 1st November to the effect that France would " remain mistress of her own security until the nations of the world shall have found effective means of realizing the organization of peace on a firm and permanent basis ", which is nothing more than a repetition of the sentiments contained in the French Memorandum of 21st July.

Indeed, rather than meeting with encouragement, French policy had suffered a definite rebuff at the hands of Senator Borah, Chairman of the Senate Committee on Foreign Relations, who, in a statement on 25th October, the date on which President Hoover and M. Laval issued their joint statement, declared himself in favour of the revision of the Peace Treaties, a sentiment which was re-echoed in a speech at Naples the same day by Signor Mussolini, who put to his audience the poignant question " how is it possible to speak of reconstruction unless there is a modification in certain clauses of certain Peace Treaties which have driven the world to the brink of material disaster and moral despair ? "

These words of the Italian Premier, taken in conjunction with those of Signor Grandi on the following day (26th October) in Berlin to the effect that the " Head of the Italian Government . . . has more than once declared that the reconstruction of Germany must be regarded as one of the most important elements in the reconstruction of Europe and the whole world ", indicate the reaffirmation of Italian support for Germany.

If the visit of M. Laval to America had no direct results, it did, however, convince the French Premier that nothing further was to be secured from the United States, and that the time had come for the necessary effort towards a *rapprochement* with Germany. The " Standstill " Agreement terminated on 29th February, 1932, and it was necessary to take some steps to meet the circumstances which would arise at the close of the Hoover Moratorium in July of the same year. It was no longer possible to refuse to realize the fact that Germany would not be capable of resuming payments, and that provision must be made for this eventuality.

With this end in view conversations were opened in Paris on 3rd November between M. Briand and Herr von Hoesch, the German Ambassador, which resulted in an agreement on 19th November whereby Germany should apply to the Bank for International Settlements for the putting into operation of the provisions of the Young Plan for the setting up of a special Advisory Committee whose function it was " to consider the circumstances and conditions which have led up to the necessity for postponement or have created a situation in which Germany considers that her exchange and economic life may be seriously endangered by further transfers of the postponable portion of the annuity, and make a full investigation of Germany's position in regard to her obligations." [31]

This Committee began its discussions at Basle on 7th December. Simultaneously with this application for a moratorium, a Committee of the creditor States met in Berlin to consider what should be done at the termination of the " Standstill " Agreement. On 23rd December, the Basle Committee signed the report endorsing strongly the views expressed by the Wiggin Committee in the previous August and calling once more for a speedy solution of the joint problems of war debts and reparations. Almost at the same moment the United States Congress in ratifying the Hoover Moratorium were adding a reservation which made it impossible for the Moratorium to be extended and virtually vetoed any potential debt settlement.[33]

A further, and much more serious complication, had arisen in the case of the Sino-Japanese dispute in Manchuria. This matter, which involved not only an infringement of the Articles of the Covenant of the League, but also of the provisions of the Kellogg Pact, had come before the Council of the League at its Session in September. The Council had adopted a Resolution calling upon Japan to withdraw her troops from the positions they had captured in Manchuria by 16th November, at which date the Council would reassemble in Paris.

When, however, this date arrived it was found that not only had Japan not withdrawn her troops, but had, in fact, extended her line and at the moment when the Paris Session of the Council opened fighting was in progress.

The subsequent deliberations of the Council, which was unable to persuade Japan to make any movement towards withdrawal, resulted only in the despatch to Manchuria of a League Commission with very restricted terms of reference.

The Manchurian dispute disclosed many of the weak points in the League machinery, and resulted in considerable loss of prestige to that body, many Powers feeling that the guarantee of security contained in the Covenant had been put to the test and found wanting.[34]

The events of the last months of the year 1931 may be said, then, to have added in no way to the hopes and chances of success of the Disarmament Conference.

NOTES TO APPENDIX I

[1] See *The Reparation Settlement*, by J. W. Wheeler-Bennett and Hugh Latimer (Allen and Unwin, 1930), pp. 65–6.

[2] These conversations had been desultorily in progress since the visit of Mr. Henderson and Mr. A. V. Alexander to Rome and Paris at the beginning of March, in an effort to secure an agreement between France and Italy which would allow of their signing the London Naval Agreement of 1930. See *Disarmament and Security*, pp. 215–239.

[3] The hint contained in this speech that France would demand as part of the price of her disarmament the revival in some form of the security of the Geneva Protocol of 1924 became stronger in subsequent speeches as the year grew older and the date of the Conference approached.

[4] Article 88 of the Treaty of St. Germain (corresponding to Article 80 of the Treaty of Versailles) declares that the independence of Austria is inalienable, otherwise than with the consent of the Council of the League ; and Austria undertakes to abstain from any act which might, directly or indirectly, compromise her independence.   The Protocol of 4th October, 1922, was the instrument under which Austria was accorded a loan under the auspices of the League to assist in her financial reconstruction.   It included an obligation undertaken by Austria not to enter into any negotiations which might, directly or indirectly, compromise her independence, and, further, not to accord to any State a special regime or exclusive advantage calculated to threaten that independence.

[5] For documents of the Austro-German *Zollunion* Case : see *Documents on International Affairs, 1931*, pp. 1–16.

[6] Writing in 1930 on the significance of this vessel, the author said that,

" Stimulated by this restriction (Article 190 of the Treaty of Versailles), the German naval architects have designed a ' pocket-battleship ', which, if its theoretical merits are borne out in practice, threatens to revolutionize naval construction and upset the existing balance of naval strength." See *The Reparation Settlement*, p. 22.

[7] The *Deutschland* was launched at Kiel on 19th May in the presence of President von Hindenburg and the Imperial Chancellor, Dr. Brüning. The circumstances of the actual launching and christening were such as might interest the superstitious reader. At the moment when the Chancellor had reached in his speech a passage containing the words. " Disarmament . . . League of Nations " . . . the vessel was inadvertently allowed to slide prematurely from the stocks into the water, leaving the President grasping an unbroken bottle of champagne and the Chancellor with his peroration in mid-air. " Like Germany, she was so tired of phrases," commented an onlooker. The ceremony of christening was performed later from a launch.

[8] The Chequers Conference marked the inauguration of a series of similar meetings between the Chief Ministers of the Great Powers. The German Minister paid subsequent visits to Paris and Rome in July and August, while the British Prime Minister and Foreign Secretary went to Berlin at the end of July. The French Premier and Foreign Minister visited Berlin and Rome in September and October, and in the latter month M. Laval went to confer with President Hoover in Washington. The United States Secretaries of the Treasury and of State were in Europe throughout the summer, and conferred with their colleagues in various capitals.

[9] The Chequers Conference also met under the shadow of the recent collapse of the important Austrian banking house, the Kreditanstalt.

[10] See *The Wreck of Reparations*, by J. W. Wheeler-Bennett (Allen and Unwin, 1933), pp. 41–4.

[11] The author was in Berlin and Bremen during these eventful June days, and was greatly impressed by the psychological effect of the announcement of the Hoover Plan. Equally impressive was the return of despair during the prolongation of the subsequent Franco-American negotiations in Paris. It was felt that if the Plan was to have its intended beneficial effect its operation must be immediate, and as the negotiations dragged on (until 6th July) so proportionately did the atmosphere of despair descend once more upon Germany, the more intensified by reason of its brief alleviation.

[12] Great Britain's loss under the Hoover Plan was estimated by Mr. Snowden at approximately £11 million.

[13] It is obviously impossible in a few lines to do anything but convey the barest outline of the important events of June and July, 1931. The full story of the Hoover Proposal and the subsequent Franco-American negotiations is to be found in *The Wreck of Reparations*, pp. 46–71.

[14] Illustrative of the critical economic situation prevailing in Germany at that moment was the failure of the North German Wool Corporation (*Nordwolle*) on 8th July and the closing of the doors of the Darmstädter und Nationalbank (Danat) on 13th July.

[15] The *Stahlhelm* rallies at Coblenz in the summer of 1930 and at Oels in June, 1931, had occasioned considerable anxiety to the French and Polish Foreign Offices respectively.

[16] An account of the Paris and London Conferences is given in *The Wreck of Reparations*, pp. 75–81.

[17] See *The Wreck of Reparations*, pp. 86–95. For text of the *Report*, see *Documents on International Affairs, 1931*, pp. 133–160.

[18] Heavy gold withdrawals from the Bank of England necessitated Great Britain's accepting a £25 million credit from France in July, 1931. In August a further credit of £40 million was obtained. Similar Agreements were reached by Great Britain with the United States. The rate

of interest was 4½ per cent in all cases. Continued withdrawals and the inability to obtain further credits necessitated the abandonment of the Gold Standard by Great Britain on 9th September, 1931 (see *The Wreck of Reparations*, pp. 97–104).

[19] See *The Wreck of Reparations*, chapter iv, " M. Laval in Wonderland " for an account of French financial policy.

[20] For text of the French Memorandum, see *Documents on International Affairs, 1931*, pp. 43–7.

[21] See above, p. 251.

[22] For text of M. Maginot's speech, see *Documents on International Affairs, 1931*, pp. 47–9.

[23] One of the principal reasons for the general depression prevalent at the opening of the Assembly was the unfortunate circumstance which attended the closing of the *affaire* of the Austro-German Customs Union. On September 5th, by eight votes to seven, the Permanent Court of International Justice made public their opinion that the proposed Union was not legally compatible with the Protocol of 1922. Two days before, however, under pressure of the necessity of French financial assistance, the Austrian Chancellor had been forced to make a public announcement abandoning the project on behalf of his country. Though it is believed that the decision of the Court was known in Geneva on 3rd September, Dr. Schober was not allowed to make use of this information in making his statement. Dr. Curtius also made a statement of renunciation on behalf of Germany, and subsequently resigned on this issue on 6th October.

[24] In his speech on 10th September, Lord Cecil declared that " No Government, let alone the British Government, would tolerate postponement ", and M. Briand was seen to applaud this statement with vigorous hand-clapping. His own speech was made on the following day.

[25] For text of Signor Grandi's speech see *Documents on International Affairs, 1931*, p. 39.

[26] Afghanistan, Argentina, Brazil, Costa Rica, Egypt, Ecuador, Turkey, the United States, and the U.S.S.R. were invited, and of these the United States, Costa Rica, Brazil, Egypt, and Turkey accepted. The Soviet Government intimated that it was prepared to support the Italian proposal provided it should be adopted in a form obligatory for all countries and concerning all categories of armaments.

[27] It will be noted that the Italian Resolution had not been drafted without taking into consideration the Franco-Italian naval discussions which were proceeding during, but outside, the Assembly, between M. Massigli and Signor Rossi. This clause would also permit Germany to continue work on the second " pocket-battleship ".

[28] In the vote on the adoption of the Resolution Persia abstained.

[29] For text of President Hoover's speech see *Documents on International Affairs, 1931*, pp. 109–111.

[30] See *The Wreck of Reparations*, pp. 118–123.

[31] See *The Wreck of Reparations*, pp. 124–7. For text of the German Government's Memorandum, see *Documents on International Affairs, 1931*, pp. 160–2.

[32] See *The Wreck of Reparations*, pp. 141–156. For text of the Basle Report, see *Documents on International Affairs, 1931*, pp. 164–202.

[33] See *The Wreck of Reparations*, chap. vi " Canutes in Congress," pp. 157–171.

[34] For full documentation of the Sino-Japanese Dispute see *Documents on International Affairs, 1932*. Edited by J. W. Wheeler-Bennett (Oxford University Press, 1933), pp. 240–398.

APPENDIX II

BRITISH DRAFT CONVENTION

Presented to the Disarmament Conference on 16th March, 1933.

PART I [1]

SECURITY

ARTICLE 1

In the event of a breach or threat of breach of the Pact of Paris, either the Council or Assembly of the League of Nations or one of the parties to the present Convention who are not Members of the League of Nations may propose immediate consultation between the Council or Assembly and any of the said parties to the present Convention.

ARTICLE 2

It shall be the object of such consultation, (*a*) in the event of a threat of a breach of the Pact, to exchange views for the purpose of preserving the peace and averting a conflict ; (*b*) in the event of a breach of the Pact to use good offices for the restoration of peace ; and (*c*) in the event that it proves impossible thus to restore the peace, then to determine which party or parties to the dispute are to be held responsible.

ARTICLE 3

The provisions of the above Article do not in any way prejudice the rights and obligations of the Members of the League, nor conflict with nor limit the powers and duties of the Assembly and Council under the Covenant.

ARTICLES 4 AND 5

ARTICLE 6

The High Contracting Parties recognize that the provisions of Annex Y of the present Convention are likely to contribute

[1] The Articles of Part I were subsequently altered several times. For details see special note on p. 292.

to the maintenance of peace, and accordingly agree to base thereon any decisions which they may have to take, particularly in the Permanent Disarmament Commission, with a view to preventing any breach of the Pact of Paris by a Power which has signed Annex Y, determining the responsibility should such a breach occur and fixing the consequences.

The High Contracting Parties agree to refrain from any action which might hamper the application of the measures to be taken in the cases provided for by Articles 4, 5, and 6 of Annex Y, and not to recognize any *de facto* situation brought about by the breach of an international obligation on the part of a State recognized as the aggressor in application of the provisions of the said annex.

The High Contracting Parties Members of the League of Nations also undertake to comply with the provisions of Article 6 of the said annex as regards the application of Article 16 of the Covenant of the League of Nations to the signatories of the said annex.

The High Contracting Parties Members of the League and signatories of the Convention for Financial Assistance signed at Geneva on 2nd October, 1930, likewise undertake to comply with the provisions of Article 6 of the said annex as regards the application of that Convention.

PART II

DISARMAMENT

ARTICLE 7

The High Contracting Parties agree to limit their respective armaments as provided in the present Convention.

SECTION I.—EFFECTIVES

CHAPTER I.—PROVISIONS AS TO NUMERICAL LIMITATIONS

ARTICLE 8

The average daily effectives in the land, sea, and air armed forces of each of the High Contracting Parties shall not exceed the figures laid down for such Party in the tables annexed to this chapter.

ARTICLE 9

It is understood that effectives consist of : (*a*) All officers, officer cadets, N.C.O.'s, soldiers, sailors, airmen, reservists, and all other persons (such as military officials of the administrative, sanitary, or veterinary services or military agents) of equivalent status who perform a day's duty in the land, sea, and air armed forces ; (b) Persons who perform a day's duty in police forces or similar formations under the conditions prescribed in Article 12 ; (c) All other persons of at least 18 years of age who receive military training under the control of the State. Military training is taken to mean any training given to persons of at least 18 years of age, under the military regulations in force in each country or under regulations containing similar provisions, with a view to preparing those who receive it for performing military duty in the armed forces.

The main characteristics of this training are as follows :—

(1) Technical and tactical training in the use of the individual and other than individual arms used in war.

(2) Training in field service over broken ground.

Furthermore, in the examination of special cases account will be taken in particular of the following criteria :—

(1) Theoretical (by map) and field training of cadres.

(2) Use of military methods of communication and signalling.

Physical and sports training in the strict sense of the term, for whatever purpose given, shall not be regarded as military training.

ARTICLE 10

The High Contracting Parties undertake to prohibit any military training whatsoever except in organizations under the control of their respective Governments.

ARTICLE 11

The average daily effectives are reckoned by dividing the total number of days' duty performed by actual effectives in each year by the number of days in such year.

In the case of continuous service, every day shall count as a day's duty. A deduction of 5 per cent may in each case be made from the total average daily effectives on account of persons sick in hospital, persons on leave for two or more days, and persons prematurely discharged on leave. Any Party for which the above-mentioned absences represent a greater percentage may make a correspondingly larger deduction after furnishing to the Permanent Disarmament Commission details as to its basis of computation.

In the case of intermittent service or instruction, attendances aggregating six hours may, for the calculation of the average daily effectives, count as the equivalent of one day's duty.

ARTICLE 12

1. Subject to the provisions of paragraph 2 of this Article, a police force or similar formation will be included in the total of effectives in Table I if it has one or more of the following characteristics :—

(a) Arms other than individual (machine pistols, Lewis guns, machine-guns, and weapons of accompaniment, etc.).
(b) Training of a military nature other than close order drill, physical training, or technical training, in the use of individual arms.
(c) Transport, signalling, or engineer equipment of a suitable nature and on a sufficient scale to enable it to be employed by units in tactical operations.

The possession by a force of one or more of the above characteristics will, in principle, determine its inclusion in whole or in part in the calculation of effectives of the land armed forces. Cases which might appear doubtful after the present Convention comes into force should be referred to the Permanent Disarmament Commission, which will give a decision by reviewing the military capacity of the force in the light of the above characteristics and taking into account, in particular, the following confirmatory conditions :—

(i) Quartering in barracks.
(ii) Training in groups of 100 men or more.
(iii) Organization on a military basis.
(iv) Previous military training.
(v) The possession of the arms referred to in sub-paragraph (a) above in such numbers as to permit of the tactical employment of the forces possessing them as military units.

2. Of the police force maintained by any High Contracting Party and possessing one or more of the characteristics set out in paragraph 1 of this Article, a number not exceeding 10 per cent (General Commission, 4th May, P.V. 56, page 2) of the figure assigned to such Party in Table I annexed to this chapter may be exempted from inclusion in the effectives of the land armed forces of such party.

ARTICLE 13

The following naval effectives should be included among the effectives of the land armed forces :—

(a) Effectives employed in land coast defence.
(b) Marines who are normally in excess of those assigned to, or destined for, service afloat.
(c) Effectives coming within the classification of similar formations (as defined in Article 12).

Naval personnel serving ashore in the fleet services (training, administrative, etc.) as well as those assigned to, or destined for, service afloat, will be included in the effectives of the sea armed forces.

TABLE 1

TABLE OF AVERAGE DAILY EFFECTIVES WHICH ARE NOT TO BE EXCEEDED IN THE LAND ARMED FORCES

(*Note.*—This table contains only the figures which are suggested for the countries of continental Europe. It would, of course, require to be completed by the addition of figures in respect of all the other Parties.)

Party.	Land armed forces.	
	Stationed in home country.	Total including overseas.
Germany . . .	200,000	200,000
Belgium . . .	60,000	75,000
Bulgaria . . .	60,000	60,000
Spain . . .	120,000	170,000
France . . .	200,000	400,000
Greece . . .	60,000	60,000
Hungary . . .	60,000	60,000
Italy	200,000	250,000
Netherlands . .	25,000	75,000
Poland . . .	200,000	200,000
Portugal . . .	50,000	60,000
Rumania . . .	150,000	150,000
Czechoslovakia . .	100,000	100,000
U.S.S.R. . . .	500,000	500,000
Yugloslavia . .	100,000	100,000
Each other continental European State	No separate figure.	50,000

TABLE 2

Table of Average Daily Effectives which are not to be exceeded in the Sea Armed Forces. (The figures will have to be related to the naval material allowed to each Party.)

TABLE 3

Table of Average Daily Effectives which are not to be exceeded in the Air Armed Forces. (The figures will have to be related to the air material allowed to each Party.)

CHAPTER II.—SPECIAL PROVISIONS AS TO THE ORGANIZATION OF THE LAND ARMED FORCES STATIONED IN CONTINENTAL EUROPE.

ARTICLE 14

The provisions of this chapter apply only to the land armed forces stationed in continental Europe.

ARTICLE 15

Troops whose primary function is to provide drafts or reinforcements for overseas garrisons are excluded from the provisions of this chapter.

ARTICLE 16

The maximum total period of service for the effectives in the land armed forces stationed in continental Europe (excluding the troops mentioned in Article 15 above and the personnel referred to in Article 18) shall not exceed eight months.

Note.—In special cases to be decided by the Conference, the maximum total period of service may be extended to twelve months.

ARTICLE 17

For each man the total period of service is the total number of days comprised in the different periods of service to which he is liable under national law or by the terms of his contract to perform.

ARTICLE 18

In the land armed forces affected by this chapter the personnel whose length of service is greater than that prescribed in Article 16 shall not at any time exceed the following proportions of the average strength throughout the year of the said forces.

Officers, officer cadets, and persons of equivalent status $\dfrac{1}{x}$

N.C.O.s, soldiers, and persons of equivalent status $\dfrac{1}{y}$

The High Contracting Parties undertake not to group in units the personnel referred to in this Article except in the case of specialized units if provided for by the present Convention.

CHAPTER III.—PROVISIONS AS TO THE METHODS BY WHICH THE REDUCTIONS AND RE-ORGANIZATIONS ENTAILED BY THE PRECEDING CHAPTERS SHALL BE EFFECTED.

ARTICLE A

The reductions in the average daily effectives in the land armed forces of the High Contracting Parties which result from Table I annexed to Chapter I shall be carried out as follows :—

By the end of the second year from the coming into force of the Convention, 30 per cent of the total reduction required.

By the end of the fourth year from the coming into force of the Convention, 75 per cent of the total reduction required.

By the end of the fifth year from the coming into force of the Convention, 100 per cent of the total reduction required.

ARTICLE B

Any increases in the average daily effectives in the land armed forces of the High Contracting Parties which may result from Table I shall be carried out at a rate not exceeding that laid down in Article A for the reductions which result from the said Table.

ARTICLE C

This Article refers only to the land armed forces to which Chapter 2 of this Section applies.

1. The High Contracting Parties concerned will effect the reductions in their existing long-service personnel necessitated by Chapter 2 in the following proportions :—

By the end of the second year from the coming into force of the Convention 30 per cent.

By the end of the fourth year from the coming into force of the Convention 70 per cent.

By the end of the fifth year from the coming into force of the Convention, 100 per cent, less the percentage allowed to them under Article 18.

By long-service personnel in this Article is understood those effectives (excluding conscripts) whose period of service exceeds that prescribed in Article 16.

2. The maximum period of service which may be performed by effectives other than long-service personnel will be reduced to the period laid down in Article 16 as follows :—

For effectives commencing their service after the end of the third year from the coming into force of the Convention, by 50 per cent of the total reduction required.

For effectives commencing their service after the end of the fifth year from the coming into force of the Convention, by 100 per cent of the total reduction required.

Note :—The columns in the Publicity Tables (Part III of the Convention) will be arranged so that the rate of the reorganization carried out annually will be available for the information of the Permanent Disarmament Commission.

SECTION II. MATERIAL. LAND ARMAMENTS

ARTICLE 19

The maximum limit for the calibre of mobile land guns for the future shall be 115 mm. Existing mobile land guns up to 155 mm. may be retained, but all replacement or new construction of guns shall be within the maximum limit of 115 mm.

As existing guns shall only be regarded those for which orders were placed before the submission of the British draft to the Conference.

The maximum limit for the calibre of coast defence guns shall be 406 mm.

ARTICLE 20

For the purposes of the present Convention a tank is defined as follows :—

"A tank is a fully armoured, armed, self-propelled vehicle designed to cross broken ground, usually by means of tracks, and to overcome obstacles encountered on the battlefield."

ARTICLE 21

The maximum limit for the unladen weight of a tank shall be 16 tons. The definition of " unladen weight " is given in Annex 1.

The number of tanks in the possession of each H.C.P. shall not exceed the figures shown for such Party in the Table annexed to this chapter.

ARTICLE 22

All mobile land guns above 155 mm. and all tanks above 16 tons shall be destroyed in the following stages :—

One-third within twelve months of the coming into force of the Convention ;

Two-thirds within three years of the coming into force of the Convention ;

All guns above 115 mm. shall be destroyed as soon as they are replaced by new guns of or below 115 mm.

Annex 1

Definition of unladen weight of a tank

The unladen weight of a tank includes the shell, with tracks, engine, and transmission machinery, but without guns and mountings, crew, fuel, oil, engine cooling water, ammunition, wireless or military equipment.

CHAPTER 2

NAVAL ARMAMENTS.

ARTICLE 23

The naval armaments of the Parties to the Treaty of Washington, signed on 6th February, 1922, and the Treaty of London, signed on 22nd April, 1930, remain subject to the limitations resulting from the said Treaties.

ARTICLE 24

Articles 25 and 26 constitute the agreement between the Parties to the Treaty of London referred to in Article 24, paragraph 4, of that Treaty. France and Italy will ratify the said Treaty not later than the date of their ratification of the present Convention.

ARTICLE 25

Until 31st December, 1936, the naval combatant vessels of France and Italy, other than capital ships, aircraft carriers, and all vessels exempt from limitation under Article 8 of the Treaty of London, shall be limited, without prejudice to Article 12 of the said Treaty, by the provisions of Articles 26 and 27 of the present Convention. The definitions adopted in Annex 1 for the purposes of the present chapter will apply.

ARTICLE 26

(a) The completed tonnage in the cruiser, destroyer, and submarine categories which is not to be exceeded by France and Italy on 31st December, 1936, is to be the completed tonnage arrived at in consequence of the provisions of Article 27.

(b) France and Italy shall have complete freedom of transfer for the purposes of replacement between cruisers of sub-category (ii) and destroyers.

ARTICLE 27

Until 31st December, 1936, the programmes of France and Italy in cruisers, destroyers, and submarines will be as follows :—

A. Cruisers with guns of more than 6·1 in. (155 mm.).

No further tonnage shall be laid down or acquired after the date of signing the present Convention.

B. Cruisers with guns of 6·1 in. (155 mm.) calibre or less, and destroyers.

The amount of further construction to be laid down or acquired by France during the period between 1st January, 1933, and 31st December, 1936, shall be limited to 34,298 (34,847 metric) standard tons as authorized in the French programme of 1932.

The amount of further construction to be laid down or acquired by Italy during the same period shall be limited to 27,173 (27,608 metric) standard tons.

Tonnage laid down or acquired in accordance with the French programme of 1931 and the Italian programme of 1931-2, and any tonnage laid down or acquired subsequently shall be devoted to the replacement of over-age cruisers of this sub-category or of over-age destroyers. Upon the completion of any replacement tonnage, a corresponding amount of over-age tonnage shall be disposed of in accordance with Annex VI to the present chapter.

C. Submarines.

Until 31st December, 1936, France and Italy will not lay down or acquire any further submarines. France will arrange her present submarine building and scrapping programme so that, on the said date, her completed tonnage will not be greater than . . . standard tons.

Any submarine tonnage under construction on that date shall be in anticipation of replacement requirements.

ARTICLE 28

No High Contracting Party shall lay down or acquire any capital ship during the period up to 31st December, 1936, except that Italy may lay down one ship not exceeding 26,500 (26,924 metric) standard tons, and carrying guns not exceeding 13 in. (330 mm.) calibre.

Except as provided in Article 7, paragraph 2, of the Treaty of London, no High Contracting Party shall, until 31st December, 1936, lay down or acquire any submarine the standard displacement of which exceeds 2,000 (2,032 metric) standard tons or carrying a gun above 5·1 in. (130 mm.) calibre.

ARTICLE 29

In order to bring about a stabilization of naval armaments until 31st December, 1936, the armaments of those High Contracting Parties to whom the Treaties of Washington and London do not apply shall, until the said date, be limited as follows :

(a) No cruisers carrying guns of a calibre above 6·1 in. (155 mm.) shall be constructed or acquired.

(b) On 31st December, 1936, the completed tonnage in cruisers of sub-category (ii), destroyers, and submarines possessed by each of the said High Contracting Parties shall not exceed the amounts specified for such Party in Annex IV. This provision does not, however, apply to vessels exempt from limitation under Annex II to this chapter, nor to the special vessels shown in Annex III. These special vessels may not be replaced.

(c) Ships in the categories subject to limitation may only be laid down or acquired in accordance with the replacement rules contained in Annex V, and only in replacement of tonnage in the same category or sub-category which is or becomes over-age in accordance with these rules.

Nevertheless, there shall be complete freedom of transfer for purposes of replacement between the cruisers of sub-category (ii) and destroyers.

Vessels which have to be disposed of as being surplus to the tonnage figures set out in Annex IV shall be disposed of in accordance with the rules set out in Annex VI.

(d) Existing ships of various types which prior to 1st April, 1933, have been used as stationary training establishments or hulks may be retained in a non-seagoing condition.

ARTICLE 30

The High Contracting Parties assent to the rules laid down in Part IV of the Treaty of London and accept them as established rules of international law.

The present article constitutes, as regards those High Contracting Parties to whom the Treaty of London does not apply, the accession contemplated by Article 25 of the said Treaty.

ARTICLE 31

It is understood that none of the provisions of the present chapter shall prejudice the attitude of any of the High Contracting Parties at the conferences referred to in Article 30. The present Convention establishes no permanent ratio in any category of ship and creates no precedent as to whether, and if so in what manner, tonnage remaining over-age on 31st December, 1936, for which replacement tonnage has not been laid down, may ultimately be replaced.

ARTICLE 32

Concurrently with the Conference in 1935 provided for under Article 23 of the Treaty of London or at least in the same year, there shall be a conference of all the High Contracting Parties possessing naval armaments with a view to the establishment of limitations to be observed after 31st December, 1936.

ARTICLE 33

The Permanent Disarmament Commission set up under Article 64 of the present Convention will take immediate steps to prepare for the Conference of 1935 referred to in Article 32, by ascertaining the opinions of the High Contracting Parties concerned. It will also examine, with a view to reporting to the said conferences, technical questions of qualitative reduction in the sizes of vessels of war in the various categories, as well as any other questions relating to the limitation of naval armaments which the Commission may consider could appropriately come before the said Conference.

ANNEXES. (See Conf. D. 157 Addendum.)

I. Definitions—Annex III of the Draft Convention, as amended by the Naval Commission.

II. Exempt vessels—Annex I of the Draft Convention, as amended by the Naval Commission.

III. List of Special Vessels.

IV. Tonnage figures for Powers other than those signatories of the Treaty of Washington. These figures will be the figures from the returns to the Secretary of the League of Nations reproduced in the Armaments Year Book, 1932, " exempt " and " special " vessels being omitted.

V. Replacement Rules—Annex IV of the Draft Convention, as amended by the Naval Commission.

VI. Rules for Disposal—Annex V of the Draft Convention, as amended by the Naval Commission.

ARTICLE 34

The High Contracting Parties accept the complete abolition of bombing from the air (except for police purposes in certain outlying regions).

ARTICLE 35

The Permanent Disarmament Commission set up under Article 64 of the present Convention shall immediately devote itself to the working out of the best possible schemes providing for : (a) The complete abolition of military and naval aircraft, which must be dependent on the effective supervision of civil aviation to prevent its misuse for military purposes.

(b) Alternatively, should it prove impossible to ensure such effective supervision, the determination of the minimum number of machines required by each High Contracting Party consistent with his national safety and obligations, and having regard to the particular circumstances of each country.

The schemes prepared by the Permanent Disarmament Commission shall be reported to the second Disarmament Conference. In any case, the measures relating to civil aviation set out in Annex II will apply during the period of the present Convention.

ARTICLE 36

With a view to effecting the reductions necessary to facilitate the attainment of the objects referred to in Article 35, the number of aeroplanes, capable of use in war, in commission in the land, sea, and air armed forces of each of the High Contracting Parties who at present possess such aeroplanes shall, by the end of the period of the present Convention, not exceed the figures laid down for such Party in the table annexed to this chapter ; as regards the other High Contracting Parties, the *status quo* existing on 1st January, 1933, shall be maintained during the said period.

Each of the High Contracting Parties mentioned in the table annexed to this chapter may keep a number of aeroplanes in immediate reserve, not exceeding in each case 25 per cent of the number of aeroplanes in commission in the land, sea, and air armed forces of such Party.

ARTICLE 37

The High Contracting Parties agree that their air armaments will not include aeroplanes exceeding 3 tons in weight. Exception, however, may be made in the case of troop-carriers and flying-boats. Complete particulars of any such machines exceeding the maximum unladen weight of 3 tons must be returned anually to the Permanent Disarmament Commission.

ARTICLE 38

No dirigible shall be constructed or acquired during the period of the present Convention by any of the High Contracting Parties for commission in their land, sea, or air armed forces. The High Contracting Parties who at present possess such dirigibles, may, however, retain but not replace them during the said period.

ARTICLE 39

The definition of unladen weight is given in Annex I.

ARTICLE 40

Aeroplanes, capable of use in war, in commission in the land, sea, and air armed forces of any of the High Contracting Parties in excess of the number indicated for such Party in the table annexed to this chapter, must have been put out of commission or otherwise disposed of by the end of the period of the present Convention. At least one-half of such excess must, in the case of each such High Contracting Party, have been so dealt with by 30th June, 1936.

ARTICLE 41

Aeroplanes exceeding the maximum unladen weight indicated in Article 37 and now existing in the armed forces of the High Contracting Parties must all, except in so far as exceptions may be made in accordance with that Article, have been destroyed by the end of the period of this Convention. At least half of their number must, in the case of each High Contracting Party, have been destroyed by 30th June, 1936.

CHAPTER III

AIR ARMAMENTS

TABLE—AEROPLANES

Belgium	. .	150	Netherlands .	150
United Kingdom		500	Norway . .	75
China	. .	100	Poland . .	200
Czechoslovakia .		200	Portugal . .	25
Denmark .	.	50	Romania . .	150
Estonia	. .	50	Siam . .	75
Finland	. .	25	Spain . .	200
France	. .	500	Sweden . .	75
Greece	. .	75	Switzerland .	75
Italy	. .	500	Turkey . .	100
Japan	. .	50	U.S.A. . .	500
Latvia	. .	50	U.S.S.R. . .	500
Lithuania	.	50	Yugoslavia .	200

(Figures will have to be inserted subsequently for the other Parties which at present possess military or naval aeroplanes.)

Annexes I and II. (See Conf. D/157, pages 9 and 10).

[Here the French delegation proposed to insert a new chapter dealing with the limitation and supervision of the manufacture of and trade in war material.]

PART III

EXCHANGE OF INFORMATION

ARTICLES 42 TO 46

(The provisions of this part will depend in the main on the limitations and restrictions imposed by the other parts of the Convention. It does not seem necessary, therefore, to attempt to draft them now. It is only necessary to note that Articles 34 and 35 of the draft Convention will have to be reproduced.)

*[Articles 34 and 35 of the draft Convention prepared by the
Preparatory Commission*

ARTICLE 34

Within one month after the date of laying down and the
date of completion respectively of each vessel of war, other
than the vessels exempt from limitation under Annex I to Chapter B of Part II, laid down or completed by or for them or within their jurisdiction after the coming into force of the present
Convention, the High Contracting Parties shall communicate
to the Secretary-General of the League of Nations the information detailed below :—

(a) The date of laying down the keel and the following
particulars :—
Classification of the vessel and for whom built (if not for the
High Contracting Party) ; standard displacement in tons and
metric tons ; principal dimensions—namely, length of water-
line, extreme beam at or below water-line ; mean draught at
standard displacement ; calibre of the largest gun.

(b) The date of completion, together with the foregoing
particulars relating to the vessel at that date.

The above information shall be immediately communicated
by the Secretary-General to all the High Contracting Parties
and shall be published by the Secretary-General not later than
. . . in each year.

ARTICLE 35

Each of the High Contracting Parties shall communicate to
the Secretariat of the League of Nations the name and tonnage
of any vessel constructed in accordance with Article 19 (Chapter
II). With regard to existing vessels of this type, this communication shall be made within two months after ratification of the
present Convention. With regard to vessels to be constructed,
the communication shall be made on the date of completion.]

PART IV

CHEMICAL WARFARE

SECTION I.—PROHIBITION OF CHEMICAL,
INCENDIARY, OR BACTERIAL WARFARE

ARTICLE 47

The following provision is accepted as an established rule of
International Law :—

The use of chemical, incendiary, or bacterial weapons as against any State, whether or not a Party to the present Convention, and in any war, whatever its character, is prohibited.

This provision does not, however, deprive any Party which has been the victim of the illegal use of chemical or incendiary weapons of the right to retaliate, subject to such conditions as may hereafter be agreed.

With a view to the application of this rule to each of these categories of weapons, the High Contracting Parties agree upon the following provisions :—

ARTICLE 48

The prohibition of the use of chemical weapons shall apply to the use, by any method whatsoever, for the purpose of injuring an adversary, of any natural or synthetic substance harmful to the human or animal organism, whether solid, liquid, or gaseous, such as toxic, asphyxiating, lachrymatory, irritant, or vesicant substances.

This prohibition shall not apply :—

(a) to explosives.

(b) to the noxious substances arising from the combustion or detonation of explosives, provided that such explosives have not been designed or used with the object of producing noxious substances.

(c) to smoke or fog used to screen objectives or for other military purposes, provided that such smoke or fog is not liable to produce harmful effects under normal conditions of use.

ARTICLE 49

The prohibition of the use of incendiary weapons shall apply to :—

(1) the use of projectiles specifically intended to cause fires. The prohibition shall not apply to :—

(a) projectiles specially constructed to give light or to be luminous, and generally to pyrotechnics not intended to cause fires, or to projectiles of all kinds capable of producing incendiary effects accidentally.

(b) incendiary projectiles designed specifically for defence against aircraft, provided that they are used exclusively for that purpose.

(2) The use of appliances designed to attack persons by fire, such as flame-projectors.

ARTICLE 50

The prohibition of the use of bacterial arms shall apply to the use for the purpose of injuring an adversary of all methods for the dissemination of pathogenic microbes, or of filter-passing viruses, or of infected substances, whether for the purpose of bringing them into immediate contact with human beings, animals, or plants, or for the purpose of affecting any of the latter in any manner—for example, by polluting the atmosphere, water, foodstuffs, or any other objects.

SECTION II.—PROHIBITION OF PREPARATIONS FOR CHEMICAL, INCENDIARY, AND BACTERIAL WARFARE

ARTICLE 51

All preparations for chemical, incendiary, or bacterial warfare shall be prohibited in time of peace as in time of war.

ARTICLE 52

In order to enforce the aforesaid general prohibition it shall in particular be prohibited :—

(1) To manufacture, import, export, or be in possession of appliances or substances exclusively suited to chemical or incendiary warfare.

The quantities of chemical substances necessary for protective experiments, therapeutic research and laboratory work shall be excepted. The High Contracting Parties shall inform the Permanent Disarmament Commission of the quantities of the said substances necessary for their protective experiments.

The manufacture of and trade in these substances may not be undertaken without Government authorization.

(2) To manufacture, import, export, or be in possession of appliances or substances suitable for both peaceful and military purposes with intent to use them in violation of the prohibition contained in Article 48.

(3) To instruct or train armed forces in the use of chemical, incendiary, or bacterial weapons and means of warfare, or to permit any instruction or training for such purposes within their jurisdiction.

ARTICLE 53

The provisions of Articles 51 and 52 shall not restrict the freedom of the High Contracting Parties in regard to material and installations intended exclusively to ensure individual or collective protection against the effects of chemical, incendiary, or bacterial weapons, or to training with a view to individual or collective protection against the effects of the said weapons.

ARTICLE 54

The High Contracting Parties shall inform the Permanent Disarmament Commission of the lachrymatory substances intended to be used by their authorities for police operations, as well as the number of the various appliances by means of which they are to be utilized.

SECTION III.—SUPERVISION OF THE OBSERVANCE OF THE PROHIBITION OF PREPARATIONS FOR CHEMICAL, INCENDIARY, OR BACTERIAL WARFARE

ARTICLE 55

The Permanent Disarmament Commission shall examine the complaints put forward by any Party which may allege that the prohibition to prepare for chemical, incendiary, or bacterial warfare has been violated.

SECTION IV.—ESTABLISHMENT OF THE FACT OF THE USE OF CHEMICAL, INCENDIARY, OR BACTERIAL WEAPONS

ARTICLE 56

Any Party claiming that chemical, incendiary, or bacterial weapons have been used against it shall notify the Permanent Disarmament Commission.

It shall, at the same time, notify the authority designated for the purpose by the Permanent Disarmament Commission or, failing such authority, the doyen of the Diplomatic Corps accredited to it, with a view to the immediate constitution of a commission of investigation.

If the above-mentioned authority has received the necessary powers, it shall itself act as a commission of investigation.

ARTICLE 57

The Commission of Investigation shall proceed with all possible speed to the inquiries necessary to determine whether chemical, incendiary, or bacterial weapons have been used.

It shall report to the Permanent Disarmament Commission.

ARTICLE 58

The Permanent Disarmament Commission shall invite the Party against which the complaint has been made to furnish explanations.

It may send commissioners to the territory under the control of that Party for the purpose of proceeding to an inquiry, to determine whether chemical, incendiary, or bacterial arms have been used.

ARTICLE 59

The Permanent Commission may also carry out any other inquiry with the same object.

ARTICLE 60

The Parties involved in the above-mentioned operations, and, in general, all the Parties to the present Convention, shall take the necessary measures to facilitate these operations, particularly as regards the rapid transport of persons and correspondence.

ARTICLE 61

According to the result of the above-mentioned operations, the Permanent Commission, acting with all possible speed, shall establish whether chemical, incendiary, or bacterial weapons have been used.

ARTICLE 62 [1]

The details of the application of the provisions of this chapter shall be fixed by regulations to be issued by the Permanent Disarmament Commission.

PART V

MISCELLANEOUS PROVISIONS

SECTION I.—PERMANENT DISARMAMENT COMMISSION

CHAPTER I.—COMPOSITION

ARTICLE 64

There shall be set up at the seat of the League of Nations a Permanent Disarmament Commission composed of representatives of the Governments of the High Contracting Parties. Each such Government shall appoint one member of the Commission. Each member may be accompanied by substitutes and experts.

The Governments of the High Contracting Parties will inform the Secretary-General of the League of Nations of the names

[1] Articles 52–63 became Articles 51–62 after redrafting of Articles 50–1 as one.

of their representatives, substitutes, and experts on their nomination and on any changes being made.

ARTICLE 65

The Commission shall set up committees, whose number, composition and functions shall be decided by the Commission.

ARTICLE 66

The Commission may be assisted by experts chosen by itself, other than any experts appointed by the High Contracting Parties to accompany their representatives.

ARTICLE 67

The members of the Commission, their substitutes, and experts, and the experts and officials of the Commission, when engaged on the business of the Commission, shall enjoy diplomatic privileges and immunities.

ARTICLE 68

The Secretary-General of the League of Nations shall provide the Secretariat of the Commission.

CHAPTER II.—FUNCTIONS

ARTICLE 69

It will be the duty of the Commission to watch the execution of the present Convention. The Commission shall receive all the information which the High Contracting Parties are bound to communicate to the Secretary-General of the League of Nations in pursuance of their international obligations in this respect. The Commission may request the High Contracting Parties to supply, in writing or verbally, any supplementary particulars or explanations in regard to the said information which it may consider necessary.

ARTICLE 70

The Commission may take into account any other information which may reach it from a responsible source and which it may consider worth attention.

ARTICLE 71

The Commission shall be entitled to have any person heard or consulted who is in a position to throw any light on the question which is being examined by the Commission.

ARTICLE 72

Any High Contracting Party whose observance of the execution of the present Convention may have been the subject of criticism shall be entitled to request the Commission to conduct in his territory such investigations as may be necessary in order to verify the execution of the obligations of the said Party under the present Convention.

On receipt of such a request, the Commission shall meet at once in order to give effect to it, to determine the scope of the investigation within the limits of the criticism which has been made, and to lay down the conditions in which the investigation is to take place.

ARTICLE 73

At the request of one or more of the High Contracting Parties, the Commission may decide to have investigations of alleged infractions of the Convention conducted on the territory of any High Contracting Party.

On the receipt of such a request, the Committee shall meet at once in order to take a decision upon it.

Its decision, which will determine the scope of the investigation, if such is decided upon, shall be taken by a two-thirds majority of all the members of the Commission, whether present at the meeting or not.

ARTICLE 74

The result of the investigations decided upon in accordance with Articles 72 and 73 shall be embodied in each case in a special report by the Commission.

The High Contracting Parties shall promptly advise as to the conclusions of the report.

ARTICLE 75

Independently of the investigations referred to in Articles 72 and 73, the Commission shall be entitled to conduct periodic investigations in regard to States which have made a special agreement to that effect.

ARTICLE 76

The Commission shall make, at least once a year, a report showing the situation as regards the execution of the present Convention and containing any observations which this situation may suggest to it.

ARTICLE 77

If one of the High Contracting Parties is of opinion that the provisions of the present Convention have been infringed, or that a threat of infringement exists, such Party may address a complaint to the Commission.

The Commission will invite the High Contracting Party whose attitude has produced the complaint to supply it with all explanations which may be useful. The Commission will proceed to investigate the matter, and may employ with this object the various methods of obtaining information provided for in the present Convention.

The Commission will draw up as soon as possible a reasoned report on the result of its investigation.

The High Contracting Parties shall promptly advise as to the conclusions of the report.

ARTICLE 78

Each member of the Commission shall be entitled to require that, in any report by the Commission, account shall be taken of the opinions or suggestions put forward by him, if necessary in the form of a separate report.

ARTICLE 79

All reports by the Commission shall be immediately communicated to the High Contracting Parties and to the Council of the League of Nations. They shall be made public as soon as possible in the conditions determined by the Commission.

ARTICLE 80

The Commission shall prepare, for submission to the High Contracting Parties, such agreements as may be necessary to ensure the execution of the present Convention.

ARTICLE 81

The Commission shall make preparations for the Conference to be held in accordance with Article 95 of the present Convention in order to facilitate the subsequent stages of disarmament.

ARTICLE 82

The Commission shall in general carry out any preliminary studies which may appear useful for the execution of its duties.

ARTICLE 83

Within the limits of its functions, the Commission shall supply the Council of the League of Nations with any information and advice which the Council may request of it.

PROPOSED NEW ARTICLE

CHAPTER III.—OPERATION

ARTICLE 84

The Commission shall meet for the first time, on being summoned by the Secretary-General of the League of Nations, within three months from the entry into force of the present Convention, to elect a provisional President and Vice-President and to draw up its Rules of Procedure.

Thereafter it shall meet at least once a year in ordinary session on the date fixed in its Rules of Procedure.

It shall also meet in extraordinary session :—

(1) when such a meeting is prescribed by the present Convention ;

(2) if its Bureau so decides, either of its own motion or on the request of one of the High Contracting Parties ;

(3) on the request of the Council of the League of Nations.

ARTICLE 85

The High Contracting Parties will furnish the delegates of the Commission who are entrusted with the investigations referred to in Articles 72, 73, and 75 with the necessary facilities for the execution of their mission. The Parties will employ the means at their disposal to secure the attendance of any witnesses whom the delegates of the Commission may wish to hear.

ARTICLE 86

Except where otherwise provided by the present Convention, the decisions of the Commission shall be taken by a majority of the members present at the meeting.

A minority report may be drawn up.

ARTICLE 87

The general expenditure of the Commission shall form the subject of a special chapter in the budget of the League of Nations.

The High Contracting Parties who are not members of the

League shall bear a reasonable share of the said expenditure. An agreement to this effect will be reached between these Parties and the Secretary-General of the Commission.

The travelling expenses and subsistence allowances of the members of the Commission, their substitutes and experts, shall be paid by their respective Governments.

The Commission shall draw up regulations relating to the expenditure necessitated by its work.

SECTION II.—DEROGATIONS

ARTICLE 88

Should any of the High Contracting Parties become engaged in war, or should a change of circumstances constitute, in the opinion of any High Contracting Party, a menace to his national security, such Party may suspend temporarily, in so far as he is concerned, any provision or provisions of the present Convention, other than those contained in Articles 30, 34, and 47 to 63, provided that :—

(a) Such High Contracting Party shall immediately notify the other High Contracting Parties, and at the same time the Permanent Disarmament Commission, of such temporary suspension and of the extent thereof.

(b) In the event of the suspension being based upon a change of circumstances, the High Contracting Party concerned shall, simultaneously with the said notification, communicate to the other High Contracting Parties and to the Permanent Disarmament Commission a full explanation of such change of circumstances.

Thereupon the other High Contracting Parties shall promptly advise as to the situation thus presented.

When the reasons for such temporary suspension have ceased to exist, the said High Contracting Party shall reduce his armaments to the level agreed upon in the Convention and shall make immediate notification to the other High Contracting Parties.

SECTION III.—FINAL PROVISIONS

ARTICLE 89

It is hereby declared that the loyal execution of the present Convention is a matter of common interest to the High Contracting Parties.

ARTICLE 90

The present Convention is not to be interpreted as restricting the provisions of the Covenant of the League of Nations—in particular, those which fix the powers of the Council and the Assembly.

ARTICLE 91

If a dispute arises between two or more of the High Contracting Parties concerning the interpretation or application of the provisions of the present Convention, and cannot be settled either directly between the Parties or by some other method of friendly settlement, the Parties will, at the request of any one of them, submit such dispute to the decision of the Permanent Court of International Justice, or to an arbitral tribunal chosen by them.

ARTICLE 92

The present Convention shall be ratified by the High Contracting Parties in accordance with their respective constitutional methods. The instruments of ratification shall be deposited with the Secretary-General of the League of Nations.

The present Convention shall come into force, for each Party whose instrument of ratification has been deposited, as soon as the instruments of ratification have been deposited by . . . (list to be drawn up by the Conference).

ARTICLE 93

Each of the High Contracting Parties will take the necessary measures for carrying the provisions of the present Convention into effect as soon as it has come into force for such Party.

ARTICLE 94

Except as provided in the following paragraphs of this Article, the present Convention shall remain in force for five years from the date on which it comes into force in accordance with the second paragraph of Article 92.

Chapter 2 of Section II of Part II (Naval Armaments), and Table II annexed to Section I of Part II (Naval Effectives) shall remain in force until 31st December, 1936.

The rules referred to in Article 30 remain in force, as provided in Article 23 of the Treaty of London, without limit of time. Article 34 and Sections I, II, and III of Part IV shall also remain in force without limit of time.

ARTICLE 95

Not later than . . . years from the date on which the present Convention comes into force, a conference of the High Contracting Parties shall meet at Geneva. It will be the duty of the said conference to prepare and conclude a new Convention, which will replace the present Convention and will carry on the work of the reduction and limitation of armaments begun by the present Convention.

ARTICLE 96

The present Convention, together with the further Conventions to be concluded in accordance with Article 95 and Article 32, will replace, as between the respective Parties to the Treaties of Versailles, St. Germain, Trianon, and Neuilly, those provisions of Part V (Military, Naval, and Air Clauses) of each of the Treaties of Versailles, St. Germain, and Trianon, and of Part IV (Military, Naval, and Air Clauses) of the Treaty of Neuilly, which at present limit the arms and armed forces of Germany, Austria, Hungary, and Bulgaria respectively.

NOTE TO APPENDIX II

Part i (Articles 1–6) of the British Draft Convention

Articles 1–5 in the original draft submitted to the Conference on 16th March, 1933, were replaced by three new articles on 24th May, 1933. These articles are those printed on page 267. In the British Disarmament Memorandum of 29th January, 1934 (see above, p. 203), it was suggested that three new articles—2 (a), 2 (b), and 2 (c)—should be inserted between the revised articles 2 and 3. The first of these—2 (a)—would be Article 89 (see above, p. 290) of the present draft Convention, which declares that " *the loyal execution of the present Convention is a matter of common interest to the High Contracting Parties* ". Article 2 (b) would declare : " *The provisions for immediate consultation contained in Article 1 will also be applicable in the event of the Permanent Disarmament Commission, to be set up in accordance with Part V, Section 1, of the present Convention, reporting the existence of facts which show that any High Contracting Party has failed to execute loyally the present Convention.*" Article 2 (c) would state : " *It shall be the object of such consultation to exchange views as to the steps to be taken for the purpose of restoring the situation and of maintaining in operation the provisions of the present Convention.*"

Under Articles 4–5 it was proposed to include the text, when agreed, of Articles relating to the definition of the aggressor, the establishment of facts constituting aggression, and the provision for a European Security Pact. The Committee on Security questions submitted on 24th May a report on these subjects and also the new text, printed on pages 267–8, for Article 6 in the original draft.

INDEX

O. K.